In the time of ancient gods, w...
... a land in turmoil crie...
She was Xena, a warrior princess forged
in the heat of battle. . . .

Veteran of the Trojan War, Comrade of Hercules and
Ulysses. Betrayed lover of Julius Caesar, and tutor to
both Hippocrates and the future King David. Archfoe
of the deadly Callisto. Boon companion (and possibly
more) to the Bard of Potidaea. Slayer of giants, Centaurs, Harpies, dryads, Bacchae, and countless warlords. Creator of CPR, kite-flying, electricity, the ruins
of Stonehenge, and the gods know what else.

Modern history books are strangely silent on this exceptional heroine, but fans of the hit television series
Xena: Warrior Princess know full well which remarkable woman fits all the descriptions above. . . .

BATTLE ON!
AN UNAUTHORIZED, IRREVERENT LOOK AT
XENA: WARRIOR PRINCESS

BATTLE ON!

AN UNAUTHORIZED, IRREVERENT LOOK AT

XENA:
WARRIOR PRINCESS

GREG COX

A ROC BOOK

ROC

Published by the Penguin Group
Penguin Putnam Inc., 375 Hudson Street,
New York, New York 10014, U.S.A.
Penguin Books Ltd, 27 Wrights Lane, London W8 5TZ, England
Penguin Books Australia Ltd, Ringwood, Victoria, Australia
Penguin Books Canada Ltd, 10 Alcorn Avenue, Toronto, Ontario, Canada M4V 3B2
Penguin Books (N.Z.) Ltd, 182–190 Wairau Road, Auckland 10, New Zealand

Penguin Books Ltd, Registered Offices: Harmondsworth, Middlesex, England

First published by Roc, an imprint of Dutton NAL,
a member of Penguin Putnam Inc.

First Printing, November, 1998
10 9 8 7 6 5 4 3 2 1

RОC   REGISTERED TRADEMARK—MARCA REGISTRADA

LIBRARY OF CONGRESS CATALOGING IN PUBLICATION DATA.

Cox, Greg, 1959–
    Battle on! : an unauthorized, irreverent look at Xena, warrior princess.
        p.   cm.
    ISBN 0-451-45731-5
    1. Xena, warrior princess (Television program)—Miscellanea.
    I. Title,
PN1992.77.X46C68   1998
791.45'72—dc21   98-8451
                                                                    CIP

Printed in the United States of America

BOOKS ARE AVAILABLE AT QUANTITY DISCOUNTS WHEN USED TO PROMOTE PRODUCTS OR SERVICES. FOR INFORMATION PLEASE WRITE TO PREMIUM MARKETING DIVISION, PENGUIN PUTNAM INC., 375 HUDSON STREET, NEW YORK, NEW YORK, 10014.

For Stephanie Cox, my favorite warrior princess

ACKNOWLEDGMENTS

Thanks to my editor, Laura Anne Gilman, for seeing the potential in this project, to Jennifer Heddle for her assistance, and to my agents, Russell Galen and Anna Ghosh, for making it happen.

Thanks also to the entire Malibu Lunch Group, not to mention my friends and family, who have listened to me ramble on about a certain television series for three years now. Also to all the enthusiastic Xena fans on the Internet for providing much stimulating discussion. Two of my favorite lurking grounds: *http://whoosh.org* and *alt.tv.xena*. My gratitude as well to the cast and crew of *Xena: Warrior Princess* for many hours of edifying entertainment; I hope they're having as good a time as it seems.

Finally, as ever, to Karen and Alex, who have lived with this book since the beginning.

SPOILER ALERT!

If you've picked up this book, chances are you're already pretty familiar with the television series *Xena: Warrior Princess*. As they say on the Internet, however, beware. It's probably impossible, and not much fun, to discuss any series at this length without giving away a plot twist or two, at least from the first three seasons.

So if you don't mind hearing the full scoop about Xena's murky parentage or finding out who first called her a Warrior Princess, read on.

CONTENTS

CHAPTER I

XENA WHO?

"In a time of ancient gods, warlords, and kings . . . a land in turmoil cried out for a hero. She was Xena, a mighty princess forged in the heat of battle."

Veteran of the Trojan War. Lover of Hercules, Ulysses, *and* Julius Caesar. Tutor to both Hippocrates and the future King David. Archfoe of the deadly Callisto. Boon companion (and possibly more) to the Bard of Potidaea. Slayer of giants, Centaurs, Harpies, dryads, Bacchae, and countless warlords. Inventor of CPR, kite-flying, bungee-jumping, electricity, the ruins of Stonehenge, and the gods know what else.

Modern history books are strangely silent on this exceptional heroine, but fans of the hit television series *Xena: Warrior Princess* know full well what remarkable woman fits all the descriptions above . . . and many more besides. Since her introduction on an episode of the companion series *Hercules: The Legendary Journeys*, Xena has turned conventional myth and history on its head while thrilling audiences with her unique combination of action, humor, and heartfelt emotion. As of this year, 4 A.X. (Age of Xena), known to the uninitiated as 1998, her weekly television series is the top-rated dramatic series in syndication, beating out such perennials as *Baywatch* and *Star Trek: Deep Space Nine*. The success of the TV show has launched an armada of merchandise and tie-ins: paperback novels, comic books, action figures, posters, T-shirts, jewelry, trading cards, a theme park attraction, and even an animated musical adventure. Xena fandom has spread out to conquer the world; the show is even a hit in Saudi Arabia, where local censors feel obliged to edit out large chunks of each episode. A trip onto the Internet reveals Xena-themed Web pages proliferating at an absolutely terrifying rate, including such intriguing sites as "The International Association of Xena Studies" (really!) and "The Bubba's Guide to *Xena: Warrior Princess*." Devout fans spin their own tales of Xena and her various friends and enemies, some of them extremely X-rated, and post them on the World Wide Web for all to see.

> *Interviewer:* What modern, indispensable comfort would Xena kill to have?
> *Lucy Lawless:* Tampons. (*TV Guide*, May 3–9, 1997)

But who is this celebrated Warrior Princess and why does she inspire such fanatical devotion?

Much remains intriguingly mysterious about Xena's past, but this much is known: After an infamous and successful career as a roving warlord, leading an army of mercenaries to sack and pillage the ancient world, Xena was reformed through her dealings with the legendary hero Hercules. Since then, she has sought to atone for her bloody past by using her incomparable fighting skills in defense of the weak and the persecuted. Despite her change of heart, she's no pacifist; indeed, she never seems truly happy except when cracking heads and fighting against overwhelming odds, at which times she flashes a wolfish smile while her ice-blue eyes light up with fierce glee. Her trademark battle cry, a high-pitched ululation that stubbornly resists phonetic transcription, cheers her allies while intimidating her foes. And all the while, the possibility that Xena might revert to her old evil ways remains a genuine source of concern to those who know her best, including Xena herself.

A woman of many talents, Xena possesses an impressive arsenal of tricks and weapons. Chief among them is her *chakram,* or "round killing thing," a sort of flying Frisbee of death that she throws with breathtaking accuracy, complete with ricochets and bank shots that rival the best efforts of the finest poolroom hustlers. When and where she acquired this distinctive weapon has yet to be revealed, but only her greatest enemy, Callisto, can fling the chakram with anything resembling Xena's skill. (More about Callisto later, I promise.) She's no slouch with a sword either, and given a swig of wine and a convenient flame, she can blow fire like a dragon—as many scorched antagonists can attest.

Even unarmed, Xena is more than a match for the average barbarian. Her acrobatics and martial arts stunts frequently defy gravity and belief; she can kick a dozen foes off their feet without touching the ground once. On her travels, she has picked up considerable medical and anatomical expertise, which she's not above using offensively. One of her favorite ploys is to cut off the flow of blood to an opponent's brain. Death follows within moments unless the unfortunate victim decides to cooperate with Xena. Few can resist her infamous "pinch interrogations." (Judging from the agonized expressions of her victims, the Xena treatment makes Mr. Spock's famous nerve pinch look like a gentle massage by comparison.)

Accompanying the Warrior Princess on her perpetual quest for redemption is Xena's sidekick and closest companion, Gabrielle, known to her fans as the Bard of Potidaea and to most of Xena's enemies as "that irritating little blonde." An aspiring storyteller and honorary Amazon, Gabby hooked up with Xena in the show's very first episode, and the two have been more or less inseparable ever since, despite a traumatic rift during the third year of their association. Gabrielle is in many ways Xena's polar opposite: idealistic and cheerful where Xena is more cynical and somber, loquacious where

Xena is laconic. Although she has gradually learned to defend herself, this selfless chatterbox would rather stop and smell the flowers, unlike her more militant partner, whose idea of a good time usually involves a battle to the death.

Despite their differences, the close bond between the two women has proved a source of strength to them both, just as their contrasting temperaments provide constant opportunities for humor. Bloody-minded rivals may wonder what the Warrior Princess sees in the good-hearted bard, but they go everywhere together . . . even if Xena does always get to ride the horse.

Xena (on Argo, her surprisingly talented steed) and Gabrielle (on foot) may travel far and wide together, but when and where exactly is an unusually thorny issue. Given Xena's connection to Hercules, the obvious answer would seem to be classical Greece (roughly 1000–200 B.C.), and certainly the gods and goddesses of Mount Olympus make frequent appearances. Yet a closer look (and your basic liberal arts education) reveals some intriguing complications.

To start with, both Greek and Roman nomenclature are applied in a fairly arbitrary manner. Thus gods like Zeus and Poseidon go by their original Greek names, but Ulysses and Hercules bear their later, Romanized appellations. And what sort of Greco-Roman name is Gabrielle, anyway?

More significantly, genuine historical figures such as Hippocrates or Julius Caesar wander into the saga, despite being separated by hundreds of years according to the precepts of conventional history, while bits and pieces of other mythologies, from the Old Testament to the Knights of the Round Table, overlap with the legends of ancient Greece in a landscape that strangely resembles New Zealand. The dialogue also has a curiously contemporary ring, as exemplified by an Aphrodite who talks like a Valley Girl, and Salmoneus, a fast-talking entrepreneur peddling seltzer water to a bygone era.

Ultimately, we discover that we have entered the Xenaverse, a bizarre but fascinating realm where myth and history blend in surprising ways—and where a certain Warrior

Princess occupies center stage in some of the world's oldest stories. (Okay, technically it's the Hercules-and-Xenaverse, but that's just too much of a mouthful.) At first this shameless mélange of widely disparate eras and worldviews can be disconcerting, and one shudders at the thought of any third-graders staking their history grades on last night's episode of *Xena*, but soon one's scholarly defenses are overwhelmed and the sheer audacity of the whole enterprise becomes all too irresistible. Spartacus? The Lost Ark? Stonehenge? Santa Claus? Everything is up for grabs, and most anything is possible, including the occasional tidbit of genuine myth or history. Just when you least expect it, the show can be remarkably faithful to the real scoop—when it wants to be, that is.

The secret to *Xena*'s success may be that the show can be enjoyed on any number of levels. On a literal level, you have an ongoing morality tale that preaches an inspiring story of personal redemption and the power of friendship. Each episode tends to have its own little moral, usually involving some guest character who is invariably inspired to a moment of personal heroism by exposure to the destiny-defying duo, like the timid toymaker in "A Solstice Carol" or the would-be warlord in "Blind Faith." The Warrior Princess can be a surprisingly positive influence, it would appear.

Furthermore, the friendship of Xena and Gabrielle has struck a nerve with many viewers, who have found it to be one of the most appealing aspects of the show. Sometimes the byplay between the grim woman warrior and her perky companion can be enough to sustain an entire episode, as in the popular "A Day in the Life." Other times the bond is tested severely, most notably during the wrenching events of the third season, but always the relationship proves strong enough to survive whatever trials the Fates (and the scripters) throw at them.

But what exactly is the nature of that relationship? On yet another level, no discussion of the show would be complete without mentioning its celebrated lesbian subtext. As a brilliant bit of fan-generated poetry put it, much effort has been expended to determine whether our heroines' partnership is "sororal or sapphistical," and such Internet newsgroups as the one at *alt.tv.xena* are filled with carefully reasoned arguments pro and con. Many viewers prefer to view this deep and abiding friendship as strictly platonic, a perfectly valid interpretation that is quite consistent with the events depicted on the screen. The gods know, both Xena and Gabrielle occasionally find romance with various manly sorts. Another segment of the audience, however, eagerly reads between the lines, looking for signs of an even closer, more physical union.

And sometimes they don't have to look very hard.

Reading homoerotic content into outwardly straight TV shows is nothing new—the Trekkies have been doing it for years—but *Xena: Warrior Princess* takes things one step further by occasionally teasing its devout (and well-publicized) lesbian following with a provocative line or scene, while simultaneously remaining open to more innocuous interpretations. Ultimately, Xenaphiles are encouraged to read as much or as little into the relationship as they wish, as long as everyone recognizes just how important these two special characters are to each other. Me, I just enjoy the subtext as a typically audacious running gag.

Of course, once Sappho herself appears, as is reportedly in the works for next season, all bets are off. Says Lucy Lawless (Xena), who intends to play the part herself, "She gets a hankering for Gabrielle, and Gabrielle doesn't know how to handle it."

I can hear the Internet chatter already . . .

It doesn't hurt, of course, that these lessons in courage and comradeship are accompanied by generous amounts of humor and jaw-dropping action scenes. The fights and stunts on *Xena*, inspired by the over-the-top excesses of today's Hong Kong action flicks, are several cuts above what passes for "action" on most TV adventure programs. Any cop or private eye can throw a mugger up against a wall; where else can you see a duel fought atop the heads of a crowd ("Sins of the Past") or a bloodthirsty band of brigands driven off by a *fish*-wielding

Subtext?

After much debate on this prickly issue, let's allow the cast and creators the final word from the front lines:

LUCY LAWLESS: "I think the characters transcend labeling, just like gay people don't want to be identified solely by their sexuality. They contribute so many things to society that to limit it to their sexuality is unimaginative." (*US*, October 1997)

RENEE O'CONNOR: "People just read into it what they choose to see." (*Starburst*, August 1997)

HUDSON LEICK: "I think Callisto has sexual feelings toward Xena. Yeah, absolutely. She has a lot of feelings toward Xena, in many different realms. But I don't think that needs to be a focus, just because America's homophobic. It's just flirting, you know. It makes it a little more razor-sharp when you mix love and hate like that." (*Realms of Fantasy*, April 1998)

ROB TAPERT, Executive Producer: "People ask me frequently about Xena's sexual orientation, especially about her relationship with Gabrielle. I tell them that she has had a string of lovers in her life and that now she is trying to get control of her emotions." (*Ms.*, August 1996)

LIZ FRIEDMAN, Coproducer: "I don't have any interest in saying they're heterosexuals. That's just bullshit, and no fun, either." (*Entertainment Weekly*, March 7, 1997)

STEVEN L. SEARS, Co-executive Producer: "(Xena and Gabrielle) have love for each other. It's up to the audience to determine what that love is." (*Entertainment Weekly*, March 7, 1997)

heroine ("Altared States")? Throw in outlandish sound effects to accompany every kick, leap, and shrug, and you have the kinetic equivalent of a sugar rush every time Xena goes into action.

Perhaps the most amazing thing about *Xena: Warrior Princess* is that you can take the show and the characters seriously at the same time that you fall off your couch laughing at the latest ridiculous sight gag or plot twist. No *Xena* viewing is truly complete unless you end up staring widemouthed at the screen, thinking, "I can't believe they just did that!" Tying history in knots, throwing in flagrant anachronisms, poking fun at their own favorite shticks, indulging in outrageous coincidences, and spinning plotlines so wacko that they don't just suspend disbelief, they send it rocketing helplessly over the moon, never to be heard from again, *Xena* the series is almost as fearless as its eponymous heroine. Rap music in ancient Greece? Sure, why not? Identical Xena look-alikes? Great, make it *three* of them. A pregnant Amazon giving birth to a Centaur? Fine and dandy. How about an episode set in the 1940s? A musical episode? An episode where Xena is a man? No problem.

Even the closing credits at the end of each new installment hold their own surprises. Buried amid the usual routine production items is a tongue-in-cheek disclaimer assuring the concerned viewer that no Harpies, Centaurs, Amazons, or whatever were harmed during the filming of the episode. (Whew, is that a relief!) Granted, these notices are in such small print and go by so quickly that they're all but impossible to read, but devout Xenaphiles end up squinting at blurry, freeze-framed images on their TV screens in hopes of finding out which mythological entity was not injured or otherwise inconvenienced this week.

How can you not love a show like this? *Xena* dares to spoof itself while demanding the viewer's total conviction and empathy. It's a tricky thing to pull off, kind of like catching an arrow in your teeth or flipping backward onto a horse, but *Xena* somehow does it week after week. Watching the show, you can't help thinking that everyone involved is having way too much fun.

And so are we.

CHAPTER II

ANCESTORS OF A
WARRIOR PRINCESS

September 28, 1997. Standing onstage in front of a packed room of *Xena* fans at the Marriott Marquis Hotel in New York's Times Square, only blocks from the Broadway theater where she was currently starring in the musical *Grease,* Lucy Lawless prepared to reveal her terrible secret. Summoning up her courage, she opened her mouth and confessed aloud that (gasp!) she had never really watched *Wonder Woman.*

The crowd took this shocking revelation as well as could be expected.

Seriously, much has been made of Xena's place in the history of TV heroines, from Emma Peel to the Bionic Woman and even Lynda Carter in her red-white-and-blue satin tights; indeed, one gets the impression from subsequent interviews and public appearances that Lawless is starting to get a bit weary of the Wonder Woman comparisons. While she may be protesting a bit too much, a case can be made that Xena's true roots lie not with Charlie's Angels and their ilk but with the classic heroines of history, mythology, and fantasy literature.

The same Greek legends that spawned Hercules also tell of remarkable women who defied the domestic servitude that was the common lot of the vast majority of Bronze Age women. Powerful goddesses like Athena and Artemis held their own against their male counterparts, often playing a

Time really *is* different in the Xenaverse. The official "Xena: Warrior Princess 1998 Calendar" is missing February and October.

vital role in the affairs of humanity. Curiously, neither goddess has appeared in the *Xena* television series, although Xena, who mistrusts most gods, seems to have a bit of faith in Athena in "Lost Mariner." The Warrior Princess certainly has little in common with the one goddess she does manage to run into fairly often: Aphrodite, the vain and self-centered Goddess of Love.

Greek myths also speak of mortal heroines, like Atalanta, who could run faster than any man and who, according to some accounts, sailed with Jason and Hercules on their quest for the Golden Fleece. Bodybuilder Cory Everson has portrayed Atalanta on several episodes of *Hercules*, but, strangely, she has yet to appear on *Xena*. (Xena and Atalanta do meet, and apparently not for the first time, in a novel, *The Huntress and the Sphinx,* by Ru Emerson.)

Also prominent in mythology are the Amazons, a fierce race of women warriors who contended against most of the major Greek heroes, including Hercules, Achilles, Bellerophon, Perseus, and Theseus. Lucy Lawless, of course, began her mythic career by playing an Amazon in the first *Hercules* TV movie, and the race of Amazons has played a major role in several episodes of *Xena*, with Gabrielle herself becoming first an honorary Amazon princess and eventually the Amazon Queen. (One is tempted to point out that Wonder Woman was also an Amazon princess, but we'll let that one go.) Powerful heroines also appear in the myths and legends of other cultures, such as the Valkyries of Norse myth or the Celtic warrior queen Scathach, who taught the art of battle to the mythic hero Cuchulainn.

Great female warriors are less well known in the real world, but history contains such notable examples as Boadicea, a

British queen who led a fierce revolt against Rome in the first century A.D., and Joan of Arc, who commanded the armies of France in the fifteenth century. The writers paid homage to these women: Boadicea allied herself with Xena in "The Deliverer," while a Xena impersonator was almost burned at the stake à la Joan in "Warrior . . . Priestess . . . Tramp." Frankly, the way *Xena* twists history around, I won't be at all surprised if Joan herself pops up any episode now.

Notorious female buccaneers like the eighteenth century's Anne Bonny and Mary Read fought beside their male crewmates, just as Xena took to the high seas as a pirate queen in "Destiny." And not unlike Xena's remarkable Chinese mentor Lao Ma, the real-life Qiu Jin (1875–1907) defied Asian tradition to become adept with horse and sword. Qiu Jin, alas, was ultimately executed for her revolutionary feminist activities, which included speaking out against arranged marriages and the cruel practice of foot-binding, just as Lao Ma was put to death by the tyrannical Green Dragon in "The Debt."

Perhaps inspired by the likes of Atalanta or Boadicea, modern fantasy fiction has already given us many strong female warriors, beginning with Jirel of Joiry in the 1930s. Created by author C. L. Moore in a series of short stories that first appeared in the classic pulp magazine *Weird Tales*, Jirel was the fiery, red-haired defender of a small province of medieval France. Prone to vows of vengeful wrath, she wielded a sword as mercilessly as any man. Here's how Moore described her in 1934: "She was a creature of wildest paradox, this warrior lady of Joiry, hot as a red coal, chill as steel, satiny of body and iron of soul. The set of her chin was firm, but her mouth betrayed a tenderness she would have died before admitting. But she was raging now."

Sound like a Warrior Princess we know? Taken as a whole, the Jirel saga is stronger on atmosphere than on plot and gets a bit repetitive when read in one sitting, but any one of the stories could be converted into a *Xena* episode with only the slightest cosmetic surgery and a bottle of hair dye.

Jirel's most famous literary descendant, prior to Xena, is

undoubtedly Red Sonja, a contemporary of Conan the Barbarian who has swung her bloody sword through comic books, novels, a feature film, television, and innumerable science-fiction-convention costume contests. Though she is often believed to be a creation of Robert T. Howard, the author of the original Conan stories, her origins are actually a bit murkier.

Howard created a number of intriguing heroines in his Conan stories, such as Belit, pirate queen of the Black Coast, and Valeria of the Red Brotherhood (memorably played by Sandahl Bergman in the first *Conan* movie), but Red Sonja was not among them. What he did do was introduce a character named Red Sonya (with a *y*) into a historical adventure, "The Shadow of the Vulture," set in sixteenth-century Vienna. First published in the January 1934 issue of *The Magic Carpet Magazine*, Howard's tale featured a red-haired she-devil intent on revenge against the Turkish invaders who destroyed her family and carried off her sister. The story suggests that there are further adventures to come, but they were never written; *The Magic Carpet* folded, and Howard eventually committed suicide. (Not because of the magazine's cancellation, mind you.)

More than forty years later, writer Roy Thomas and artist Barry Smith converted Howard's old story into an issue of the *Conan the Barbarian* comic book, in the process transforming Red Sonya of Rogatino into Red Sonja of ancient Hykrania. Sonja was popular enough that she was granted her own comic book series, which eventually begot a series of paperback novels and a 1985 movie starring Brigitte Nielsen as a rather wooden Sonja. The movie was not a success either artistically or financially, and Red Sonja has kept a low profile since, although she still shows up in Marvel Comics now and then, even guest-starring with Spider-Man on at least one occasion. Most recently, Sonja had appeared in the new syndicated *Conan* television series, now played with all the warrior spirit of a snitty receptionist by Angelica Bridges, whose stiff performance reminds you just how easy Lucy Lawless makes it look.

Xena producer Rob Tapert has publicly admitted his fondness for the old Sonja comics, and there are definite similarities between that character and today's Warrior Princess. Like Xena, Red Sonja embarked on her sword-and-sorcery career after heartless raiders attacked her simple peasant family, and she too later faced all manner of ancient gods, warlords, and kings. Unlike Xena, however, Sonja was bound by a sacred oath of celibacy that not even Conan could overcome. Nor were there ever any rumors about Sonja and a chatty young bard . . .

Appropriately, scribe Roy Thomas, who originally brought Red Sonja to comics, is now the primary scripter of the popular *Xena: Warrior Princess* comic books, published by Topps. He also cowrote the story for an episode of the *Xena* television show. What goes around comes around . . . just like a chakram.

Another major influence on Xena's creation was the entire genre of hyperactive Hong Kong action flicks. Tapert was particularly inspired by *The Bride with White Hair*, a 1993 fantasy adventure directed by Ronny Yu and starring Brigitte Lin Ching Hsia as the Bride, a feral wolf girl who grows up to be a one-woman killing machine. Director Yu described his movie as "a period swordplay drama with a contemporary flavor," which could also serve as a good description of *Xena: Warrior Princess*. The deadly heroine of *Bride* lacks a chakram, but she wields a nasty whip, much as Xena has been known to do. The comparisons with *Bride* can be seen most clearly in Xena's second episode on *Hercules*, "The Gauntlet," which borrows the eponymous ordeal from the earliest film, transforming it into a major turning point in the life of the Warrior Princess.

Proof that Trekkies Have Too Much Spare Time . . .

Lucy Lawless comes in second to Jeri Ryan of *Star Trek: Voyager* in a poll of the sexiest stars on television. (*TV Guide,* December 27, 1997)

And just as Jirel and Sonja inspired Xena, the tremendous success of *Xena: Warrior Princess* has led to a bold new era of unapologetic action heroines on television, including *Buffy, the Vampire Slayer* (yay, Buffy!), *La Femme Nikita*, and the indomitable Seven of Nine on *Star Trek: Voyager*. Even the syndicated *New Adventures of Robin Hood* shamelessly transformed its Maid Marian into a leather-clad Xena clone. Needless to say, this fascinating flurry of female fighters has sparked much intense on-line discussion on who would win in a fair fight, Buffy vs. Xena or Xena vs. Nikita. (The outcome, it is generally conceded, depends on whether the twentieth-century heroines can bring modern automatic weapons to the fray.) Even Disney got into the act, with the 1998 animated feature *Mulan*, featuring a young Asian heroine who defies tradition to become a mighty warrior.

And there's more to come. The folks behind the long-running cult favorite *Highlander* are already gearing up a spin-off series, tentatively titled *Highlander: The Raven*, and starring an immortal swordswoman played by former Miss America Elizabeth Gracen.

Finally, in a development that can only be seen as eerily in-evitable, Warner Bros. is conducting a worldwide talent search to find an exciting new actress to star in a brand-new television version of . . . *Wonder Woman*!

No word yet on whether Lucy intends to watch.

CHAPTER III

THE ROAD TO XENA

"Here, you fall at our feet," snarls Lysia the Amazon to Hercules, son of Zeus, seconds before delivering a vicious kick to his privates. Actress Lucy Lawless, billed sixth in the credits of *Hercules and the Amazon Women*, probably had no idea how far that kick would take her.

Hercules and the Amazon Women (1994) was the first of five TV movies starring Kevin Sorbo as Hercules. Loosely based on the original Greek myths, the films were produced by Renaissance Pictures for Universal Television and sold as part of a self-described "Action Pack" of syndicated adventure programs. Renaissance' founders Sam Raimi and Rob Tapert, perhaps best known for the wildly energetic *Evil Dead* series of comic horror films, worked with screenwriter Christian Williams to adapt the ancient legends for modern TV audiences, emphasizing spectacular action sequences along with a certain irreverent humor. Williams eventually left the project after the first batch of movies, but Raimi, and especially Tapert, have continued to oversee both *Hercules* and *Xena* to this day.

With the rugged—and less expensive—landscapes of New Zealand subbing for ancient Greece, the Hercules movies offered acting opportunities to a number of local talents—including a young actress with the unlikely name of Lucy

Lawless. Born Lucy Ryan, Lawless was a former Mrs. New Zealand and onetime aspiring opera singer, with only a handful of acting credits, most notably a guest appearance on the cable series *Ray Bradbury Theater* and a two-year stint as the cohost of a popular New Zealand travel program. Originally considered, along with many other candidates, for the meaty role of Hippolyta, Queen of the Amazons, Lawless ended up playing Hippolyta's most dangerous lieutenant, the lethal female warrior Lysia.

Looking back with the benefit of flawless hindsight, it's easy to see the early glimmerings of Xena in Lawless's portrayal of Lysia, who has a similarly take-no-prisoners approach to life. "No small talk, just sex," she orders none other than Zeus himself (played by movie legend Anthony Quinn) before ravishing the king of the gods in between fierce battles against Hercules and others. It's perhaps not surprising that the Amazons whom Xena later encounters regard the Warrior Princess as a true sister in spirit.

(In terms of future plot continuity, we should note that the twist ending of *Hercules and the Amazon Women* has Zeus reversing time and undoing the events of the movie, so that technically *Amazon Women* did not happen and Hercules and Lysia have never met. No wonder he didn't recognize the face when he ran into Xena later on!)

Lawless was not involved with the second Hercules movie, *Hercules and the Lost Kingdom* (1994), but that film introduces another face that would become just as familiar to *Xena* fans, that of American actress Renee O'Connor, who a few years later would be cast as Xena's faithful sidekick and partner, Gabrielle. O'Connor had previously appeared on television in everything from *The Mickey Mouse Club* to *Tales from the Crypt*, before flying down to New Zealand to play opposite Kevin Sorbo's Hercules. Just as Lysia prefigures Xena, O'Connor's character in *Lost Kingdom* is strikingly similar to Gabrielle; Deianeira is a scrappy, talkative young virgin who decides to tag along with Hercules despite his initial efforts to discourage her. A future-sidekick-in-training, in other words.

"Ten Years Ago . . ."

Have you noticed yet that almost everything interesting that ever happened to Xena took place "ten years ago"? Even allowing for plus or minus a year or two to adjust for this or that season, Xena was awfully busy a decade ago. Consider, ten years ago she

—befriended the young girl who would grow up to be the Black Wolf,

—nearly died fighting the giant Gareth somewhere near Corinth,

—led her army in battle against Bacchus, leading to the death of Eurydice,

—learned the secrets of M'Lila, captured and loved Julius Caesar, survived crucifixion,

—traveled to Chin, joined forces with Borias, accepted (for a time) the guidance of Lao Ma,

—waged war against the Centaurs, sought the Ixion Stone, and gave birth to Solan.

That's not a year, that's a miniseries!

Deianeira is not quite as sunny as Gabrielle, having grown up orphaned and alone, but she gets herself into and out of trouble with as much ease. She also looks astonishingly like the young Melissa Gilbert in *Little House on the Prairie*, but that's neither here nor there. Another amazing coincidence: Deianeira eventually ends up as the rightful queen of the lost kingdom of Troy; Gabrielle would someday claim the title Queen of the Amazons.

(To avoid confusion, the character in *Lost Kingdom* is apparently not the same Deianeira, played by Tawny Kitaen, who would later marry Hercules and bear his children.)

Also showing up in the second movie was Robert Trebor, playing a comical slave who indignantly insists that he is *not* a eunuch. Trebor would be seen in both *Hercules* and *Xena* as the comically greedy Salmoneus, who presumably isn't a

eunuch either. So much for the movies. A year later, when
Hercules returned to television as the star of a weekly syndi-
cated series, Lucy Lawless returned as well . . . but not yet as
Xena.

In "As Darkness Falls," the sixth episode of *Hercules: The
Legendary Journeys*, Lawless played Lyla, a reckless and wild
young woman who scandalizes her neighbors by consorting
openly with Centaurs. Although not nearly as fierce as Lysia
the Amazon, Lawless is hardly playing an ingenue or mere
damsel in distress; before the episode is half over, Lyla has attempted to seduce Hercules, then poisoned him. Like the
Warrior Princess to come, however, Lyla eventually sees the
error of her ways—and in less than half the time it would take
Xena.

Lawless played Lyla one more time in a second-season *Hercules* episode titled "Outcast." Now the mother of a Centaur
child, Lyla is killed by a racist gang but is inexplicably brought
back to life by Zeus to provide a somewhat forced happy ending. Unfortunately, motherhood seems to have mellowed
Lyla, who makes less of an impact this time around. (Being
dead most of the episode might also have something to do
with that.) Like Lyla, Xena would cope with anti-Centaur
prejudice in future episodes of her own series, eventually becoming the godmother of another half-breed Centaur child.
Robert Trebor also guest-stars as Salmoneus in "Outcast," as
he does in many of Xena's early appearances on *Hercules*.

And what about those appearances? Well, the story of how
Lucy Lawless lucked into the part of Xena when actress
Vanessa Angel (*Weird Science*) fell ill at the last moment has
been widely reported elsewhere. In retrospect, however,
from Lysia to Lyla to Xena, and from Deianeira to Gabrielle,
the road to Xena seems predestined by Syndicatia, the fabled
Muse of television.

Now all that remained was for the son of Zeus to meet up
with a Warrior Princess . . .

CHAPTER IV

THE XENA CHRONICLES

In the beginning, there were the episodes. All hype and hoopla aside, the heart of the Warrior Princess and her adventures can be found in the more than sixty hour-long episodes of *Xena: Warrior Princess*, plus the occasional installment of *Hercules: The Legendary Journeys*. What follows is an unauthorized, opinionated, and arguably obsessive* look at the saga as it has developed, beginning with the three *Hercules* episodes that introduced the character of Xena and proceeding through to the end of the third season.

As noted earlier, *Xena* often does to history and mythology what Xena herself does to the mangled bodies of her victims. This is all part of the fun, but in the best interests of civilization as we know it, each entry here attempts to compare the individual episodes with the actual historical record. If some readers decide afterward that they prefer the World According to Xena . . . well, that's up to them. My hands are clean.

Rating the episodes against each other is a dangerous game, but it's also irresistible. Someone is bound to disagree, and the Spartan judge will automatically deduct one sword from any episode that mentions Athens, but arguing vehemently about what are ultimately subjective opinions is a large

*Editor's note: no argument, it's obsessive.

part of what fandom is all about. Thus, please take heed of the highly scientific rating system below:

⚔⚔⚔⚔	Divinely inspired by the Muses
⚔⚔⚔	A tale fit for a bard
⚔⚔	Good enough for a night around the campfire
⚔	Even a Warrior Princess can have an off day.

Finally, just to really go out on a limb, as Xena herself has been known to do, the Xena chronicles concludes with my personal list of the top ten *Xena* episodes of the first three seasons. Screams of protest ("I can't believe he included that one!" "But what about . . . ?") can be directed at me care of the publisher, but I'm already planning to run for safety, especially since I listed a couple of Joxer episodes.

Who's Joxer, you ask? Keep reading . . .

Hercules: The Legendary Journeys: The Warrior Princess

WRITTEN BY JOHN SCHULIAN
DIRECTED BY BRUCE SETH GREEN

It's that murdering warrior, Xena!
—Unnamed soldier, soon to be deceased

What Happens

A mysterious Warrior Princess comes between Hercules and his best friend, Iolaus. History will never be the same . . .

Remarks

Xena makes a memorable first impression on TV viewers, and boy, is she nasty! It's hard to spot a future heroine in this scheming, duplicitous, homicidal femme fatale who seduces Iolaus (Michael Hurst) as part of her diabolical scheme to destroy the Son of Zeus and conquer the Arcadian highlands. Certainly the screenplay minces no words about her less-than-sterling character, describing her as "a murdering harlot," "a crazy woman," and "a monster just like the Hydra." She's responsible for the deaths of at least six people in this episode alone, including her lover, Theodorus, whom she sends on a suicide mission, and another lieutenant, Estragon, whom she casually executes for failing to kill Hercules, and she relies on deceit and treachery as much as on her formidable fighting skills. She even beats herself up, then tells the gullible Iolaus that Hercules attacked her. This is a future feminist role model? If the idea of eventually reforming Xena was indeed lurking in the minds of her creators, then they certainly set themselves a challenge.

This Xena makes much more use of her feminine wiles to maintain the loyalty of her followers than the later Xena would. (Far be it from me to invoke a comparison between the bewitched Theodorus and a certain blond storyteller.) She also seems to be in possession of her own fortress, unlike the rootless wanderer she would eventually become. Her skin looks paler, too, and her voice sounds somewhat different from the Xena of the future.

Still, many of Xena's basic attributes are already in place: the chakram (identified in the original script as "a razor-sharp round throwing device"), the murderous rages, the chanting Bulgarian choir in the background. Although originally attired in a series of seductive gowns, she eventually dons a slightly more elaborate version of what would become her standard armor, complete with ornate shoulder-pieces that perch atop her arms like gargoyle wings. All that's missing now is the neck pinch, the battle cry, the sidekick, and an improved attitude toward the rest of the world. Oh, yeah, and Argo, too. (The Xena we know would never intentionally injure Argo the way she cripples an anonymous horse here.)

Xena's steamy hot tub scene with Iolaus (actually, it was filmed in the distinctly unerotic atmosphere of a chilly warehouse in Auckland City) sets a precedent for love scenes to come; as we'll see, warm and cozy baths will repeatedly serve as preludes to seduction and/or subtext. (See also "The Path Not Taken," "A Day in the Life," "A Comedy of Eros," "The Debt," and "King of Assassins.") Makes sense to me. Traipsing all over the countryside fighting evil is probably dirty, sweaty work. I'd want to wash up before a hot date, too.

In retrospect, it's intriguing that Xena tells Iolaus that her father and all three brothers died in battle. She's lying, of course, but why *three* brothers? After all, we would later learn that Xena actually has two brothers, only one of whom, Lyceus, is pushing up daisies . . . so far. And her father is still alive, at least as far as she knows. (See "The Furies" for the full scoop on Xena's mysterious parentage.)

Oddly enough, for all that Xena is built up here as a fighter to rival Hercules, she and Herc never battle each other in this episode, much as Luke Skywalker never fought Darth Vader in the first *Star Wars* movie. A genuine physical confrontation would have to wait until "The Gauntlet." Little did the Son of Zeus dream that the villainess who escapes on her horse at the end of this first encounter would someday eclipse him in popularity.

Schulian and Green would later collaborate on "Unchained Heart," the third chapter of the original Xena trilogy. Green has since gone on to direct episodes of *Xena*, *seaQuest DSV*, and *Buffy the Vampire Slayer*.

Reality Check

Unlike Hercules and Iolaus, Xena cannot be found in classical mythology. The name "Xena" means "guest" in Greek, a rather innocuous appellation for such a fierce character. Hercules' mother, Alcmene, seemed to be of the opinion that it was a reasonably common name in that place and time. "There must be lots of other Xenas in the world," she tells Hercules, although we have yet to meet any such namesake on either *Hercules* or *Xena*.

The chakram is an authentic historical weapon used primarily by the Sikhs of India, who wore them around their turbans. How and where the Warrior Princess became so proficient in its use has yet to be revealed.

Rating: ⟨⟨⟨

Hercules: The Legendary Journeys: The Gauntlet

WRITTEN BY ROBERT BIELAK
DIRECTED BY JACK PEREZ

Oh, proud warrioress? —Salmoneus

What Happens

Xena's troops turn on her after she commits an unexpected act of mercy. Later, Hercules and Xena join forces to stop her former army from conquering Parthia.

Remarks

Lucy Lawless first heard rumors of a spin-off series while filming this episode, and by the time "The Gauntlet" first aired, *Xena: Warrior Princess* was already in the works. The big question then was, Could such a nefarious character really be transformed into a true heroine?

Xena's redemption does not come easily. The character shows her debt to *The Bride with White Hair* most clearly in this episode's brutal gauntlet sequence, which is lifted from an almost identical scene in *Bride*, when that movie's female warrior must endure the same ordeal in order to leave the evil cult that has taught her to be a lethal killing machine. Similarly, Xena must be symbolically punished for her crimes before getting her own series.

Already, it can be noted, Xena is more honorable and less duplicitous than she was in her previous appearance. She may still be a ruthless warrior, but she at least offers besieged villages a chance to surrender before she annihilates them, slaying all the men but sparing the women and children . . . unlike her even more vicious, not to mention uglier, successor, Darphus (Matthew Chamberlain). Looking back, we see that the scene in which she displays the bodies of her victims contains chilling echoes of her own crucifixion at the hands of Caesar—as we would learn a couple of years later.

Curiously, the first character to see faint glimmerings of good in Xena, thus encouraging the viewer to do the same, is Salmoneus, a comic-relief character who had previously appeared in a number of *Hercules* episodes, beginning with "The Road of Calydon." Played by Robert Trebor, Salmoneus is drafted into service as Xena's personal jester and confidant, and he goes a long way toward uniting Hercules and Xena against Darphus. He must be a better salesman than he appears, given how quickly Herc comes around to the pro-Xena camp, which is not entirely convincing, considering all the atrocities and treachery that Xena has been responsible for. It's probably just as well, though, that Iolaus did not tag along on this adventure; he would have brought too many bad memories with him. Salmoneus would stick around for Part 3 of the trilogy, then make a handful of appearances on *Xena*. (See "The Black Wolf," "The Greater Good," and "Here She Comes . . . Miss Amphipolis.")

Despite Salmoneus's efforts at peacemaking, we still get the first no-holds-barred battle between Xena and Hercules, pitting Herc's strength and skill against Xena's acrobatics and chakram. The Son of Zeus wins, naturally—it's still his show—but Xena partisans can take comfort in the notion that the Warrior Princess had not yet fully recovered from the harrowing ordeal of the gauntlet. Unfortunately, Xena's subsequent reformation makes any true rematch unlikely.

The recipe, we see, for successfully turning a bad guy into a good guy is a simple one: Make her pay, throw her up against someone worse, then let her be accepted by someone the audience knows they can trust. If Hercules can forgive Xena, then so can the rest of us.

On the fashion front, Xena is still wearing those wild shoulder-pieces, along with an unwieldy cape, but she eventually picks up a·suit of tacky golden armor that looks more like something from a Vegas floor show than a Parthian battlefield. Thankfully, it has not been seen since.

If you listen carefully during the opening battle, you can hear, despite the pounding music, the first rendition of Xena's soon-to-be infamous battle cry. *Yi-yi-yi-yi!*

In an ominous epilogue, a cloaked figure identified only as an "emissary" of Ares appears to resurrect Darphus (now dead at Xena's hand) and send him forth in search of revenge. To date, the true identity of this emissary has yet to be revealed, although we are free to speculate. Strife? Hades? Ares himself? If the last, then he has given up on Xena with surprising speed; she has barely turned over her new leaf and Ares is already lining up a replacement? Later adventures would reveal that the Warrior Princess and the God of War have a much more complicated love/hate relationship than this brief scene implies.

Darphus is the first of Xena's vanquished foes to return from the grave, but he's far from the last. See "Callisto" for the holder of the current world record.

Reality Check

Xena's army is wandering far afield. Not only was the kingdom of Parthia, founded in 251 B.C., not a peninsula, as described here, it wasn't even in Greece, but closer to what is now modern-day Iran. In any event, there are no known accounts of its being invaded by a fearless female warlord.

Rating: ⅔⅔⅔

Hercules: The Legendary Journeys: Unchained Heart

WRITTEN BY JOHN SCHULIAN
DIRECTED BY BRUCE SETH GREEN

She's a warrior in the truest sense of the word.
—Hercules

What Happens

Xena and Hercules find time for romance before battling both Darphus and his monstrous "dog." Xena feeds Darphus to the doggie, then heads off to her own series.

Remarks

Probably the weakest chapter of the Xena trilogy, despite the big love scene between Kevin Sorbo and Lucy Lawless, which is reputedly even more intense on the video release. To be honest, Xena seems to have mellowed too much. Along with a conscience, she has acquired poufy big hair and a more girlish air. Thoroughly smitten with Hercules, she gazes at him adoringly and appears to have lost much of her edge.

> "I'm not a sex symbol in my own house. I'm boring old Mom."
> —Lucy Lawless (*TV Guide*, November 22–28, 1997)

Xena unchained bears only a slight resemblance to the formidable and intimidating she-devil seen in her first two appearances; fortunately, she would get back to her old self by the time her own series came along. (See "Sins of the Past.") Still, even here, Xena hasn't been completely domesticated. She refuses to cook dinner for Hercules and the others, in what would be only the first of many references to her dubious culinary skills.

If Herc and Xena have gotten awfully chummy all of a sudden, considering she was a "murdering harlot" only two episodes ago, Iolaus still holds an understandable grudge after Xena's vampish trickery in "The Warrior Princess." He eventually comes around after Xena saves his life, although they would not achieve a full reconciliation until "Prometheus" a season later. Hercules and Xena would meet next in "Prometheus" as well, but the romantic sparks between them would never again ignite as they do here. Despite graduating to her own series, Xena would continue to make occasional guest appearances on *Hercules* in such episodes as "Judgment Day," "Stranger in a Strange World," and "Armageddon Now II."

Costumers should note that Xena's armor still includes the cape and shoulder-pieces, but not for much longer.

Although the villainous Darphus goes to Hades for good this time, he would briefly reappear in the fourth-season *Hercules* episode "Armageddon Now II," which depicted an alternate time line in which Xena never reformed and Darphus never usurped her army. Guess she didn't save any babies that time around . . .

Reality Check

The man-eating "Graegus," given to Darphus by Ares' emissary, is consistently described as a monstrous dog, even though the computer-generated creature seen on the screen looks more like a relative of Godzilla. Graegus had been introduced in a previous *Hercules* episode, "The Vanishing Dead." If he has any basis in history or mythology, I've been unable to find it.

Rating: ⚡⚡

YEAR 1 A.X.

Personally, *Hercules* infected me with the Xenaverse virus. Like many viewers who stumble onto either show for the first time, I didn't get *Hercules* for a while. What was with the contemporary slang and the shameless anachronism? Why did Aphrodite talk like she had just surfed in from California? Didn't these "Action Pack" people know anything about history or mythology? I grumped indignantly, just as certain friends and acquaintances still do when confronted with the televised exploits of the Warrior Princess.

Eventually—I'm not sure when—I realized that not only did the show's creators know what they were doing, they were doing it on purpose. Furthermore, they were working from a surprisingly broad knowledge of myth and history that they deliberately twisted and tweaked to suit their purposes. *Hercules* wasn't *supposed* to be historically accurate; anyone who couldn't get past that was missing out on a lot of good, clean fun.

Thus enlightened, I was able to fully appreciate *Xena: Warrior Princess* from the very beginning.

Sins of the Past

STORY BY ROBERT TAPERT
WRITTEN BY R. J. STEWART
DIRECTED BY DOUG LEFLER

Celebrate your dark side. Don't run away from it.
—Draco to Xena

What Happens

Xena gets a hostile reception when she returns to her native Amphipolis, now menaced by one of her old warlord buddies. But a young would-be bard is determined to befriend the Warrior Princess, whether she likes it or not.

Remarks

The solo adventures of *Xena: Warrior Princess* get off to a strong start, effectively showcasing the series' distinctive mixture of action, humor, drama, special effects, and striking New Zealand scenery while simultaneously fleshing out Xena's murky past and pairing her up with a new and appealing sidekick all her own. Renee O'Connor as Gabrielle now looks shockingly young in her first appearance, but the character's natural ebullience already plays nicely off Xena's battle-hardened toughness. Despite her naiveté, Gabby proves her smarts (and won over this viewer right here) by talking her way out of the cannibalistic clutches of a hungry cyclops in a scene forever immortalized in the opening credits.

As for Xena herself, the show's creators bravely chose to follow the advice of the warlord Draco, quoted above: They did not run away from Xena's bloodthirsty history. One supposes that it must have been tempting, after successfully reforming the character on *Hercules*, to whitewash their new heroine's villainous roots and never refer to them again. Instead, "Sins of the Past" finds Xena confronted by those sins everywhere she turns; even her own mother does not trust her, pulling a sword on her the moment they're reunited. Perhaps symbolically, the episode begins with Xena's attempting to bury her past—literally—consigning her armor and weapons to a hole in the ground, before taking them up again to defend Gabrielle and her fellow villagers.

From the beginning, Xena's problematic origins have been transformed from a potential liability to a rich source of dramatic possibilities. As Lawless has said of her character, "The day she finds peace with herself will be the last day of the series" (*TV Guide,* May 3–9, 1997).

We learn a good deal more about Xena's past, meeting her estranged mother, Cyrene (Darien Takle), who blames Xena for the death of her own brother, killed in one of Xena's wars—along with many of the young men of Amphipolis—but many mysteries remain. If her mother runs a tavern, where did the "Princess" in "Warrior Princess" come from? And how did an ordinary peasant girl like Xena become the terror of the ancient world? Many of these questions would not be answered until such second- and third-season episodes as "Destiny" and "The Debt." Despite Xena's seemingly humble roots, her martyred brother, who would not receive a name until "Death Mask," has a tomb worthy of minor nobility, although I suppose we can assume that Xena the warlord had the tomb constructed with the spoils of her conquests. Curiously, neither Xena nor her mom mentions Xena's *other* brother, whose existence would also be revealed in "Death Mask," or her father, whom we would encounter (sort of) in "Ties That Bind."

With all this dysfunctional family stuff going on, perhaps it's not surprising that we hear a bit about the problems of Oedipus, which apparently took place only a few years earlier and a couple of miles down the road. Other tidbits of Xena lore to file away: Xena once blinded a man-eating cyclops, and she gave the warlord Draco a nasty scar on his face when he tried to "get rough" with her. Her soon-to-be-legendary pinch interrogation is demonstrated here for the first time.

Besides Gabrielle and Cyrene, this premiere episode also introduces a number of friends and relations whom we would meet again, including Gabrielle's sister Lila (Willa O'Neill), her jilted fiancé Perdicas (as played by Anton Bentley, much larger and homelier than he would be in subsequent appearances), and the fierce Draco (charismatically played by Jay Laga'aia), undoubtedly the most appealing of the various warlords Xena has run into before or since. Lila would be seen next in "The Prodigal," Perdicas would return, greatly changed, in "Beware of Greeks Bearing Gifts," while Draco, alas, would stay away until the second-season closer, "A Comedy of Eros." (He appears prominently, however, in the first Xena novel, *The Empty Throne*, by Ru Emerson.)

The blinded cyclops who let Gabrielle get away has been too ashamed to show his face again.

Speaking of recurring characters, Xena's horse still doesn't have a name, but judging from its apparent gender, the stallion in this episode may not be Argo after all.

The climactic battle between Xena and Draco, conducted atop the heads of the hapless spectators, anticipates many equally imaginative fights on precarious perches, including treetops ("Hooves and Harlots"), ladders ("Callisto"), hanging vines ("The Quest"), and flagpoles ("The Furies").

Reality Check

Like Xena herself, Gabrielle was created without reference to any actual historical personage. Her name, derived from the Hebrew "Gabrielle," meaning "man of God" or "God is mighty," is more than a little anachronistic for a girl from a Grecian backwater. (Funny, she doesn't look Jewish.) As far as we know, Gabby would not even meet a Hebrew until she went on the road with Xena. Then again, when you think about it, there aren't a lot of female names in Greek literature that come with the same angelic, innocent connotations. Electra, Jocasta, Medea . . . not a lot of sweet young ingenues there.

Ironically, the barbaric Draco may have been named after his polar opposite, an Athenian statesman noted for composing Athens's first written code of laws during the seventh century B.C.

Rating: ϤϤϤϤ

Chariots of War

WRITTEN BY ADAM ARMUS & NORA KAY FOSTER
STORY BY J. BECKER AND J. PEREZ
DIRECTED BY HARLEY COKELESS

I'm not very good at this horse thing. —Gabrielle

What Happens

Xena defends a family of settlers from yet another warlord, while Gabrielle bonds with a young warrior troubled by career and family problems. But a stray arrow almost brings the Warrior Princess's own career to an abrupt halt.

Remarks

To be honest, this episode left little or no impression on my memory the first time around, but subsequent viewings reveal an enjoyable Greco-Roman version of *Shane*, with both Xena and Gabby finding a bit of romance along the way. (No, not with each other.) Still, the "berserk warlord threatens helpless village" plot is already starting to get a bit stale. Darphus, Draco, Cycnus ... where are all these guys coming from? This time the marauders wear vaguely Mongol-looking helmets, but they invoke Ares, the god of war, just as their predecessors have. (See "The Reckoning" for more on Ares.)

The rewards of this episode lie mostly in some nice character touches, along with a rousing finale featuring the eponymous chariots. Xena finds herself briefly tempted by the cozy pleasures of domesticity in the form of a good-looking settler and his three cute kids, while Gabrielle, having ditched her hulking betrothed last episode, meets the first of several sensitive young hunks who would catch her eye this season.

In hindsight, it's also fun to watch Xena and Gabrielle at the very beginning of their partnership. At this point Xena still doesn't seem to know what to make of this cheery, chatty tagalong. Not surprisingly, she goes out of her way to keep her self-appointed sidekick away from the bulk of the action until the very end—when Gabby proves just how bad a horsewoman she really is.

Another highlight, in a wince-worthy way, comes when Xena, with the kindly settler's queasy assistance, pushes that nasty arrow out through her back, then cauterizes the gaping wound with a hot poker. She tersely claims to have done this before, and she would in fact subject Gabrielle to the same ordeal a few years later in "One Against an Army," when the sidekick receives a similar wound.

More crumbs of Xena's colorful past are doled out, including the revelation that she once fought a giant (Gareth from

"Giant Killer" and "A Day in the Life"?) and took part in a fierce battle in Corinth a few years before. As in the previous episode, Xena's infamous reputation precedes her and she finds herself viewed with fear and suspicion by the very people she is trying to save. Except for Darius the handsome farmer, of course.

"Chariots of War" is the first installment penned by the writing team of Armus and Foster, who would later provide some of the series' most humorous episodes, including "For Him the Bell Tolls" and "The Xena Scrolls."

Reality Check

Darius and his fellow settlers are refugees from the Trojan War, which sounds as though it has been going on for some time. The real Trojan War came to its celebrated end in 1193 B.C., an event that Xena and Gabrielle would witness later this season in "Beware of Greeks Bearing Gifts."

Shane, starring Alan Ladd as a reluctant gunslinger who comes to the aid of a frontier family, was released in 1953. "Chariots of War" also bears a familial resemblance to any number of episodes of *The Fugitive*, *Kung Fu*, *The Incredible Hulk*, etc.

Rating: ХХ

Dreamworker

WRITTEN BY STEVEN L. SEARS
DIRECTED BY BRUCE SETH GREEN

Blood innocence?   —Xena

What Happens

A cult of evil mystics kidnaps Gabrielle and tries to force her to take a life. To rescue Gabby before the innocent girl must kill or be killed, Xena travels through a magical "dreamscape passage," where she is confronted by specters from her bloody past.

Remarks

More overtly fantastical than the preceding episodes, "Dreamworker" provides a welcome relief from marauding warlords while testing the ingenuity and character of both our heroines. Writer Sears, who would work on numerous future episodes, saw his story as "a huge chance to immediately explore the difference between these two characters." Gabrielle, who has never killed another human being, learns that, on second thought, maybe she doesn't really want to be the fierce warrior that Xena is, while the Warrior Princess, brought face-to-face with her guilty conscience, becomes determined to preserve the younger woman's "blood innocence," a theme that would be further explored in such episodes as "Return of Callisto" and (especially) "The Deliverer."

More foreshadowing can be found in the oriental robes that Xena inexplicably wears on her journey through her own psyche. An astonishingly prescient hint at Xena's lost years in China, which would stay hidden until well into the third season? Or merely homage to the Hong Kong movies that inspired her creators? Gabrielle also anticipates her future weapon of choice by defending herself with an improvised staff that she creates by breaking off the tip of a spear. The "breast dagger" that Xena confiscates from Gabrielle near the beginning of this episode would also find a use in days to come, most notably in "Death Mask."

Turning from the future to the past, "Dreamworker" reveals a couple of absolutely first-rate bits of trivia. Did you know that the first man Xena ever killed was a scruffy raider named Termin, or that Gabby was born with six toes on her right foot? Well, now you do. (Don't bother looking for the extra digit; it's not there anymore.)

An intriguing loose end: After his defeat, the evil high priest warns Xena that she has made an enemy of Morpheus, the God of Dreams. Morpheus must be taking his time since, to date, this threat has not been carried out—unless Xena's having a lot of nightmares we don't know about. She would suffer through some bad dreams in "Intimate Stranger," but that was pretty clearly Ares' fault.

The script for "Dreamworker" is one of about half a dozen *Xena* scripts that have been offered for sale. They can be purchased via the mail, on the Internet, or at Xena conventions.

Needless to say, this would not be the last time Gabby is abducted, held hostage, and/or threatened with human sacrifice, execution, a forced marriage, or all of the above. Ah, well, such is the life of a sidekick . . .

Reality Check

Morpheus, the Greek god of dreams, was indeed one of three dream brothers, as explained in this episode. A fairly abstract and esoteric deity, he doesn't have much personality in the old stories, although, as far as I know, there's nothing in the mythology to suggest that he was particularly darker than his brothers or that he had any special interest in the blood innocence of his brides. These days, Morpheus is probably best known as the enigmatic protagonist of the award-winning *Sandman* comic book series, written by Neil Gaiman. *Xena* fans may want to check out some of the *Sandman* comics and graphic novels, as the series frequently touches on many of the same mythological elements found in *Xena*.

Rating: ⵣⵣⵣⵣ

Cradle of Hope

WRITTEN BY TERRENCE WINTER
DIRECTED BY MICHAEL LEVINE

Imagine sending a baby down a river. —Gabrielle

What Happens

When an oracle proclaims that a newborn baby will one day claim the throne of a powerful king, Xena must defend the orphaned infant from those who would harm him. Her task is not made any easier when a woman named Pandora misplaces her box.

Remarks

It was the uproarious climax of this episode that hooked me on *Xena* once and for all. As Xena battles half a dozen armed guards while simultaneously hurling the wide-eyed baby around like a football, the scene plays like some crazed mutant hybrid of *Raising Arizona* and *The Three Musketeers*, hitting a hilarious peak when the outnumbered Warrior Princess tosses the baby skyward, dispatches her foes with a few swift thrusts of her sword, then catches the kid on his way down. To me, this remains one of the archetypal, jaw-dropping *Xena* moments.

The rest of the episode's not bad either, although Gabrielle has little to do except keep Pandora and the baby company while Xena dons a harem costume to infiltrate the king's palace. The inclusion of Pandora and her box, or, more specifically, the granddaughter of the original Pandora, launches a *Xena* tradition of reworking classic stories from myth and history, just as the discovery of a baby set adrift in a basket is only the first time the show would borrow from the Old Testament, most notably in "Altared States" and "Giant Killer."

Edward Newborn as King Gregor gets a nice close-up in the credit sequence every week as the "king" in "ancient gods, warlords, and kings," but otherwise has not been seen since, although his character is mentioned both in the next episode and in "The Dirty Half Dozen" a few years later. (King Gregor is also prominently featured in a *Xena vs. Callisto* comic book series published in 1998.)

Is it just me, though, or does the king's evil adviser Nemos, played by Simon Prast, look like Tom Hanks with a bad goatee? I kept expecting him to offer Xena a box of chocolates or a trip on *Apollo 13*.

"Cradle of Hope" reveals that Xena's many talents include exotic dancing and fire-breathing, talents shared in real life by Lucy Lawless, who performs the latter stunt again in several upcoming episodes. "I use milk to coat the membranes of my mouth and stomach," she told readers of *The Chakram*, the official Xena Fan Club newsletter. "I don't do it every day. And I don't try to do anything fancy."

Another baby would be sent down a river, under far more harrowing circumstances, in "Gabrielle's Hope." Gabby's cheery observation here, in reference to the contents of Pandora's Box, that hope is "inside every one of us" would take on eerie (and perhaps unintended) resonances in the third season.

Reality Check

According to Greek mythology, the original Pandora was the first woman, created by Zeus to punish mankind. Pandora was given a box and told never to open it, but, like Eve with the apple, she succumbed to temptation and opened the box, releasing all the evils of the world. Only hope remained within.

"Cradle of Hope" embellishes the original myth by establishing that Pandora's descendants have been cursed to guard the box ever since, although it seems unlikely that the Pandora whom Xena encounters is only two generations removed from the first woman on Earth, which may be why Gabrielle doesn't mention that aspect of the story. The episode throws in a final twist by revealing, through Gabby's klutziness, that the box is actually empty.

The baby placed in the river to avoid execution echoes the biblical story of Moses, believed to have taken place sometime between 1500 and 1000 B.C. The child in this story is clearly not meant to be Moses, although the timing is about right. I guess there were a lot of babies floating around back then.

Rating: ⵣⵣⵣ

The Path Not Taken

WRITTEN BY JULE SHERMAN
DIRECTED BY STEPHEN L. POSEY

I don't want to stand over your grave.
—Xena to Marcus

What Happens

To rescue a kidnapped princess and prevent a war, Xena infiltrates the fortress of a notorious arms dealer. Her quest is complicated by the presence of an old lover, Marcus, who ultimately sacrifices his life for her sake.

Remarks

Near the beginning of this episode, Xena refuses to accept payment for rescuing the princess, just as she declined a reward from King Gregor the week before. All of which raises an interesting question: Where do Xena and Gabrielle get their money? They always seem to have enough dinars for supplies and the occasional meal. Granted, they probably save a fortune by sleeping under the stars, but where is the cash coming from? Does Xena have secret caches of gold and silver, squirreled away during her warlord days? And, if so, did she trust Gabby with the map?

Moving from money to sex, are we surprised that Marcus initially tries to renew his amorous relationship with Xena while the two of them are alone by the hot tub? The Warrior Princess's ill-fated romance with Marcus, whom she would encounter again in "Mortal Beloved," remains one of the series' most affecting love stories (not counting Xena and Gabrielle). The interracial union attracted praise from so unlikely a source as *Ms.* magazine, not exactly known for its coverage of fantasy adventure shows, which described Xena as "one of the first white women in TV history to passionately kiss a black man onscreen. Several times, in fact."

Xena puts her dubious reputation to good use here, although rumors of her shifted priorities are already circulating among her old cronies. The events of both "Sins of the Past" and "Cradle of Hope" come under discussion, with the latter adventure seeming to have taken place only a few weeks before. We also learn that the evil Xena once stole a large supply of weapons from someone named Escalus, then ransomed them back to him. Marcus assures Xena that she "never killed defenseless people," but we would discover later this season that this wasn't entirely true. (See "Callisto.")

With the emphasis on Xena and Marcus, little time is devoted to Gabby, who manages to talk her way *into* a dungeon. A nice touch, though, has Gabrielle worrying aloud about the possibility that Xena will revert to her old ways.

Xena's horse, still lacking a name, begins to acquire a bit of a personality, deftly disarming a knife-wielding thug with his rear hooves and hiding himself at Xena's instruction while she enters the fortress.

The plot device of a royal marriage bringing peace to two warring kingdoms would be employed again in "For Him the Bell Tolls" and "Been There, Done That." Mezentius, killed by Xena here, would return next season in "Remember Nothing." The dirge that Xena sings over Marcus's flaming bier can be found on Volume 1 of the *Xena* sound-track albums, as well as in subsequent episodes.

Sherman's script was adapted into a children's book, *Princess in Peril,* by Kerry Milliron (Random House, 1996). The simplified script replaces Mezentius with Draco and leaves out Marcus entirely!

Reality Check

"What we have here is a failure to communicate," Gabby informs her jailer, anticipating Strother Martin in *Cool Hand Luke* (1967) by a millennium or so.

Rating: ϫϫϫϫ

The Reckoning

WRITTEN BY PETER ALLAN FIELDS
DIRECTED BY CHARLES SIEBERT

I used to wonder what you looked like.
—Xena to Ares

What Happens

How's this for irony? Xena, who is responsible for the deaths of hundreds, is put on trial for the murder of three peasants whom she *didn't* kill—by the only village in Greece that apparently hasn't heard about the infamous Warrior Princess. Although Gabrielle tries to muster a defense, only Xena knows that the real killer is none other than Ares, the god of war.

Remarks

Up until now, the God of War has been frequently invoked by every warlord Xena has run up against, but this marks his first personal appearance and, judging from the quote above, the first time Xena has met Ares in the flesh. Actor Kevin Smith, who had previously played Hercules' envious brother, Iphicles, on *Hercules*, makes the first of several guest appearances as the cunning and seductive Ares. Having previously ordered Xena's death in "The Gauntlet," he now wants the Warrior Princess to get back to the business of carnage and conquest; like many men, divine or otherwise, he apparently did not truly appreciate what he had until he lost it.

Ares' repeated attempts to cajole Xena into returning to the dark side of the Force make for a slightly slow and talky episode, without a lot of humor and with only a couple of action scenes. Still, Gabrielle, after cooling her heels in the last two episodes, gets a chance to shine: facing down an enraged lynch mob, defending Xena in court, and playing detective in hopes of proving her friend's innocence (a task that might have been easier if Xena had bothered to tell Gabby what was going on). For her pains, she gets smacked around by Xena, who is temporarily consumed by a berserker fury, but she surprises Xena by standing by the Warrior Princess nonetheless. As before, Xena tries to shoo her new sidekick away at the first sign of trouble, but their nascent friendship achieves a minor breakthrough as Xena admits for the first time that she didn't really want Gabby to leave.

In an even more important development, Xena's faithful palomino horse finally gets a name: Argo.

You have to wonder, though, what happened to Xena's newly acquired army after she came to her senses? Did they all just shrug, pick up their swords, and go home?

Reality Check

Ares, known to the Romans as Mars, was the son of Zeus and Hera, making him the half brother of Hercules. Perhaps the least likable of the major Olympian deities, he is probably best known for his adulterous affair with Aphrodite, the goddess of love,

"You gotta a lesbo thing going on? " —New York hardhat to Ted Raimi (Joxer), according to Raimi. (New York Convention, February 21, 1998)

although this aspect of the myth has been avoided by both *Hercules* and *Xena*, where Ares and Aphrodite are usually portrayed as squabbling siblings. Prior to "The Reckoning," Ares had been depicted on a single episode of *Hercules* as a grotesque, skull-headed monster. From now on, the God of War would be consistently played by Smith, who would return to *Xena* shortly in "Ties That Bind."

During a discussion of legendary warriors of the past, Xena and Ares refer to Hector, Achilles, and Agamemnon—all heroes of the Trojan War—as long dead, even though it has been previously implied that the war is still going on.

Rating: ⭐⭐

The Titans

WRITTEN BY R. J. STEWART
DIRECTED BY ERIC BREVIG

If anyone can stall, it's Gabrielle.   —Xena

What Happens

Gabrielle accidentally releases three Titans from their stony prison, with catastrophic results. Xena is a bit annoyed, but she manages to keep Gabby alive long enough to reverse the spell and change the gigantic Titans back to stone.

Remarks

A fun episode with impressive special effects. The nastiest of the revived Titans, Hyperion, tears through a peasant village like Godzilla through Tokyo, accompanied by reverberating sound effects that add a convincing extra dimension to the illusion. Best of all, this makes four episodes in a row without any rampaging warlords to contend with, proving that the series has indeed managed to avoid the rut it seemed heading for.

Beyond the larger-than-life menace, the emphasis is on Gabrielle as we learn that this simple village girl possesses a surprising degree of scholarship, including a thorough knowledge of the difference between Dorian and Ionic rhythms. Also revealed, to Gabby's slight embarrassment, is her status as a virgin, although she flirts with the notion of changing this situation by means of Phyleus, an idealistic, if ineffectual, youth of the village. In the end, however, Gabrielle's virginity would remain inviolate until "Return of Callisto," midway through the second season.

Gabrielle and Xena have their first falling-out in this episode, beginning when Xena snappishly criticizes Gabby for slowing her down during the pursuit of a murderous criminal and resulting in a tense moment when Xena (and the viewer) are led to believe that Gabrielle may have impulsively slept with Phyleus. Xena claims the latter is none of her business, but she doesn't look too happy about it. Subtext fans may read into this what they wish.

Needless to say, our heroines reconcile before leaving the rescued village behind, but Xena still warns Gabby, "Don't you ever touch my horse again." I guess raising the Titans and almost destroying the world is one thing; messing with Argo is, well, a horse of a different color.

Reality Check

The ancient myths tell us that the Titans were a race of giants who ruled Earth and the heavens before the rise of the gods of Mount Olympus. Zeus overthrew his father, Cronus, the ruler of the Titans, and banished all but a few of the Titans to Tartarus, the lowest and bleakest level of the Underworld. The ranks of the Titans vary slightly from one account to another, but the three giants seen here—Crias, Theia, and Hyperion—are usually among their number. Xena would encounter another Titan, Prometheus, in the very next episode. The Titans would return, in a radically reconceived form, in the upcoming animated video, *Hercules & Xena: The Battle for Mount Olympus,* to be discussed later.

Edward Campbell, who plays Crias, the kindest of the three Titans, had previously appeared as a worried villager back in "The Warrior Princess."

Rating: ⟨⟨⟨

Prometheus

WRITTEN BY R. J. STEWART
DIRECTED BY STEPHEN POSEY

You're not much for girl talk, are you?
—Gabrielle to Xena

What Happens

When the Titan Prometheus is captured and chained by the gods, humanity begins to lose his gifts to mankind, including fire and the ability to heal. Hercules and Xena, along with Iolaus and Gabrielle, join forces to free Prometheus with the Sword of Hephaestus but face various obstacles dispatched by the wrathful Hera.

Remarks

Hercules and Iolaus make their debuts on *Xena,* reuniting with the Warrior Princess for the first time since "Unchained Heart," in this spectacular adventure featuring larger-than-life special effects. Beyond the giant flying eagle and bloodthirsty green warriors, what's most interesting here is the interaction between the two casts. Gabrielle meets Herc and bonds big time with her opposite number, Iolaus, while Xena and Iolaus find time to allude to their own "complicated" history, with Iolaus finally forgiving Xena for the way she used him way back when. "Tell her there's no hard feelings," he assures Gabrielle when it looks like he might never see the Warrior Princess again.

Romance also sparks between Hercules and Xena, for what would turn out to be the last time. From a strictly narrative point of view, it's not at all clear why they feel compelled to go their separate ways; in the real world, of course, the demands of headlining two different series pose a challenge that not even Cupid could overcome. The whole gang, Xena and Herc and Gabrielle and Iolaus, would reunite next year in an episode of *Hercules* titled "Judgment Day."

Gabrielle's interest in attending the Academy in Athens, mentioned a couple times here, foreshadows "Athens City Academy of the Performing Bards," aired later this season and cowritten by Stewart.

The script for "Prometheus" was among the first offered for sale to *Xena* fans via catalogs and conventions.

Reality Check

Prometheus is famous in myth for stealing fire from the gods and giving it to mankind, for which he was punished by Zeus, who chained him to Mount Caucasus and set a giant eagle (or vulture, depending on the account) to gnaw at his liver. (Ick!) Some stories also credit him with the very creation of mortal men and women. Hercules had previously liberated Prometheus, portrayed as a bearded figure quite unlike the hairless Titan seen here, in the 1994 TV movie *Hercules and the Circle of Fire*. The *Xena* version gets the basics right, although Hera, as Hercules' recurring nemesis, takes most of the blame for Prometheus's renewed captivity and torment. (Zeus remains a largely offscreen presence in the Xenaverse.) At least the giant bird is there, although it seems a lot more interested in chowing down on a fresh Warrior Princess than on Prometheus's liver.

As further punishment for the theft of fire, according to the myths, Zeus sent Pandora and her box of woes to Earth, which "Cradle of Hope" suggests took place a few generations before this episode.

The parable that Gabrielle tells the dying Iolaus, about how each of us is searching for our other half, dates back to Plato's *Symposium* (387 B.C.), and Plato attributes the story to the comic playwright Aristophanes (450–387 B.C.).

Hephaestus was the Greek god of the forge, brother to Ares and husband of Aphrodite. Although he has yet to appear on *Xena*, both the sword and the chains in this story are said to have been forged by him. The miraculous metal of Hephaestus would later figure in "The Dirty Half Dozen" and (briefly) "The Deliverer." Hephaestus himself was seen in a *Hercules* episode, "Love Takes a Holiday."

Rating: ⵜⵜⵜ

Death in Chains

WRITTEN BY ADAM ARMUS & NORA KAY FOSTER
STORY BY BABS GREYHOSKY, ADAM ARMUS, AND NORA KAY FOSTER
DIRECTED BY CHARLES SIEBERT

> *Hey, relax. I'm a big fan.*
>
> —Hades to Xena

What Happens

Death takes a forced holiday when the wily King Sisyphus captures Celesta, the sister of Hades, God of the Underworld. Xena's quest to liberate Death is opposed by the evil Toxeus and his band of undying warriors. And, oh yeah, Gabby meets another cute guy . . . but not for long.

Remarks

Last week mankind temporarily lost the ability to heal. Now we lose the ability to die. It must have been a very disorienting month for healers throughout the world, not to mention their patients.

On a more serious note, "Death in Chains" raises an important question of chronology. Namely, when did Gabrielle ditch her homespun peasant blouse and skirt for the snazzier, skimpier outfit she is suddenly wearing here? Gabby's unexpected costume change strongly suggests that this episode actually takes place *after* the next episode, "Hooves and Harlots," when she acquires what is revealed to be her new Amazon garb.

"Nice outfit. What's the matter, Heidi Fleiss couldn't show up?"
—Alleged comedian Gilbert Gottfried, shortly before Xena chops off his head in a *Tonight Show* sketch

---

As a rule, it seems best to work under the assumption that the episodes take place in roughly the same order in which they initially aired, but here and there we will find a few instances in which this is obviously not the case. See also· "One Against an Army." (Just to confuse matters further, the boxed set of first-season episodes, which does rearrange the sequence to some extent, nonetheless explicitly identifies "Death" as taking place before "Hooves," despite the obvious glitch with Gabby's costume. Was somebody not paying attention?)

Xena and Sisyphus speak as though they've met before, so much so that a viewer new to the series could be forgiven for thinking that the crafty king had previously appeared on the show. Sisyphus would return in a *Hercules* episode, "Highway to Hades," then come back to *Xena*, albeit played by a different actor, next season in "Ten Little Warlords."

Gabrielle's new boyfriend, whom she describes as "warm and sensitive," is more appealing than, say, Phyleus in "The Titans," but this tendency to pair Gabby up with someone every other show is becoming annoyingly predictable. Counting Iolaus in the last episode, this makes five this season—with more to come. No wonder Xena seems ready to roll her eyes when Gabby starts gushing about her latest crush.

On the other hand, you've got to like a kid who admires our favorite bard because "she knows every line of Sophocles by heart."

Kate Hodge, who portrays Celesta, the spirit of death, doesn't have much to do besides look wan and ethereal, plus glide across the sets without moving her legs, but she is perhaps best known to fantasy fans for starring as the lycanthropic heroine of the cult TV series *She-Wolf of London*, also known as *Love and Curses*. She later returned as Celesta in a fourth-season episode of *Hercules*.

Erik Thomson as Hades had previously appeared on a couple of episodes of *Hercules*, presenting the grim lord of the Underworld as a surprisingly amiable fellow who never quite seems to have matters under control, thus requiring the assistance of Xena or Hercules to sort out the living and the dead.

A sequence in which Xena must crawl through a rat-infested tunnel provided a highlight for the *Xena* blooper reel, as Lucy Lawless comes understandably unglued when dozens of squirming gray vermin are dropped onto her head. Said blooper reel can be ordered via the Official Xena Fan Club, c/o 411 N. Central Avenue, Suite #300, Glendale, CA 91203.

Reality Check

Hades, also known as Pluto (no, not Mickey Mouse's dog!), was the brother of Zeus and Poseidon and the ruler of the land of the dead. His sister, Celesta, cannot be found in mythology and is apparently the invention of *Xena*'s devil-may-care writers.

The myth of Sisyphus, however, is surprisingly close to what is depicted here. According to legend, King Sisyphus of Corinth angered Zeus by informing the river god Asopus that Zeus had raped his daughter; in exchange, Corinth got a fresh spring from Asopus, but Sisyphus got a death sentence from Zeus. The wily king then trapped Thanatos, the spirit of death, until Zeus sent Ares to liberate Thanatos. "Death in Chains" substitutes Celesta for Thanatos and Xena for Ares, but otherwise follows the gist of the tale. The episode never actually explains how Sisyphus angered Zeus (perhaps to protect Hercules' father's reputation), but it does allow Sisyphus to make a cryptic reference to providing his kingdom with water, a line that presumably left numerous viewers scratching their heads—or leafing through a dog-eared copy of Bulfinch.

Speaking of which, imagine my surprise when I discovered in those very same pages that there really was a Toxeus, a minor warrior who was eventually killed by Meleager in a dispute over a boar trophy. Silly me, I had assumed that "Toxeus" was just a tongue-in-cheek invention of the *Xena* writers. See "The Prodigal" for more on Meleager.

Rating: ⅄⅄

Hooves and Harlots

WRITTEN BY STEVEN L. SEARS
DIRECTED BY JACE ALEXANDER

Excuse me, you must be confusing me with a pet.
—Gabrielle to Ephiny

What Happens
While Xena tries to avert a brewing war between the Amazons and the Centaurs, Gabrielle becomes a full-fledged Amazon princess, acquiring a wooden staff, a new costume, and some long overdue lessons in self-defense.

Remarks
A classic episode that sets a lot of balls rolling. This was also the installment that turned me into an evangelical proponent of the show among my unsuspecting friends and coworkers, breathlessly narrating the plot to whomever I could corner. I had never seen anything like this on television before; after

all, when was the last time you saw a TV heroine prove the innocence of a condemned Centaur by presenting the queen of the Amazons with a handful of straw-infested horse dung? ("Centaurs don't eat hay.") Talk about Must-See TV.

> "Hey, baby, I'm queen now!" —Danielle Cormack (Ephiny) to a faux "Gabrielle" (New York Convention, February 21, 1998)

After playing both Lysia the Amazon and Lyla the Centaur lover, it's not surprising that Lawless takes both Centaurs and Amazons in stride. The Amazons here are portrayed much as they were in *Hercules and the Amazon Women*, except that they now apparently worship Artemis and not Hera, as they did in the TV movie. Kiwi actress Danielle Cormack makes the first of several appearances as Ephiny, initially the most hostile of the Amazons, who eventually overcomes her mistrust of Xena, Gabrielle, and even the Centaurs. Now a veteran of the Xena convention circuit, Cormack had no idea that this one-episode role would balloon into a recurring presence on both *Hercules* and *Xena*. "Hooves and Harlots" (love that title!) remains Cormack's favorite episode, mainly because Ephiny had the most edge then; she regrets that the character has mellowed so much over the years. (Cormack can also be seen as "The Chartreuse Fox," a Scarlet Pimpernel–like heroine of the French Revolution, in an unusually bizarre *Hercules* episode titled "Les Contemptibles.") Ephiny appears next in "Is There a Doctor in the House?"

Gabrielle starts off the episode in her old peasant garb, confirming that this episode occurs before "Death in Chains." Her adoption into the Amazon nation marks a turning point for the character, who no longer needs to be shooed away every time the fighting starts. Gabby takes to the staff with remarkable speed, considering, even as the nonlethal nature of her chosen weapon preserves her blood innocence, at least for the time being. Sequels to Gabby's Amazon adventure include "The Quest," "A Necessary Evil," and, in a broader sense, every episode in which Gabby whacks someone with a stick.

Despite the major changes in Gabrielle, Xena gets to show her stuff as well, with more of her eventful past revealed. We learn not only that the Warrior Princess is familiar with secret Amazon lore (maybe she picked it up from Lysia) but also that she fought a tremendous war against the Centaurs several years before. The famous Battle of Corinth, mentioned briefly in "Chariots of War," turns out to be a bloody affair in which Xena's army fought the Centaurs to a standstill, never quite defeating them. Xena's long-ago war against the Centaurs would figure prominently in the plot of next season's "Orphan of War," while this episode's evil warlord, Krykus, would reappear in "Remember Nothing."

The Centaur effects, including the spectacular visual of Centaur-drawn chariots carrying defiant Amazons to battle, are impressive and amusing, although I have to confess that every time I see Xena or Hercules carrying on an urgent discussion with some Centaur or other, part of me always visualizes the poor actor playing the Centaur as he rocks from side to side, striving manfully to simulate an appropriate horsey gait while trying to deliver compelling dialogue at the same time. I mean, what kind of auditions do they hold for these parts? ("Okay, now let's see you *trot* . . .")

"Hooves and Harlots" was adapted as a children's book, *Queen of the Amazons*, by Kerri Milliron (Random House, 1996). It also inspired the title—*Centaurs Don't Eat Hay*—of a netzine devoted to Xena humor and parodies. It can be found at *www.concentric.net/~Errorlog*. ("Callisto: The Barbara Walters Interview" in Issue 7 is particularly recommended.)

Reality Check

"Amazon" actually means "without breast," referring to the legendary Amazon custom of cutting off one breast, the better to employ a bow. Not too surprisingly, every filmmaker since the beginning of Hollywood, including the good folks at

Renaissance Pictures, has chosen to overlook this part of the myth, much to the relief of generations of actresses and casting directors. The Amazons of ancient Greece figure prominently in many of the old stories, although I don't believe they were ever known for any special enmity against Centaurs. *Hercules and the Amazon Women* notwithstanding, it seems much more probable that these fierce women warriors, who lived without the company of men, would worship the virgin huntress, Artemis, rather than Hera, the goddess of marriage. (*Amazon Women* no doubt linked its Amazons to Hera simply to perpetuate the theme of Hera's hatred of Hercules, which is not quite as relevant on *Xena*.)

Centaurs, half-man and half-horse, were generally portrayed in the ancient myths as rowdy, barbaric creatures, with the notable exception of Chiron, tutor of Hercules and other heroes, who eventually attained immortality in the night skies as the constellation Sagittarius. Chiron appeared in the third Hercules TV movie, *Hercules and the Circle of Fire*. In general, Centaurs are consistently portrayed on both *Hercules* and *Xena* as a persecuted minority, more sinned against than sinning.

According to mythology, the Centaurs lived primarily in Thessaly while the Amazons were located somewhere in Asia Minor, making it unlikely that they ever fought over shared hunting grounds—even assuming there really were any Centaurs.

Rating: ϗϗϗϗ

The Black Wolf

WRITTEN BY ALAN JAY GLUECKMAN
DIRECTED BY MARIO DI LEO

You have a friend? —Salmoneus to Xena

What Happens

Xena promises to rescue the daughter of an old friend from the dungeon of a cruel tyrant, eventually discovering that the daughter is now the mysterious rebel leader known as the Black Wolf. Salmoneus and Gabrielle end up in the dungeon, too, before Xena stages their great escape.

Remarks

Not a terribly memorable episode, really, with most of the action confined to an overcrowded cell packed with squabbling prisoners. Still, Xena gets to exploit her notoriety again, plus demonstrate that she can deliver her battle cry even while underwater . . . *yi-yi-yi—glub!*

No neighborhood hunks for Gabrielle this time; instead, she meets Salmoneus for the first time, while the Black Wolf (not to be confused with the Chartreuse Fox) gets the good-looking guy in the end. Emma Turner, who looks about as fearsome as Winona Ryder, is not entirely convincing as the dreaded rebel commander, a.k.a. Flora, daughter of Hermia. One of the small disappointments of this episode is that Xena spends more time bonding with Flora, whom we would never hear of again, than with either Gabrielle or Salmoneus. It's interesting to note, however, that the Xena whom Flora recalls from their last meeting, some ten years before, sounds surprisingly benign: climbing trees with the children, defending their village from marauders, teaching little Flora both to swing a sword and to embroider. Maybe the old Xena wasn't always a bloodthirsty monster? (In hindsight, it seems safe to assume that Xena's friendship with Hermia and her child occurred before Xena's fateful encounter with Julius Caesar in "Destiny," roughly nine years before this episode.)

Xena's remark "I have many skills," made in reference to her reported talent for embroidery, would become something of a running joke throughout the series, with those skills eventually including surgery ("Is There a Doctor in the House?"), curtseying ("Blind Faith"), singing ("Ulysses"), and cardsharping ("King Con"). Everything, in short, except cooking!

She also brags to her captors about killing Mezentius back in "The Path Not Taken."

Reality Check

The nasty King Xerxes whom Xena overthrows in this episode is presumably not the same Xerxes who ruled the Persian Empire from 485 to 465 B.C. Xena would later have a much harder time against the historical Persians in "One Against an Army."

Rating: ﾏ

Beware of Greeks Bearing Gifts

WRITTEN BY ADAM ARMUS & NORA KAY FOSTER
STORY BY ROY THOMAS AND JANIS HENDLER
DIRECTED BY T. J. SCOTT

I thought you were a farmer?

—Xena to Perdicas

What Happens

Xena does *The Iliad* as an urgent summons from Helen of Troy draws our heroines to the embattled city. But while Xena falls under suspicion from her new Trojan allies, Gabrielle is surprised to find a (sort of) familiar face upon the ramparts.

Remarks

You know, for a heartless warlord, the old Xena seems to have made an awful lot of friends. Granted, she admits to having "had some differences" with the fabled Helen, but she still comes running when the most beautiful woman in the world starts having Cassandra-like visions of Troy's downfall. As it turns out, Xena cannot change the outcome of the Trojan War, but she does manage to smuggle Helen and a few others out of the city by means of the famous wooden horse, including none other than Perdicas, Gabrielle's abandoned fiancé from "Sins of the Past," now a valiant soldier risking his life in defense of Helen and Troy.

(How exactly a Greek farmer from Potidaea ended up fighting on the side of the Trojans is a bit puzzling, especially considering all the grief Paris and the other Trojans give Xena because of her Greek roots.)

Gabby is amazed by the change in her old beau, as well she should be, considering that he is now played by a completely different actor! American actor Scott Garrison takes over the role of Perdicas, previously played as a hulking oaf by Anton Bentley. Elevated from a punch line to a potential love interest for Gabrielle, Perdicas is now much more presentable. Even Xena, preoccupied with other matters, seems to like him; subtext notwithstanding, she shows no sign of jealousy regarding Gabby's once and future betrothed. Garrison would return as Perdicas, to meet a tragic fate, in "Return of Callisto."

The plot of this episode was partially devised by well-known comic book writer Roy Thomas, who had previously introduced both Conan and Red Sonja to the comics. Thomas would eventually write the first several *Xena* and *Hercules* comics, as well as pen a humorous essay on his role in the creation of "Beware of Greeks Bearing Gifts" (a line traditionally attributed to Aeneas in Virgil's *Aeneid* but delivered by Xena in this version). By necessity, the hour-long segment simplifies the sprawling plot of Homer's original epic, concentrating on Helen's dilemma as the unwilling trophy of the conflict. *Ms.* magazine praised Xena's feminist take on the classic tale, although one has to wonder why, if the treacherous Deiphobus can sneak in and out of Troy via a secret passage, his Greek allies had to bother with the whole wooden horse trick anyway?

If nothing else, the war provides Gabrielle with several opportunities to put her brand-new staff and Amazon training to good use. Strangely enough, though, the staff (a sacred heirloom from Ephiny's mother, remember) is shattered halfway through the episode, but a few scenes later has magically repaired itself.

Galyn Gorg, who plays the tormented but ultimately triumphant Helen, has also guest-starred on both *Star Trek: Deep Space Nine* ("The Visitor") and *Star Trek: Voyager* ("Warlord"). Coming next season: "Ulysses."

Reality Check

Up until now, Xena, like Hercules, has existed largely in the mythic neverland of Greco-Roman legendry, but this episode finally links the Xenaverse to a specific historical event, namely the Fall of Troy in 1193 B.C. I started to write that this episode "tied" the series to that particular time and place, but, as we'll soon see, that tie turned out to be no restraint at all when it came to pillaging the rest of history. The Fall of Troy is just the first stop on an extremely bumpy ride back and forth down the time line. Just wait until the next episode!

The Iliad, by Homer, is, of course, the best-known account of the closing days of the Trojan War, previously alluded to in "Chariots of War." Homer's epic poem involved most of the major gods, goddesses, and heroes of the age, the majority of whom did not make the cut in the *Xena* version. Conspicuously absent are Ares and Aphrodite, both of whom sided with the Trojans during the war, as well as such notable figures as Achilles, Agamemnon, Hector, Ulysses, and Cassandra. As noted before, Hector, Agamemnon, and Achilles were all described as long dead in "The Reckoning," despite the fact that Agamemnon survived the war, as confirmed in "The Furies" two seasons later, when his homecoming (and subsequent murder) are mentioned by Gabrielle and others. Ulysses, unseen here, would enter the Xenaverse next season in an equally Xena-centric take on *The Odyssey*, while Cassandra, who is said to have prophesied Troy's downfall, showed up on *Hercules* a few years later, just in time for the sinking of Atlantis! According to Roy Thomas, the first few drafts of the script had Xena getting involved with Aeneas, the legendary founder of Rome, but that idea was done in by a rewrite.

Just to confuse matters further, we should note that Xena's most noted contemporary, Hercules himself, was already dead by the time of the Trojan War and that the Troy seen here is apparently not the same "lost kingdom of Troy" that Renee O'Connor was ruling over in *Hercules and the Lost Kingdom*. Got that? Good. Hang on, it only gets more complicated from here.

"Beware of Greeks Bearing Gifts" differs from previous accounts mostly in its depiction of Helen's fate, as well as by casting Deiphobus, a distinctly minor character in *The Iliad*, as the primary villain of the piece, betraying Troy and eventually murdering Paris, his own brother, out of unrequited lust for Helen.

While this Helen escapes to a new life free of war and intrigue, traditional versions have her returning to Greece with Menelaus, although she was briefly married to Deiphobus after Paris's death. *The Iliad* is curiously silent on the subject of that death, but later accounts have him killed not by his brother but by the Greek archer Philoctetes, said to have been, like Xena, a former lover of Hercules. (See, I told you it got more complicated.)

Finally, Gabby's description of Helen as "the face that launched a thousand ships" actually comes from Christopher Marlow's play *Dr. Faustus*, first performed in 1604 A.D., close to three millennia after the events portrayed here.

Rating: ﾑﾑ

Athens City Academy of the Performing Bards

WRITTEN BY R. J. STEWART AND STEVEN L. SEARS
DIRECTED BY JACE ALEXANDER

No one should pass up their dreams.   —Xena

What Happens
Our favorite bard competes in a prestigious storytelling contest, regaling her fellow bards with tales of the Warrior Princess and bonding (of course) with a sensitive young bard uncertain of his own talent.

Remarks
Despite the wholesale recycling of old footage from previous episodes, not to mention the general absence of Xena herself (off dealing with a cattle-stealing cyclops somewhere), this is a surprisingly enjoyable hour. The folks at Renaissance Pictures demonstrate a knack for finding amusing ways to cope with the inevitable "clip show." In this, the first but far from the last such *Xena* episode, they spice up clips from "The Warrior Princess," "The Gauntlet," "Sins of the Past," "Chariots of War," "Dreamworker," "Cradle of Hope," "The Path Not Taken," "Death in Chains," and "Prometheus" by throwing in bits and pieces of some cheesy Italian *Hercules* movie, as well as, astoundingly, two or three minutes from the 1960 film classic *Spartacus*. (Look close—this may be the only time you'll ever see Kirk Douglas, Sir Laurence Olivier, Tony Curtis, and Jean Simmons guest-star in an episode of *Xena*.)

The mystery of Xena and Gabrielle's finances may be partially dispelled by an early scene in which Gabby earns a few coins doing the bard thing in a village tavern. Hmmm, could it be that Gabrielle may actually be the breadwinner in this partnership?

Having survived a few marathon writing workshops myself,

I can testify that the episode captures some of the anxiety, creative stimulation, and camaraderie that such an experience brings about, although how Gabby and the others managed it without caffeine I'll never know. The title is presumably a takeoff on the famous New York City High School for the Performing Arts, immortalized in the movie *Fame* (1980).

Gabrielle and Homer are reunited in the second Xena novel, *The Huntress and the Sphinx*.

Reality Check

One week after the Fall of Troy, along comes Homer, who lived a mere three or four centuries later, between 900 and 800 B.C. That's the least of it, though; history as we know it is dealt a death blow when Homer tells Gabby and the others of Spartacus's inspiring revolt against Rome, which didn't take place until 71 B.C., nearly a millennium *after* Homer practiced his art. Not only is the chronology wrong, but it's *backward* as well. After this, conventional history never stood a chance. From now on, everything was fair game—and the gods help the poor students who treat *Xena* as the video equivalent of Cliffs Notes where real history is concerned.

Little is known of the historical Homer, if he ever truly existed, although tradition holds that he was blind. *Xena* gives that legend a typically wacky spin by revealing that, no, he just liked to recite his stories with his eyes shut. Homer almost abandons his art, but carries on after a pep talk from Gabrielle—not the last time she would come to the rescue of Western literature. (See "Giant Killer.")

Also attending the competition is Euripides (484–406 B.C.), who wasn't exactly a contemporary of Homer's, although they both wrote of the Trojan War. As for "Stallonus," a bard overly fond of fight scenes, his works appear to have been lost to history.

Rating: ⟨⟨

A Fistful of Dinars

WRITTEN BY STEVEN L. SEARS AND R. J. STEWART
DIRECTED BY JOSH BECKER

Godhood. What a great job.   —Thersites

What Happens

Xena, Gabrielle, a warlord, and a master assassin join forces to find the Lost Treasure of the Sumerians. That the warlord is also Xena's former fiancé does not make things any simpler.

Remarks

Xena had a fiancé? Chances are, the viewer is just as surprised by this little newsflash as Gabrielle is. Petracles turns out to be a sweet-talking warlord who dumped Xena as soon as she agreed to marry him; apparently even in the Bronze Age some men had problems with commitment. (One can only speculate about when exactly this relationship occurred, but Xena would later admit, in "Forgiven" two seasons later, that she started hanging out with the wrong kind of boys as early as her teens.) Gabrielle, who so far has never met a handsome guest star she didn't like, finds Petracles attractive enough, despite Xena's heartfelt warnings to stay away from him.

Actor Peter Daube is not bad as Petracles, but he is undeniably upstaged by the assassin, Thersites, played in a humorously sinister, Peter Lorre fashion by Jeremy Roberts. For those who are counting, Petracles's tragic demise racks up three dead boyfriends on Xena's romantic scorecard: Theodorus, Marcus, and Petracles. (We don't know about Borias yet). Iolaus should be thanking his lucky stars . . .

The decaying skeletons that Xena and crew pass on their way to the treasure look suspiciously similar to the rotting casualties outside Troy in "Beware of Greeks Bearing Gifts," right down to the grisly close-up of spiders crawling out of a skull's eye sockets. Gosh, we wouldn't want to miss seeing *that* again.

Although the title plays off an old Clint Eastwood western, this episode was actually inspired by *The Treasure of the Sierra Madre* (1948).

Reality Check

Ambrosia, seen here for the first time, was indeed the food of the gods, said to taste like honey. I'm not sure if the fact that the ambrosia of the Xenaverse looks a lot like orange Jell-O is supposed to be funny, but it cracks me up every time. (Does Bill Cosby know about this?) Ambrosia, and its supernatural properties, would later figure prominently in the plots of "The Quest" and "A Necessary Evil."

Sumerian civilization, as in the Lost Treasure of, was at its height from 3500 to 3000 B.C., almost two thousand years before the Trojan War, which gives it exactly the sort of antiquity that this episode implies. I'm not sure if anyone in Xena's era (whenever that is) would still identify himself as a Sumerian, as Thersites does, but I suppose there are people around today who are inordinately proud of their ancestral roots. Just look at all the Celtic and Egyptian gewgaws on sale at any science fiction convention.

Rating: ⚔⚔

Warrior . . . Princess

WRITTEN BY BRENDA LILLY
DIRECTED BY MICHAEL LEVINE

*It's like looking in a mirror, before I've brushed
my hair.*   —Princess Diana

What Happens

Xena trades places with a sheltered princess who just happens to be her identical twin. Hilarity ensues, while Argo's tail gets its most thorough brushing ever.

Remarks

Xena episodes tend to fall into three categories (with a fair amount of overlap): lighthearted adventure, heavy drama, or flat-out comedy.

"I don't think Xena ever thinks she's funny." —Lucy Lawless (*Starlog*, May 1997)

"Warrior . . . Princess" is the series' first purely comic installment, unless you consider the prospect of Xena's playing a harp the essence of Greek tragedy. Lucy Lawless has a ball playing Xena, Diana, Xena-as-Diana, and Diana-as-Xena, with the last providing the biggest laughs. The mere sight of the misplaced ingenue, in full Warrior Princess garb, fleeing in terror or riding Argo sidesaddle is worth taping the episode. Diana also manages to coin the deathless phrase "round killing thing" with reference to Xena's deadly chakram.

Not counting Lysia and Lyla, who are theoretically still running around the Xenaverse somewhere, poor Princess Diana is the first of Xena's amazingly coincidental look-alikes, but far from the last. See also "Warrior . . . Princess . . . Tramp" and "Warrior . . . Priestess . . . Tramp," not to mention a few less obvious examples. (Don't worry, I'll point them out eventually.)

More fun with statistics: This now makes *two* royal marriages saved by Xena and Gabby. We should also note that the kindly King Lias in this episode is apparently the cousin of the soon-to-be-deceased King Sisyphus of "Death in Chains." I guess royal bloodlines are just as close-knit in the Xenaverse as they are in real life. No word yet on where or how King Gregor fits in.

Xena's many talents, we learn, do not include harp playing, although she does manage to fire four arrows from the same instrument in another highlight of the episode.

Reality Check

The real Princess Diana, who died in 1997, could have used a Warrior Princess of her own. At the risk of irking Lucy Lawless, please note also that Princess Diana was the real name of Wonder Woman. A coincidence? I think not.

"You got that right, Plato," Xena snarls at one point, implying a passing familiarity with the Greek philosopher (427–347 B.C.), who came along centuries after both Homer and Helen of Troy.

Finally, the idea that Princess Diana and her new hubby would abolish slavery throughout their respective kingdoms is appealing but also anachronistic. Slavery was ubiquitous throughout the ancient world, enough so that it's kind of surprising that Gabrielle is never mistaken for Xena's slave. She walks beside the horse, does most of the shopping and cooking, occasionally does what she's told . . .

Rating: ⵣⵣⵣ

Mortal Beloved

WRITTEN BY R. J. STEWART
DIRECTED BY GARTH MAXWELL

It's great to be wicked and dead.   —Toxeus

What Happens

Xena is reunited, briefly, with her dead lover Marcus, who helps her restore order and justice to the Underworld after a dead murderer steals Hades' helmet of invisibility.

Remarks

An unusually ambitious episode that manages to combine a trip to the land of the dead, computer-generated Harpies, deceased warlords, a depressed god, an invisible serial killer, a funny cameo by Michael (Iolaus) Hurst as Charon, and a tearjerker of a love story to boot. Okay, there's no sign of Argo, but I guess you can't have everything.

Bobby Hosea, returning after his unfortunate demise in "The Path Not Taken," generates a convincing rapport with Xena even in the midst of frequent action scenes. Xena reacts to his initial reappearance with remarkable calm; I guess it takes more than the ghost of a dead boyfriend to rattle a Warrior Princess. She's much more broken up, affectingly so, when she has to kill him all over again to send him on to his just reward.

Also showing his face again is the warlord Toxeus, whom Xena killed back in "Death in Chains." He loses his head quite literally this time, but that doesn't necessarily rule out another guest shot; as we'll see next season in "Girls Just Wanna Have Fun," a severed head can be quite active in the Xenaverse.

Hades returns as well, looking even more ineffectual than usual. Surprisingly, Xena doesn't call in any favors for rescuing Celesta a few weeks back when she pleads Marcus's case to the god of the Underworld.

The main baddie, Atyminius, a sort of Hellenic Hannibal Lecter, is genuinely creepy, producing some actual shudders when he sneaks up on Gabby halfway through. Otherwise, our favorite bard spends most of the story sitting around on a beach without even the usual teenage boy to keep her company.

Xena's cover story among the dead, that she broke her neck after being thrown from a horse, now seems eerily prophetic of her equestrian accident on the set of *The Tonight Show* some months later.

Reality Check

You can *swim* to the Underworld? That's a new one on me, although otherwise this episode presents a fairly accurate depiction of the traditional Greco-Roman afterlife, with the wicked consigned to Tartarus and the virtuous rewarded in the Elysian Fields. Hades' helmet of invisibility is also mentioned in the ancient myths.

Presenting the Harpies as the guardians of Hades' infernal palace, as seen here, is taking greater liberties with the old stories. The Harpies, birdlike monsters with the faces of women, were found on a distant island in the mortal realm, where they plagued first Jason and the Argonauts (whose quest, according to *Hercules*, took place several years before Xena's reformation) and later Aeneas and his fellow refugees from Troy. Neither the Argonauts nor Aeneas ever managed to do more than drive the Harpies away, unlike Xena, who effectively reduces two Harpies to ashes.

The obvious moral: Never send a hero to do a Warrior Princess's job.

Rating: ⚡⚡⚡⚡

The Royal Couple of Thieves

WRITTEN BY STEVEN L. SEARS
DIRECTED BY JOHN CAMERON

Funny, Hercules never mentioned you.
—Autolycus to Xena

What Happens

The Warrior Princess joins forces with the King of Thieves to steal a mysterious weapon of frightening power, which turns out to be (attention, Indiana Jones!) the Lost Ark of the Covenant.

Remarks

Enter Autolycus, the self-proclaimed King of Thieves, a sort of Bronze Age Robin Hood with more ego and (slightly) less scruples. Previously introduced on *Hercules*, Autolycus is played by fan favorite Bruce Campbell, star of both the *Evil Dead* movie trilogy and, on television, the short-lived western spoof *The Adventures of Brisco County, Jr.* (Ironically, considering *Xena*'s fondness for subtext, he also played Ellen DeGeneres's homophobic boss for one season on *Ellen*.) A longtime friend and colleague of both Rob Tapert and the Raimi brothers, Campbell was always destined to enter the Xenaverse, but his appearance is no less enjoyable because of that.

"The Royal Couple of Thieves" is not quite as funny as "Warrior Princess," but it offers a similar comic tone. Having impersonated a princess only two weeks ago, Xena must now pose as a concubine named Cherish. Judging from the angry cloud hovering over her head most of the time, especially when she's forced to perform the seductive Dance of the Three Veils—with only two veils, it seems safe to assume that she liked being royalty a whole lot more!

Unfortunately, the plot doesn't introduce its best villain until halfway through: Lord Sinteres, a philosopher-assassin who shares Xena's extensive knowledge of pressure points. An intriguing character, from a different mold than the usual warlord. It's too bad they killed him off—not that this has ever stopped anyone in the Xenaverse from popping up again. The sound effects get a real workout during Xena's finger-to-finger duel with Sinteres; even an adjustment to his turban gets a *whoosh*.

More old friends from Xena's past show up, this time a wandering tribe whose biblical origins are not revealed until a climax taken straight from the end of *Raiders of the Lost Ark*. Whereas Indy and Marion survived, however, by averting their eyes from the unleashed glory of the Ark, Xena and Co. realize that only by looking straight at the divine truth can they hope to endure. (Great. Now I have *no* idea what to do if faced with the open Ark.) This would not be the only time the Warrior Princess would take a cue from *Raiders*. Just wait until we get to "The Xena Scrolls," not to mention a brief gag in "The Debt."

With Xena partnered with Autolycus, there's even less Gabby than usual this time around, although she does wind up at the wrong end of a Xena-style pressure point pinch, thanks to Sinteres.

Autolycus would meet our heroines next in "The Quest."

(Note: The boxed set reverses the order of "Mortal Beloved" and "Royal Couple," possibly to put the latter on the same tape as the even more humorous "Warrior . . . Princess.")

Reality Check

The ancient Israelites received the Ten Commandments, on tablets that Xena finds in the Ark, somewhere between 1500 and 1000 B.C. Chronologically, this is within a century or three of the Trojan War, although what these Hebrews are doing wandering around in Xena's backyard at a point when they should be returning from Egypt to Canaan is puzzling. They took one hell of a detour during the Exodus, I guess. Too bad they left that part out of the Charlton Heston movie.

Rating: 折折

The Prodigal

WRITTEN BY CHRIS MANHEIM
DIRECTED BY JOHN T. KRETCHMER

But you're coming back, right? —Xena to Gabrielle

What Happens

Suffering a crisis of confidence, Gabrielle returns to her village, now threatened by another warlord. Xena is nowhere nearby, and the only hero around is an old drunk who's lost his nerve.

Remarks

For an almost Xena-free episode, this is surprisingly fun. After playing third wheel to first Xena and Marcus, then Xena and Autolycus, Gabby finally gets a chance to shine, demonstrating her musical abilities with a set of panpipes and honing her hitchhiking skills (in a hilarious sequence) before coming home to Potidaea, which looks somewhat larger and more prosperous than it did in "Sins of the Past." Curiously, no one comments on her spiffy new Amazon threads, although I suppose they do have other things to worry about. (A nice touch: Check out the road signs printed in what I assume is Greek.)

Tim Thomerson, who guest-stars as the perpetually inebriated Meleager the Mighty, has starred in numerous low-budget science fiction and fantasy movies, most notably as a time-traveling cop in the *Trancers* series. Meleager, who eventually bonds with Gabrielle, would meet Xena herself next season in "The Execution."

Willa O'Neill returns as Gabby's sister, Lila, now more than a little jealous of Xena, "the woman wonder." Perdicas, last seen beating a hasty retreat from Troy, is nowhere to be seen, although actor Anton Bentley (the original Perdicas) is still lurking around, now playing another minor character. Also offstage are Gabrielle's parents, briefly glimpsed in "Sins of the Past." Perhaps they headed for the hills at the first sign of trouble. It seems we'll never know how they reacted to the return of their prodigal daughter. (For all the drama frequently surrounding Xena's family connections, Gabby's mother and father have never made much of an impression on the series; I had to go back and rewatch the first episode just to see if they'd ever been shown at all. Gabby might just as well be an orphan.)

As for the Warrior Princess, her raven tresses look a good deal shaggier than usual. For some reason, she's got a real cavewoman look going here. Maybe the King of Thieves pinched her best comb?

Come to think of it, whatever happened to Gabby's panpipes?

Her Hairdo Would Change the World . . .

"Many of television's best-dressed actresses, from Brooke Shields to Lucy Lawless . . . are making bangs the hottest look in Hollywood hair." (*TV Guide*, December 13, 1997)

Reality Check

Meleager was one of the Argonauts who joined Jason on his Quest for the Golden Fleece, although he was not mentioned as being among their number when they held a reunion in the *Hercules* episode "Once a Hero." Meleager was also the lover of the great female athlete Atalanta, although this has not been reflected by events in the Xenaverse. According to some accounts, he was the son of Ares, which would probably come as a shock to Kevin Smith. As if that isn't tangled enough, the legends also claim that he killed Toxeus, who was either his brother or his uncle, even though we saw Xena kill Toxeus earlier this season. He's also supposed to have married Cleopatra, who would eventually show up, apparently unattached, in "King of Assassins."

Basically, the powers that be seemed to have picked up the name "Meleager" and left most of its mythological context behind.

Gabby also mentions Orpheus (whom she would meet next season) and Sophocles (496–406 B.C.), who would have known Meleager only as a legendary hero of the distant past.

Rating: ⅄⅄

Altared States

WRITTEN BY CHRIS MANHEIM
DIRECTED BY MICHAEL LEVINE

By the gods, you are beautiful! —Gabrielle to Xena

What Happens

Our heroines sneak up on the Old Testament, while the subtext starts to creep out of the closet. Xena tries to stop a strangely familiar patriarch from sacrificing his favorite son on the altar of God. Gabby gets stoned, and not in the biblical sense, on some very special nutbread.

Remarks

Up until now, the celebrated lesbian subtext has been just that: subtext. On the surface, the relationship between Xena and Gabby has been no more overtly sexual than that of any other hero and sidekick. Even *Ms.* admitted that "if they are lovers, it is mostly in the covert Batman and Robin way." With "Altared States," however, the show starts deliberately teasing the viewer, and tantalizing various demographic segments of the audience, with hints and innuendo, raising the burning question of just how "sub" this subtext is going to be. It's nothing concrete, mind you, and on a sheer narrative level, it

seems fairly clear that Xena and Gabby are *not* sleeping together. But are we supposed to think that maybe, just maybe,
they want to? Well, take a look at this episode . . .

Before the opening credits even roll, the camera pans over
our heroines' discarded clothing while some mildly sugges-
tive dialogue, which could be misconstrued with hardly any
difficulty at all, is heard coming from nearby. Surprise! It's not
what you think (and shame on you, anyway); Xena is just in-
structing Gabby in the fine art of nude fish-catching. Shortly
thereafter, a religious fanatic with a secret agenda describes
Xena, a woman traveling alone with only "a scrawny little companion," as "unnatural" and "an abomination." Then Gabby,
flying high on henbane, sees Xena with new eyes, resulting in
the quote above, and finally, when Xena and Gabrielle are
hanging by a thread over a bottomless pit, the Warrior Princess instructs her young friend to "climb up my body," later
muttering "loving every moment of it" while Gabby clings to
her for dear life.

Okay, all these bits are taken out of context, more or less,
but are we really supposed to think they're not there on purpose? Yeah, right—and I've got a bridge over the Rubicon I'd
like to sell you. Things are not always as obvious as they are
here, but the sapphic genie is out of the bottle and will continue to pop up in the most surprising places from here on,
the exact nature of her features barely hidden behind wispy
veils of ambiguity.

Beyond alternative lifestyles, "Altared States" is a first-rate
episode that audaciously lifts its plot from Chapter 22 of the
Book of Genesis, while still finding time for such amusing di-
versions as a Warrior Princess wielding fish as weapons and a
dazed and confused Gabby leading a choir of stalagmites in
song. Even God Himself shows up, sort of. I'm tempted to
deduct one sword for not using the original biblical names
(see below), but Gabrielle drugged is just too darn funny. It's
odd, though, that neither woman relates this tribe of devoted
monotheists to the tribe of unnamed Israelites they met a few
weeks ago with Autolycus.

Karl Urban, who plays the intended sacrifice's treacherous older brother, meets a spectacular end here, but would return next season as both Julius Caesar *and* Cupid, proving that maybe he really was the chosen one after all.

Reality Check

Okay, this one's a judgment call. Are Anteus and Icus, as they're called here, literally supposed to be Abraham and Isaac from the Old Testament? The story's the same, mostly, but they're a long way from Canaan and that's Hestia, the Greek goddess of the hearth, that Anteus's wife is worshiping on the sly. Maybe this is all just one enormous coincidence?

For the record, the historical Abraham left Ur for the Holy Land around 2100 B.C., or a little under a thousand years before the Fall of Troy. Of course, if Anteus *is* Abraham, that means that Moses and the Ten Commandments came *before* Abraham in the Xenaverse, but if we can have Spartacus before Homer, then why stand on ceremony here?

Coming next year: David and Goliath. Oy!

Rating: ⵣⵣⵣⵣ

Ties That Bind

WRITTEN BY ADAM ARMUS & NORA KAY FOSTER
DIRECTED BY CHARLES SIEBERT

There's a reason why I play the part of Atrius so well.   —Ares

What Happens

Father's Day comes early for Xena when an aging warrior claims to be her long-lost dad. The Warrior Princess is skeptical at first, but the growing bond between father and daughter eventually pits Gabrielle against Xena.

Remarks

So, who is Xena's dad, anyway? Watching this episode again, for the first time in a year or so, I was struck by just how strongly it hints that Xena's real father is the God of War, an issue that would be explored further in the third-season opener, "The Furies." Kind of makes you wonder why he was so quick to order her death back in "The Gauntlet." Maybe that was just a temporary overreaction to her conversion. (Yeah, yeah, I realize that the real explanation is that the writers hadn't thought that far ahead yet, but that kind of practical, realistic reasoning is no fun.)

On the other hand, Atrius, as played by Tom Atkins, comes off as exactly the kind of hot-tempered, fearless old soldier that you'd expect Xena's father to be if he really was a mortal warrior . . . and assuming that Ares was doing a reasonable approximation of the real thing. Me, I still lean toward the Ares paternity theory, but it would be interesting to see Xena run into the real Atrius someday, if only in the Underworld.

Xena's brief reversion to "kill them all" mode is scarily convincing and leads to a great confrontation between Gabrielle and the temporarily berserk Warrior Princess, one much more intense than their little spat in "The Titans." A subplot involving Gabby and a disgraced slave girl (hmm, sounds like an X-rated fan fiction plot) is not too compelling, but that final confrontation, arguably Gabrielle's first good look at the bloodthirsty Xena of old, makes up for it, while also setting up a later scene in "Callisto" when Gabrielle worries aloud about the possibility of her own death turning Xena back into a monster, just as Atrius's apparent ˇ" i Äeˇê KåÄe

A nice bit of continuity has a pensive Xena humming her dirge from Marcus's funeral, while the funniest moment in a generally serious episode comes when she turns the tables on an assassin with a blowpipe. Let's just say Xena makes him swallow his words, among other things.

At one point, Ares/Atrius appears to be in two places at once, riding with Xena as Atrius while conferring with yet another warlord as Ares, but I guess if you're a god you can do that sort of thing.

Reality Check

The most notable Atreus in Greek lore was the king of Mycenae, father of Agamemnon and Menelaus (seen by Xena at Troy) and grandfather of Orestes (whom Gabrielle would meet later on). There is no indication, however, that Cyrene's husband, an ordinary mercenary soldier, is meant to be that Atreus.

Ares, like most of the Olympian gods, fathered numerous children by mortal women, most notably Meleager. Interestingly, he also had a son by a water nymph named Cyrene, but presumably not the same Cyrene who runs a bar in Amphipolis!

Rating: ⅄⅄⅄

The Greater Good

WRITTEN BY STEVEN L. SEARS
DIRECTED BY GARY JONES

I wish the two of you would just get along.
—Xena to Gabrielle and Argo

What Happens

With Xena down but not out, the victim of a poison dart, it's up to Gabrielle and Argo to save . . . a seltzer bottling factory?

Remarks

Callisto's arrival next episode is foreshadowed via a poison dart that leaves Xena at the brink of death. "The Greater

Good" is great fun in its own right, though, deftly mixing humor with tear-jerking near-tragedy. Forced to impersonate Xena, Gabrielle is a hoot, especially when she dons Xena's battle armor in a dead-on parody of the opening credits, complete with background music. But the real star of the show is Argo, now definitely established as the "daughter of a mare," who turns into the most able animal sidekick this side of Cheetah, saving both Xena's life and Gabrielle's at various points and even talking an enemy horse over to the side of good. Argo and Gabby achieve a truce of sorts, although not enough that the horse would have any compunction later on about nearly dragging Gabby to her death in "The Bitter Suite."

Salmoneus, last seen hawking Black Wolf merchandise, shows up again as "Lord Seltzer," proud bottler of carbonated water to the thirsty masses of ancient Greece. (Come again?) Given how ambitious and profitable this enterprise seems to be, one wonders why he ever gave it up. Perhaps the business lost its fizz? In any event, Salmoneus would have moved on to beauty contests by next season ("Here She Comes . . . Miss Amphipolis.")

Poor Gabrielle. After Xena apparently dies, a distraught Gabby tells her, "Don't ever do that again!" No such luck; Xena would die again in "Destiny" and in "The Quest." (Amazingly, Xena managed to get through the entire third season without dying once.) An intriguing detail: With Xena ailing, Gabrielle briefly considers going to Iolaus for help. I guess Hercules was on vacation that week.

Reality Check

Never mind that soda factory business. What's with this mystery metal, "talgamite," that supposedly dissolves in the rain? It's not enough that history is different in the Xenaverse, now they're making up brand-new elements too? What is this, the planet Mongo or something?

Rating: 𝄡𝄡𝄡

Callisto

WRITTEN BY R. J. STEWART
DIRECTED BY T. J. SCOTT

*As a villain, you were awesome. As a hero, you're a
sentimental fool.*   —Callisto to Xena

What Happens

Xena encounters her worst nightmare in the form of a
vengeful warrior woman from her past, while Gabrielle meets
some fans' worst nightmare, a bumbling would-be warrior
named Joxer.

Remarks

Call her what you will: killer bimbo, Malibu Xena, or Warrior Queen. The crazed blond psycho named Callisto is undeniably Xena's most popular and personal foe. Ares may
tempt her, Caesar will seduce her, but Callisto invariably hits
Xena where she's most vulnerable: her guilty conscience. Callisto present Xena with a no-win moral dilemma: Show mercy
to Callisto, herself a victim of Xena's bloody past, and more in-
nocents will suffer, something Callisto is all too happy to rub
in Xena's face every chance she gets. That she's nearly Xena's
equal in battle (and later much more), only makes her even
more dangerous.

And, unlike Xena, Callisto is not above killing women and
children, as is brutally demonstrated in the opening sequence. (Omigod, they killed the kid . . .)

American actress Hudson Leick has become a fan favorite,
making numerous appearances on both *Xena* and *Hercules*,
not to mention at the occasional convention. Ironically, given
Callisto's flamboyant evil, Leick has also appeared on such
wholesome, family-friendly TV shows as *Seventh Heaven* and
Touched by an Angel (as an angel, no less). She has even
played *Xena* producer Liz Friedman in a spoofy *Hercules*

episode titled "Yes, Virginia, There Is a Hercules." Not surprisingly, Leick as Friedman was not above plotting the deaths of Rob Tapert and her fellow staffers.

"Callisto" does a good job of introducing the character, while also foreshadowing future events. In a retrospectively ominous moment, the father of one of Callisto's victims, now intent on revenge, tells the merciful Gabrielle, "You'd feel the same way if you lost what I did." Later on, Gabby even praises Xena for sparing Callisto's life, words that no doubt came back to haunt her next season when the grieving father's abstract hypothesis becomes all too real. (Say good-bye, Perdicas.)

In real life, Hudson Leick is less than two years younger than Lucy Lawless, making one wonder exactly how old Callisto was when Xena slaughtered her family. Subsequent flashbacks to Callisto's youth, in "Destiny" and "Armageddon Now II," suggest that she was somewhere between twelve and fourteen when Xena's army torched her village, leading us to conclude that either Xena is a few years older than the actress who plays her or the Warrior Princess was sacking the countryside in her teens. How exactly a traumatized village girl acquired fighting skills to rival Xena's has yet to be revealed. Perhaps she was trained by Lord Sinteres? Or maybe Ares had another daughter?

More foreshadowing: Callisto threatens to kill Argo, something she almost manages in "Intimate Stranger" next season.

And now for something completely different . . . "Callisto" also introduces another major character to the mythos, Joxer the Mighty, who makes several incompetent attempts at kidnapping Gabrielle and joining Callisto's army, getting the

---

High Praise Indeed:

"If I were a ten-year-old, I'd bite anyone who tried to keep me away from an episode of Xena." —A. J. Jacobs (*Entertainment Weekly*, November 24, 1995)

stuffing beaten out of him each time. Little did he suspect that he would eventually fall in love with the same "irritating little blonde" who repeatedly trounces him this episode, although he ultimately cannot bring himself to slice Gabby's throat when Callisto gives him the opportunity, which must mean something.

In Xena fandom, the character of Joxer is more controversial than the subtext. Some fans find him annoying and unnecessary, others find him annoying but funny, while still others vigorously defend his every annoying action. Me, I'm not sure *Xena* necessarily needed any extra comic relief, but such episodes as "A Comedy of Eros" and "Been There, Done That" would not have been as funny without him.

The producers originally wanted Joxer to be played by comic actor Wallace Shawn, perhaps best known to fans as "The Grand Nagus" on *Star Trek: Deep Space Nine*, but the part was ultimately played by Ted Raimi, the younger brother of producer Sam Raimi, who had previously starred as "Communications Officer Mack O'Neill" on *seaQuest DSV*. Raimi has also appeared in numerous feature films, including *Patriot Games*, *Darkman*, *Candyman*, and *Evil Dead II* (where he played a bloated female corpse). An avid science fiction fan whose favorite authors include Orson Scott Card, Isaac Asimov, Ray Bradbury, and Richard Matheson, Raimi has admitted that he "had a rough time in high school," no doubt perfect training for his role as the Xenaverse's designated dweeb.

Despite and/or because of the fan response, Joxer's role would steadily expand over the course of the series, especially after Lucy Lawless's accident during the second season resulted in a flurry of Joxer-heavy episodes. Recent rumors, some of them stemming from Raimi himself, that Joxer had been signed for *every* episode in the fourth season have only fanned the flames of the Great Joxer Controversy. Hell, I like the character, but even I get a little nervous at the prospect of twenty-two straight hours of the Mighty One.

Joxer's comment to Gabby that he comes from a long line of warriors would be confirmed in "King of Assassins."

Highlights of the episode include the climactic ladder fight between Xena and Callisto, plus a quieter campfire scene between Xena and Gabrielle. "You promise me," Gabby says, "if something happens to me, you will not become a monster." Probably a valid concern, given the way Xena lost control when her father was killed only two episodes ago.

Joxer would return next in "Girls Just Wanna Have Fun," one episode before "Return of Callisto." David Te Rare makes the first of three appearances as Callisto's lieutenant Theodorus, not to be confused with the Theodorus that Xena sicced on Hercules back in "Warrior Princess."

Reality Check

Xena's archfoe bears no resemblance to the Callisto of mythology, a nymph raped by Zeus, then transformed into first a bear, then a constellation. That Callisto was a follower of Artemis, unlike the new Callisto, who eventually becomes a goddess herself.

The Temple of Apollo at Delphi, sanctuary of the famous Oracle, whom Callisto attempts to assassinate with Xena's chakram, was indeed one of the most sacred sites of the ancient world, attracting pilgrims from all over the world, just as seen here. Although its roots stretch deep into antiquity, with several successive temples built on the same site at the foot of Greece's Mount Parnassus, the Temple of Delphi reached the height of its fame and reverence around the fifth century B.C. It was eventually destroyed not by Callisto but by the Goths, in 396 A.D.

Finally, what's with all these crossbows? Callisto had a miniature one last episode, Joxer breaks his here. Correct me if I'm wrong, but I believe crossbows were developed in Europe in the ninth century.

Rating: ⳤⳤⳤ

Death Mask

WRITTEN BY PETER ALLAN FIELDS
DIRECTED BY STEWART MAIN

Fight now, talk later.   —Xena

What Happens

Talk about old home week. Xena stumbles onto not only Cortese, the warlord who attacked her village years ago, but her estranged older brother as well. Meanwhile, Gabby practices blocking arrows with her staff . . . with mixed results.

Remarks

So, contrary to what Xena told Iolaus when they met, not all of her brothers are dead after all. Seems the older sibling, Toris, took to the hills when Xena and their younger brother, now identified as Lyceus, fought back against Cortese. Funny that neither Xena nor her mom mentioned Toris back in "Sins of the Past," nor would they ever in the future. Truth be told, though, as played by Joseph Kell, he's not terribly interesting.

In fact, despite new details about Xena's early years, plus a few amusing stunts, "Death Mask" is not all that memorable. Cortese, the warlord who "created" Xena long ago, turns out to be a cowardly schemer of no particular distinction, while her brother is just a so-so warrior who learns a fairly predictable lesson about the folly of revenge. Some insight into the Warrior Princess's own code of ethics is revealed when she lectures Toris on the difference between killing in the heat of battle and killing in cold blood; she considers herself a warrior, not an assassin. (This scene takes on added significance when considered after the events of "The Debt.")

Although otherwise forgettable, this episode does contain one classic Xena moment as our heroine finally demonstrates a creative use for that breast dagger she took off Gabrielle in

"Dreamworker," inventing possibly the world's first and only cleavage-powered missile.

Incidentally, despite various efforts to establish Argo's gender as female, Gabby clearly refers to the horse as "he" during the campfire scene.

So, whatever happened to Xena's big brother, who has never been seen or mentioned again? We may never know, but perhaps he just realizes that if he keeps out of sight he stands a better chance of not getting killed off by a blood-thirsty writer. Look what happens later to her father and her son . . .

Reality Check

At first, I thought that messenger doves employed by Cortese and his minions might be a historical anachronism, but I was assured by numerous correspondents on the Net that this time *Xena* got it right, even if it's a bit unlikely that birds released from the king's castle would be able to locate a roving band of raiders; as an Aethelrede at *alt.tv.xena* helpfully explained to me, carrier pigeons and such are only good for delivering messages to fixed locations. It's possible, I suppose, that Malik and his mercenaries never moved their camp, but that doesn't reflect well on the honorable army captain out searching for them.

Rating: א א

Is There a Doctor in the House?

WRITTEN BY PATRICIA MANNEY
DIRECTED BY T. J. SCOTT

Maybe I'll make them take an oath. —Hippocrates

What Happens

Xena does *M*A*S*H*, complete with shelling (catapults, naturally), as the Warrior Princess turns a temple of healing into an emergency room during a bloody civil war. But her revolutionary medical savvy reaches its limit as Gabrielle lies dying . . .

Remarks

You know you're in for something dramatic from the opening shots, which make the woods of New Zealand . . . I mean, ancient Thessaly . . . look as ominous as *The X-Files*. Then things get intense.

This episode is a perfect example of how *Xena* can work on your brain in completely different ways simultaneously. On the one hand, it's hard not to get caught up in the gritty, gory human drama on the screen. People bleed, limbs are severed, and, omigod, someone stabbed Gabrielle. At the same time, though, there's something outrageously funny about the fact that a TV superheroine in leather armor is teaching first aid to Hippocrates . . . and delivering a baby Centaur by caesarean section! I mean, you can't take this entirely seriously, and yet you do.

Anyway, Xena proves to be a one-woman paramedic team, performing a tracheotomy with her breast dagger, suturing open wounds, demonstrating the essentials of medical triage, amputating the diseased leg of a character identified in the closing credits as "Gangrene Man" (his parents must be so proud), administering anesthesia by both pressure points and hypnosis, playing midwife to a pregnant Amazon, giving Gabby mouth-to-mouth, and ultimately discovering CPR by accident. Wow. Take that, Dr. Quinn, Medicine Woman. True, Xena didn't manage to transfuse blood or cure polio, but I guess they had to save something for season four. Oh, yeah, and she ends the war, too.

"He doesn't have four legs." —Danielle Cormack (Ephiny, mother of Xenan) on her real-life son. (New York Convention, February 21, 1998)

Returning from "Hooves and Harlots" is Ephiny the Amazon. Alas, we learn that her Centaur consort, Phantes, whose life Xena saved earlier this season, has been torn apart by hunting dogs (ick!), but not before starting a family with his former adversary, Ephiny. Recalled Danielle Cormack at a recent convention, "Having to give birth on camera to a Centaur child is pretty embarrassing." Before disaster befell them, Ephiny and Phantes were on their way to Athens, which is apparently more tolerant of mixed Centaur-Amazon marriages. Really.

Ephiny would be seen next in "The Quest." Her four-legged offspring, to be named Xenan, would reappear in "Maternal Instincts," as well as in a fourth-season *Hercules* episode, "Prodigal Sister."

According to Lawless, who considers this one of her favorite episodes, an earlier version was even bloodier, but it was toned down before its first airing.

Reality Check

Hippocrates, regarded as the father of medicine, lived from 460 to 377 B.C., although combat medicine was described by Homer as early as 800 B.C. or so. The Hippocratic Oath is still taken by physicians today.

Asclepius, whose temple Xena commandeers, was the son of Apollo and the god of healing and medicine. Intriguingly, the mythical Asclepius was tutored by the Centaur Chiron, who also educated Hercules, Jason, and Achilles. His temple at Epidaurus was one of history's first major hospitals, attracting patients from 400 B.C. to the sixth century A.D. Although many miraculous cures were attributed to the god, the healers at the temple often used their own skills to treat the patients as well.

Poor Galen, portrayed here as a closed-minded zealot, much older than Hippocrates, gets a particularly bum rap. The real Galen was a distinguished Greek physician and writer, known for extracting plant juices for medicinal purposes, who lived during the second century A.D., close to five hundred years after Hippocrates.

Catapults were introduced as weapons of war around 400 to 350 B.C., or at roughly the time of Hippocrates. Score one for the Xenaverse.

Rating: ХХХХ

Year 2 a.x.

Xena's second season might be best remembered as the Year of the Accidents, as a couple of unplanned mishaps caused complications, raised eyebrows, and generated still more publicity for the now hugely popular series.

First, in October 1996, while filming a comedy skit for *The Tonight Show* with Jay Leno, Lucy Lawless (in full Xena regalia) fell off a horse in the parking lot outside the studio, fracturing her pelvis. With their star temporarily sidelined, the writers and producers were forced to new heights of creativity and off-the-wall plotting, as seen in such episodes as "Ten Little Warlords," in which the part of Xena was played by Hudson Leick, and "The Quest," in which Xena was played in part by . . . Bruce Campbell? Fortunately, Lawless soon returned triumphantly to both *Xena* and *The Tonight Show*, on the latter being carried onstage by a pair of largely naked slave boys, before demonstrating her recovery with an enthusiastic shimmy before the cheering audience.

Moving from the excruciating to the merely embarrassing, Lawless made headlines again in May 1997 while performing "The Star-Spangled Banner" at a Mighty Ducks hockey game in Anaheim. Clad in an eye-catching combination of a fringed red cheerleader's costume and an Uncle Sam top hat, she caught the world's attention when her left breast escaped her costume as she belted out the national anthem. Video footage of the titillating incident, censored and otherwise, was soon zipping around the Internet at the speed of lightning. The story of Xena's accidental exposure even made *Newsweek* magazine ("Her Cup Runneth Over"), prompting one to recall Gabrielle's prophetic words at the beginning of last season's "Dreamworker": "It's not like your breasts aren't dangerous enough . . ."

Not that the show really needed more publicity. Now a certified hit, the number one action series in syndication, the *Xena* phenomenon yielded press coverage in everything from *TV Guide* to *Entertainment Weekly*, with the celebrated subtext attracting perhaps the lioness's share of the spotlight.

Meow Mix, a lesbian bar in Manhattan's East Village, received national attention for its monthly "Xena Nights," even holding a Xena look-alike contest as part of the 1997 Gay Pride Celebration. (Hmmm, I wonder if Princess Diana knew about this?) But back in the Xenaverse, where things really matter, Gabrielle was about to learn a shocking secret from the Warrior Princess's past.

Xena Invades Pop Culture . . .

"Sorry, girls, she's taken." —Jay Leno on Lucy Lawless's wedding (*The Tonight Show*, April 2, 1998)

Orphan of War

WRITTEN BY STEVEN L. SEARS
DIRECTED BY CHARLES SIEBERT

Your mother would be very proud of you.
                                    —Xena to Solan

What Happens

Surprise! Xena has a ten-year-old son, a revelation that complicates her mission to save some old enemies, the Centaurs, from a former lieutenant of hers, now a ruthless warlord intent on finding a mystical stone.

Remarks

The second season gets off to a dramatic start with more details about Xena's colorful past. Seems that ten years ago, during her war with the Centaurs, she had a child by her lover, Borias, who later switched sides to help defend the noble Centaurs from Xena's rapacity. Borias ended up dead under mysterious circumstances, but not long thereafter, Xena gave up her infant son to be raised by the Centaurs, hoping both to protect the child from her enemies and to keep him from growing up like her. It seems to have worked, too; certainly, the kid's accent is nothing like hers. (In fact, since Borias eventually turns out to be a dark-haired Mongol warrior, how come his child by Xena is a blond kid with fair skin and a Kiwi accent?)

> "You can't be a warrior princess all your life." (Poster advertising Lucy Lawless's Broadway debut in *Grease*.)

According to Sears, speaking in *Starlog* magazine, "What I was writing was a story I had read about a woman who was a crack mother and a prostitute and had a child that she gave up for adoption. She got her story straight, redeemed herself, got off crack, got a job, and three years later, wanted her child back. . . . That's what I wanted to write: Xena as the crack mother."

It's somewhat unclear if these are the same Centaurs, likewise old foes of the Warrior Princess, with whom Xena made peace in "Hooves and Harlots," also by Sears. There is no sign of Tyldus, the leader of the Centaurs in that episode, or any reference to those events. Furthermore, this is apparently the first time Xena has encountered these particular Centaurs since giving up her child, now named Solan, a decade before.

One has to wonder, too, if the old Xena was indeed in search of the Ixion Stone, as the evil Dagnine is now, had she actually intended to use its magical power to turn herself into a monster Centaur, like Dagnine does here? Doesn't really seem like her style.

Gabrielle's only role in these events is basically to provide a friendly ear and a shoulder to cry on for both Xena and Solan, but she does manage to overcome her aversion to horses long enough to take a ride on the back of a Centaur, which probably is as much fun as it looks to be. (Xena gets to ride a Centaur, too. Let's hope Argo wasn't too jealous.)

An evil alchemist working for Dagnine reminds me that in three seasons, Xena has never faced off against an evil sorcerer or sorceress, a curious omission given that evil wizards tend to be a staple foe of most fantasy heroes and heroines. I mean, Red Sonja used to run into diabolical spell-casters every other comic or so. Guess things are different in the Xenaverse. Maybe Ares and the other gods don't like competition?

Borias, long dead here, would be seen in the flesh in "The Debt." We do hear that he and Xena liked to sing together, among other things. Solan would come to a bad end in "Maternal Instincts" but make a brief return in "The Bitter Suite."

Reality Check

Such notable figures as Asclepius, Hercules, Jason, and Achilles were all raised, at least in part, by a Centaur, placing Solan in fairly illustrious company, which may be what Xena had in mind when she picked out her son's foster parent.

Ixion, after whom the mystical Ixion Stone is named, was indeed the father of the Centaurs (by making love to a cloud?), as well as the first murderer, whose crimes condemned him to Tartarus. That he concentrated all the potential evil of the Centaurs into a stone, thus granting them nobility, seems to be an invention of the Xenaverse.

Xena also constructs the world's biggest, if anachronistic, crossbow.

Rating: ⚡⚡⚡

Remember Nothing

STORY BY STEVEN L. SEARS
WRITTEN BY CHRIS MANHEIM
DIRECTED BY ANSON WILLIAMS

The hardest thing is losing you and Gabrielle.
—Xena, over her mother's tomb

What Happens

The Fates offer Xena a chance at a world without a Warrior Princess, where her brother is still alive, her mother is dead, Gabrielle is a hardened slave girl, and Lucy Lawless looks like Snow White. But is the world ready for the adventures of "Xena: Peasant Innkeeper"?

Remarks

At the beginning of "Sins of the Past," Xena tried to hang up her sword for good, only to pick it up again to defend Gabrielle. "Remember Nothing" basically replays that scenario by way of the Twilight Zone (not to mention Frank Capra). Xena's ultimate decision, when she sacrifices her peaceful new existence (and Lyceus's life) to preserve Gabrielle's blood innocence, provoked much discussion on the Net, up to and including thoughtful analysis of Xena-as-Christ-figure, taking the sins of the world upon her own conscience (and that was *before* she got crucified in "Destiny").

Along the way, we finally meet Xena's martyred brother, played with cheerful good spirits by Aaron Devitt. Mysteriously, their older brother, Toris (from "Death Mask"), is neither seen nor mentioned; Lyceus even tells Xena that she's "all the family I've got," which you'd think would inspire our heroine at least to inquire what's happened to Toris in this alternate Xenaverse—but, no, the subject never comes up. Parallel history takes a peculiar turn with a mutual crush between Lyceus and this reality's Gabrielle, a development that Xena seems to approve of—before she is forced to nip the new time line in the bud with a bloody sword.

Lucy Lawless remains the same old Xena, even dressed like a Disney heroine, but Renee O'Connor does a painfully effective job of differentiating this Gabrielle, downtrodden and bitter, from the effervescent young bard we know and love, while still allowing hints of the real Gabby to show through. It's too bad there wasn't time to show us the alternate Callisto, possibly now a cheerful bard, happy bride, or maybe even a heroic warrior princess.

Instead Xena picks up her *second* fiancé, this time a good-looking villager with quick wits but questionable backbone, whose real-world counterpart may still be running around Amphipolis. Xena never seems terribly keen on marrying this Mathias, whom she seems distinctly surprised to find herself involved with; one suspects that even if she hadn't called off the entire what-if scenario, the new, peaceful Xena would have eventually given Mathias his walking papers, perhaps wandering out in search of the alternate Marcus or Petracles.

Without a Warrior Princess to bring them to heel, two old villains form an alliance to menace the world: Mezentius ("The Path Not Taken") and Krykus ("Hooves and Harlots"). The latter, we learn, succeeded in his scheme to pit the Centaurs and the Amazons against each other, while Mezentius, killed by Xena in "our" reality, is run through by a bloodthirsty Gabrielle, who never even met Mezentius in the real Xenaverse.

But who is this third warlord who teams up with Mezentius and Krykus and also attacks the temple of the Fates in the prologue? *The Official Guide to the Xenaverse* identifies him as Caputius, but I swear on the episode it sounds like his name is "Confucius," which would be pushing historical inaccuracy even for *Xena*. Either way, why introduce a new warlord when there are so many other nasties from Xena's past who could have been resurrected just as the other two were?

Finally, there obviously wasn't sufficient time to give us a complete accounting of everything Xena *didn't* do in this reality, but who do you think rescued Death from her chains, or freed Prometheus from captivity? (Hey, they started this by bringing up that whole Amazon/Centaur thing . . . !) I guess maybe Hercules had to work overtime.

Reality Check

Dwelling apart from the gods of Olympus, the three Fates— Clotho, Lachesis, and Atropos—controlled the destinies of every man and woman. They are often portrayed, just as here, as a trio consisting of a maiden, a mother, and a crone. Not even Zeus could overrule the decrees of the Fates, which probably explains why Ares lets them take Xena's warlike past away. Or maybe he just knew that Xena wouldn't be able to put down her sword for long. The Fates are briefly seen again in "Judgment Day," a *Hercules* episode guest-starring Xena and Gabrielle.

It's a Wonderful Life (1946) tells a similar story, but Jimmy Stewart never swings a sword at anybody, let alone does any nifty backflips.

Rating: ⲭⲭⲭ

The Giant Killer

WRITTEN BY TERRENCE WINTER
DIRECTED BY GARY JONES

This one-god stuff is a new concept for me.
—Gabrielle

What Happens
Xena and Gabrielle wander back into the Bible when they discover that Xena's old comrade, a giant named Goliath, is working as a mercenary for the Philistines in their ongoing war against the children of Abraham. While Xena tries to convince Goliath that he's on the wrong side, Gabrielle bonds with King Saul's second son, David, a sensitive young poet talented with both psalms and a sling.

Remarks
We learn a bit more about Xena's shadowy past, specifically that she and Goliath fought in a massive battle against another giant, Gareth, ten years previous to this episode. Goliath saved Xena's life when she was wounded, just as the ancient Hebrews in "Royal Couple" once did, but he was thus unable to defend his family against Gareth, leaving both Xena and Goliath with plenty of guilt to go around. Exactly what was being fought over in this great battle remains unclear, but apparently Zeus himself was involved, slaying several giants with his thunderbolts.

Also included are useful bits of giant lore, such as the facts that giants leave their dead above the ground as a sign of respect and, more important, that all giants have a fatal weakness in their skulls just above the bridge of the nose.

The giant effects, including a boneyard full of oversized skeletons, are eye-catching, but the real fun here is the audaciousness with which our heroines are inserted into the well-known biblical tale. Not only does Xena provide the crucial edge that David needs to bring down his massive foe, but

Gabrielle encourages the insecure young poet to share his psalms with the world, just as she gave Homer a boost last season. (Where would Western literature be without her?) The scene in which David, christened "the warrior-poet of Israel" by Gabrielle, nervously recites his latest poem, beginning with "The Lord is my shepherd," is an irreverent hoot. Indeed, Gabby comes close to entering the genealogies of the prophets, but the inconvenient arrival of Sarah, David's betrothed, cuts short her budding romance with the future king of Israel. (Just as well; Xena probably would have ended up killing Bathsheba in a battle to the death or something.)

David seems to have a curiously flexible definition of monotheism, by the way. As he explains it to Gabrielle, the God of Abraham ranks above Zeus and Ares and the other "lesser gods," an interpretation that certainly sounds valid for the Xenaverse, even though I'm not sure how it would fly with most contemporary theologians.

Xena eventually catches up with Gareth in "A Day in the Life," exacting vengeance in Goliath's name. In fact, Xena's battle with Gareth in that episode was originally filmed as the conclusion to "Giant Killer," but the footage was held over for later use when the David and Goliath story line ran overtime.

Meanwhile, the evil leader of the Philistines, Dagon, escapes with his life in this episode, vowing "This is far from over!" (Despite this promise, he has yet to be seen again.) The show previously touched on Old Testament themes, though not quite as flagrantly, in "The Royal Couple of Thieves" and "Altared States."

Reality Check

In the episode, David decides to challenge Goliath after his older brother, Jonathan, is killed by the Philistines. According to the Old Testament, specifically Samuel I, Jonathan and David were brothers in spirit only. Jonathan was indeed King Saul's son, but David did not join the family until he married one of Saul's daughters, named Michol, not Sarah, all of which took place *after* the death of Goliath, who, rather than being a wandering mercenary as depicted here, is specifically identified as a Philistine. The biblical Goliath stood "six cubits and a span," roughly ten feet tall, not nearly as large as Xena's old comrade, nor was he responsible for the eventual death of Jonathan, which also happened several chapters after the famous battle with the sling. "Dagon," incidentally, was not a warlord but a major Philistine deity.

As always, the question of geography is a thorny one. Both the Philistines and the Israelites spend a lot of time making claim to "the land" in this episode. And that would be . . . ancient Greece? New Zealand?

David reigned as king of Israel from 1000 to 960 B.C., about a thousand years after Abraham, whom Xena met (sort of) last season.

Rating: ⲭⲭⲭ

Girls Just Wanna Have Fun

WRITTEN BY ADAM ARMUS & NORA KAY FOSTER
DIRECTED BY T. J. SCOTT

I would know a Bacchae if I saw one.   —Gabrielle

What Happens
Children of the night, what subtext they make! Ancient Greece goes Transylvanian as Xena, Gabrielle, and Joxer take on the blood-sucking Bacchae and their intoxicating master.

Remarks
Just in time for Halloween, this episode represents a fairly ingenious (or shameless, depending on your point of view) attempt to superimpose vampire lore and iconography, as handed down over the last two hundred years by books and

movies, on a typically *Xena*-fied version of various Greek myths. "Girls" has got it all: bats, fangs, wolves, blood, graves, stakes, even one shot taken straight from the 1922 silent classic *Nosferatu*. Only the *v*-word remains unspoken.

And speaking of themes that dare not speak their name, the subtext content of this episode, especially when Gabby goes out dancing with a group of suspiciously goth-looking Greeks, was overt enough to warrant a special mention in *Girlfriends,* "America's Fastest-Growing Lesbian Magazine." This should come as no surprise; lesbians and vampires have been linked since at least "Carmilla," a celebrated vampire story by J. Sheridan Le Fanu, first published in 1871. (Judging from the scene in question, Gabby has apparently gotten over her phobia about dancing in public, which she had confessed to Ephiny in "Hooves and Harlots.")

As a vampire enthusiast from way back, I naturally enjoyed this episode. The story's on the convoluted side, and the plot logic required to bring things to a point where Xena willingly lets Gabrielle drink her blood is nothing short of torturous, but how can you object to an episode that turns both Xena and Gabby into vampires . . . I mean, Bacchae . . . if only for a little while? (One of the highlights of the first *Xena* blooper reel, shown at conventions and sold via the mail to members of the official Xena Fan Club, is the sight of Lucy Lawless and Renee O'Connor, in full undead makeup, vamping it up while singing an enthusiastic rendition of "Deep in the Heart of Texas." Reba McEntire, eat your heart out.)

Xena Hits the Tabloids!

"Six-foot tall, athletic LUCY LAWLESS, star of *Xena: Warrior Princess*, is the hero of gay women everywhere, who love the lesbian overtones of her relationship with sidekick Gabrielle . . . But women who fantasize about dating Lucy should know that when it comes to romance, she prefers the company of men." (*Star*, "Who's Gay and Who's Not on TV," September 2, 1997)

As stylishly directed by T. J. Scott, complete with quasi-spooky double exposures, strobe lighting, and flashy MTV editing, "Girls" looks like no other *Xena* episode, except maybe the opening of "Is There a Doctor in the House?," also directed by Scott. It gets exhausting after a while, and I'm glad the show's not always so visually jarring, but it gives this particular episode an effectively nightmarish tone that not even the return of Joxer can entirely dispel.

Previously seen in "Callisto," the Mighty seems to have abandoned his career as an incompetent mercenary to pursue a higher calling as an incompetent hero. We also learn that his mother wanted him to be a musician and that he (unlike Xena, whose many fabled skills do not—as in "Warrior . . . Princess"—seem to include musical instruments) can also play the lyre, sort of. His climactic recital is to be charitable, of the *plink-plink-plink* school of musical artistry. Strangely, this performance has never been immortalized on any of the *Xena* sound-track albums.

Meanwhile, more of Xena's backstory is revealed as she informs us that ten years ago her army fought Bacchus in a massive battle that resulted in one unfortunate bit of collateral damage: the death of Eurydice, friend of Xena and bride of Orpheus. Actor Matthew Chamberlain, previously seen as Darphus in "The Gauntlet" and "Unchained Heart," is unrecognizable as the severed, but still quite lively, head of Orpheus.

How exactly Joxer gets his boots back after they're stolen by the skeletal Dryads is unclear, but check out the way that transforming from human to Bacchae (and back again) completely changes Gabby's clothing and hair. I guess the kiss . . . er, bite . . . of one of the Bacchae automatically combs back your bangs and dresses you for a night on the town. I can see the fan T-shirts already: I WAS BIT BY A BACCHAE—AND ALL I GOT WAS A TWO-PIECE BLACK COSTUME AND A PAIR OF SILVER EARRINGS.

Reality Check
Whew. Let me take a deep breath here. This is going to take some sorting out . . .

The Roman deity Bacchus, called Dionysus by the Greeks, was the god of wine, ecstasy, and the irrational; he was also one of the patron gods of comedy and drama in whose names plays were performed at Delphi (see "Callisto"). *Xena* focuses exclusively on the darker aspects of the god, casting him as a demonic figure who bears a startling resemblance to the Darkness portrayed by Tim Curry in the movie *Legend* (1985). His female followers, the Bacchae, were indeed capable of acts of extreme violence, as depicted in *The Bacchae*, an ancient drama by Euripides, Gabby's old classmate from the Athens Academy. Equating the wine of Dionysus with the blood of Dracula has a certain perverse, if vaguely sacrilegious, logic, although one has to wonder why the writers bothered to turn the Bacchae into vampires when Greek mythology provides a closer analogue in the form of the lamia, a female serpent-woman who drank the blood of her victims. (Oh, well, there's always the fourth season . . .)

The classical Bacchae were most often found in the woods and on the hilltops, as opposed to in the moldering catacombs seen here. The cult of the Bacchae was banned by the Roman senate in 186 B.C.

Orpheus, son of Apollo, was the greatest poet and musician in the Greek myths, perhaps best known for his unsuccessful attempt to retrieve his lost love, Eurydice, from the Underworld. Most stories have Eurydice dying from a snakebite, but making the Warrior Princess responsible for her death, however indirectly, gives the myth a suitably *Xena*-ish twist. As related here, Orpheus was eventually torn apart by the Bacchae, leaving only his semi-divine head to sing on. The severed head of Orpheus also figured prominently in the award-winning comic series *Sandman*, previously recommended in conjunction with "Dreamworker."

The Dryads, portrayed as winged skeletons bearing a definite familial resemblance to the Harpies in "Mortal Beloved," have little in common with their mythological namesakes, who were tree-dwelling wood nymphs. The ideas that Dryads are the sworn enemies of Bacchus and that only the sharp bone of a Dryad can kill a Bacchae, seem unique to the Xenaverse.

Legends involving blood-drinking spirits date back at least as far as Homer's *Odyssey*, but much of what we now consider standard vampire lore comes to us from Eastern Europe by way of such Victorian fictions as "Carmilla" and Bram Stoker's *Dracula* (1897). For more on this fascinating topic, I humbly refer the reader to my previous nonfiction work, *The Transylvanian Library,* still available here and there.

The title is an obvious allusion to the work of Cyndi Lauper. Never mind the rap music playing while Gabby dances the night away . . . What strange music, indeed.

Rating: ⵌⵌⵌ

Return of Callisto

WRITTEN BY R. J. STEWART
DIRECTED BY T. J. SCOTT

You never wrote.   —Xena to Callisto

What Happens

The Warrior Queen's escape from prison proves fatal for poor Perdicas, the morning after his and Gabrielle's wedding night, leaving Xena to cope with both her archenemy and a sidekick intent on vengeance.

Remarks

Talk about an eventful episode. Gabrielle weds Perdicas, loses her virginity, and gets widowed—all in less than ten minutes of air time! The episode itself quickly moves on to the consequences of Perdicas's death, focusing on Gabrielle's grief and anger, as well as on Callisto's shocking fate, but let's linger on the wedding for a moment or two.

Countless pages of fannish commentary and fiction have been devoted to explaining, justifying, rationalizing, and dismissing why exactly Gabby decides to marry Perdicas all of a sudden. Remember, this is the same guy—well, the same character—that she called dull and stupid back in the first episode. His transformation during the Trojan War (into an entirely different actor) helps account for her change in attitude, but it still plays as kind of abrupt. She even says no the first time he proposes to her here, but she comes around when he demonstrates his sensitivity by succumbing to combat fatigue in the middle of a fight. Maybe this was the first time she really thought he needed her . . . or something.

Anyway, Xena is a remarkably good sport about the whole thing, giving Gabby her blessing in a scene that would later be echoed in "Ulysses." She puts up a brave front at the wedding, attended only by her and Joxer, of all people, but falters when no one is looking. Grieving subtext fans can take solace in Xena and Gabrielle's poignant good-bye kiss after the ceremony, although Gabby's ecstatic morning-after declaration that at last she "knows what love is" must have really rubbed salt in their wounds. (A scene in which our favorite bard compares her wedding night with Perdicas unfavorably to the rapture she eventually finds in the Warrior Princess's arms appears to be a staple of lesbian fan fiction about the characters.)

After Perdicas's cremation, accompanied by Xena's now traditional funeral dirge, the big question is whether Gabrielle's idealism and blood innocence can survive this tragedy. In a touchingly atypical moment, Xena privately prays for Gabrielle's soul, and, although we don't know if Zeus and Co. heard her, Gabby does manage to overcome her newfound bloodlust in the end, helped along by a well-timed flashback to the "don't become a monster" scene in "Callisto." Nice to know that Gabrielle can take her own advice, although her blood innocence would not survive the next season.

As for the Warrior Queen herself, she's crazier and creepier, than ever. Initially trussed up like a Hellenic Hannibal Lecter, she soon sets out to torture Xena by killing Gabrielle, but settles for Perdicas instead. Preoccupied with her own torment and need for revenge, she abstains from alcohol and shuns the romantic overtures of the faithful Theodorus, only to drown in a pool of quicksand, pleading for her life while Xena looks on. Alas, Xena could have probably spared herself that particular moral dilemma; Callisto would be back from the dead in no time at all ("Intimate Stranger").

Theodorus, also returning from "Callisto," turns into something of a punching bag here: rebuffed by Callisto, pinched by Xena (for the *second* time), belted by Gabby with her staff . . . It's a miracle Joxer doesn't clean his clock, although Theodorus stays intact to return one last time in "Intimate Stranger."

Joxer, on the other hand, actually justifies his existence, maybe, by providing a much-needed distraction at a crucial moment, giving Xena a chance to save Gabrielle's life and taking an arrow in the shoulder for his pains. Fortunately, for his sake at least, Callisto still seems to find him too worthless to kill.

Intense and brutal, "Return of Callisto" is an episode that I would think twice before showing to any underage *Xena* fans. Director T. J. Scott brings his trademark visual flair to this episode, filming a drunken debauch among Callisto's soldiers much like the revels of the Bacchae. In fact, it looks like it might even be the same cave.

Reality Check

The wedding ceremony is noticeably nondenominational, invoking no specific Olympian deities, not even Aphrodite, whom Gabby would meet in person later on this season. This may have been a wise decision; given Hera's embarrassing defeat in "Prometheus," it probably would have been asking for trouble to call upon the goddess of marriage, no matter how historically appropriate.

Rating: ⚔⚔⚔⚔

Warrior . . . Princess . . . Tramp

WRITTEN BY R. J. STEWART
DIRECTED BY JOSH BECKER

Don't listen to anything Gabrielle says. I'm seriously considering having her executed.   —Meg as Xena

What Happens

Remember Xena's remarkably coincidental double, Diana? Turns out Xena also looks amazingly like a scatterbrained tramp named Meg, the reluctant centerpiece of a diabolical plot to kill Diana and impersonate the princess. Then Xena shows up . . . or does she?

Remarks

The uproarious sequel to "Warrior . . . Princess" doesn't give the princess much to do, but Lucy Lawless steals the show as the klutzy and frequently amorous Meg, who gets most of the good lines. There are too many funny bits to cite, but I have to point out her description of Xena's round killing thing as her "trusty shamrock," not to mention her enthusiastic rendition of "Ninety-nine Bottles of Beer on the Wall." There's even a subtext joke, as Meg reacts indignantly to the suggestion that she become a thespian: "You never said nothing about no kinky stuff!"

Meanwhile, both Gabrielle and Joxer end up understandably confused, especially considering Meg's unaccountable attraction to the Mighty One. Gabby does a great not-so-slow burn as her best friend (or so she thinks) keeps her locked in a dungeon for most of the episode. The climax, with another helpless infant suspended over a blazing fire, then sent flying through the air, calls up distinct memories of the tossed-baby hijinks in "Cradle of Hope."

By the end, Lawless has played just about everyone playing everyone else—but what's with all these doubles anyway? Let's not forget, Lysia and Lyla (from those early *Hercules* adventures) are still running around the Xenaverse, too. This is stretching coincidence pretty far, and we're not through with the Xena doubles yet. The best explanation I can think of is that Xena's father, Atrius (or maybe Ares), sowed an awful lot of wild oats a few decades back.

Coming next year: "Warrior . . . Priestess . . . Tramp."

Reality Check

Dolly the sheep was reportedly cloned in Scotland in 1997. Human cloning remains a few years away, at least in the real world . . .

Rating: ⅄⅄⅄

Intimate Stranger

WRITTEN BY STEVEN L. SEARS
DIRECTED BY GARY JONES

Of all the bodies to be stuck in, why did it have to be Callisto?   —Gabrielle to Xena

What Happens

Hades lets another one get away as Callisto escapes the Underworld (with a little help from Ares) by trading bodies with Xena. Trapped in the body of her nemesis, Xena races to protect her friends and family from the ersatz Warrior Princess.

Remarks

Boy, that didn't take long. Callisto is dead for all of one episode before sneaking back into world of the living by way of Xena's guilty conscience. Right after the multiple mistaken identities of last week's show, we now get Hudson Leick as Xena and Lucy Lawless playing Callisto playing Xena. It's like "Warrior . . . Princess" but with fewer laughs and more blood. "Warrior . . . Psycho," maybe.

Besides the lately late Callisto, this ep also brings return appearances by Cyrene, Ares, Joxer, Hades, and even the unfortunate Theodorus, who finally ends up at the wrong end of "Xena's" blade, joining his namesake from "The Warrior Princess" in death before becoming a punch line in "A Day in the Life."

Ares eventually discovers that Callisto is too crazy even for his taste, although he does take advantage of her new body to consummate his long-standing desire for the Warrior Princess, something Xena is none too happy to hear about when he mentions it to her in the next episode. In an unnerving moment, Ares, who impersonated Xena's dad last season, briefly takes the form of Cyrene to confront Xena. More foreshadowing of the familial revelations to come or just proof that Ares has a weird sense of humor?

Having previously lost track of Darphus and Sisyphus and Atyminius, Hades is almost as useless here. "I can't believe Ares would do this," he whines indignantly, not that this stops Hera from liberating Callisto *again* later this season. He doesn't even offer to switch Xena's body back, despite his debt to her from the last two times the Warrior Princess pulled his Plutonian fat out of the fire. Geez, what a schmuck.

Sears's script contains a few subtle nods to some of his earlier episodes. Callisto, now intent on stealing Gabrielle's blood innocence, gives Gabby back the breast dagger that Xena took from her in "Dreamworker," while the drugged dart that Xena uses to dispatch Callisto back to the Underworld recalls the poison dart that Callisto announced her arrival with in "The Greater Good." The dart even strikes home at the same place: the neck.

(Watch enough episodes in a row, over and over, and it's amazing how these recurring images start to pop out at you. . . . Life? Did someone mention a life?)

Anyone who wonders why Xena puts up with Joxer need only check out the scene here where the Mighty One risks his life to protect Argo. Okay, he fails miserably, but it's the thought that counts. Callisto's brutal attack on the fearful horse remains one of the series' more disturbing moments; it's hard to watch if you're any sort of animal lover. The Warrior Queen is just following through with her promises, though; she threatened to kill Argo as early as "Callisto." Fortunately, Xena turns out to be as good a vet as she is a combat surgeon.

The biggest surprise of the episode, and the one that set tongues wagging at work the next week, comes at the very end—when Xena doesn't get her body back! Was Xena doomed to spend the rest of her life as a bleached blonde in a leather bikini?

I sure couldn't wait to find out.

Reality Check

Is there any precedent for Greek gods springing deceased mortals from Tartarus by way of unsupervised soul transplants? Not in any myth that I recall, although the Underworld of the Xenaverse obviously has slacker regulations than most.

Rating: ⚡⚡⚡

Ten Little Warlords

WRITTEN BY PAUL ROBERT COYLE
DIRECTED BY CHARLES SIEBERT

Can you dye your hair?
—Gabrielle to the newly blond Xena

What Happens

Still residing in the body of Callisto, Xena discovers that Ares' godhood has been stolen by the no-longer deceased Sisyphus, who has invited ten vicious warlords (including Callisto) to a lonely island to compete for the position and powers of God of War. But what are Joxer and Gabrielle doing here?

Remarks

Let's see, last episode Lucy Lawless played Callisto pretending to be Xena. Now Hudson Leick gets to play Xena pretending to be Callisto. Lord, to what tangled plots we're forced, when the star falls off a horse. . . .

Seriously, the casting of Leick as a spiritually transmigrated Xena was an ingenious and typically audacious way for the series to cope with the fall-out from Lawless's equine accident. Nor was this the only such ploy; as we see in "The Quest," the Warrior Princess's soul ends up in the strangest places this season. Oh, well, at least Gabby gets to call someone else an "irritating blonde" for a change.

In the meantime, there's a disenfranchised war god and a resurrected Sisyphus to deal with, the latter making you wonder just who *can't* get out of Tartarus these days? The party responsible this time is Hades himself, who is apparently willing to cut Sisyphus a deal in exchange for the souls of (aha!) ten warlords; not surprisingly, the god of the Underworld declines to show his face after this petty bit of plea bargaining and remains offstage for the entire episode.

This rematch between Xena and Sisyphus, who last clashed

in "Death in Chains," gains a surreal twist when you realize that neither character is being played by the same actor as before! Director Siebert, who also helmed "Death," takes over the part here from Ray Henwood, who played Sisyphus the first time. Neither death nor recasting has improved the wily king's character, which is overtly sinister here, whereas he was merely misguided before—although I suppose you could rationalize that disposing of ten ambitious warlords to save your own life is not the worst thing to do. After all, Sisyphus doesn't know that "Callisto" is really Xena.

As before, however, the king has not thought out the full cosmological implications of his trickery. Just as his capture of Death almost doomed humanity to an eternity of suffering, the absence of a war god to regulate human aggression somehow causes peaceful people to go berserk. (Come again?) Frankly, the logic seems a little murky there, but at least it gives Joxer and Gabby something to do as they bicker and storm in a cloud of rage that never seems quite as funny as it should be.

The plot itself, a sword-and-sorcery variation on Agatha Christie's *And Then There Were None* is not too compelling, possibly because the other eight warlords don't get much in the way of characterization. Given the time constraints of episodic TV, maybe Hades should have settled for "Five Little Warlords." (Let it never be said, though, that the powers that be don't learn from their mistakes. See "The Dirty *Half* Dozen" next season.)

More entertaining is Kevin Smith as the suddenly vulnerable and eventually sympathetic Ares. His loss of humanity when he ultimately regains his godhood, just as Xena predicts, contains the tiniest bit of pathos, even if he does retain enough vestigial decency to give Xena her old body back.

"Ten Little Warlords" ends up being mostly just a curiosity in the grand saga of the Warrior Princess, kind of like the old *Batman* episodes in which anybody besides Julie Newmar played Catwoman. Hudson Leick does as well as she can, considering the circumstances, but one experiences a definite sense of relief when the *real* Xena finally shows up on the beach beside Gabrielle. Let's face it. Callisto is much more fun when she's out of her mind, and only Lucy Lawless *is* Xena.

Reality Check

After his death, which takes place between this episode and "Death in Chains," Sisyphus was indeed condemned to roll the same rock endlessly uphill, eventually becoming the subject of a famous 1955 existentialist essay by Albert Camus. We should also note that he has apparently constructed a primitive phonograph, beating Thomas Edison (who did it in 1877) by at least a millennium or two.

Xena displays similar foresight. "Rumors of my demise have been greatly exaggerated," she says as Callisto, anticipating a later remark by Mark Twain (1835–1910 A.D.).

Rating: ⑃⑃

A Solstice Carol

WRITTEN BY CHRIS MANHEIM
DIRECTED BY JOHN T. KRETCHMER

I didn't know you did gift-wrapping.
—Gabrielle to Xena

What Happens

Miserly King Silvas bans the celebration of the winter solstice—until Xena shows him the error of his ways. She also inspires a timid toymaker named Senticles to climb down a chimney for the first time.

Remarks

Let it never be said that the folks behind *Xena* aren't willing to push a gag as far as it can go—and then some. Take this particular installment, for instance. You have to be impressed by a Christmas . . . er, Solstice . . . episode that manages to work in Scrooge, Santa Claus, *and* Mary and Joseph. "A Solstice Carol" doesn't miss a trick, from candy canes and stuffed stockings to a choir of singing orphans. Gabrielle even plays "Jingle Bells" on the helmets of some unlucky guards, and the chakram ends up crowning the top of a decorated pine tree. In the gleefully giddy conclusion, Xena and Gabby and Senticles defend the orphanage with a battery of borrowed toys and ornaments, including a hand-carved Hercules marionette that bears a marked resemblance to Kevin Sorbo, as a deluge of downy feathers from battered stuffed animals yields a white solstice after all.

Silly, yes, but also irresistible if you're in the right frame of mind. Xena seems to have fun impersonating the Ghosts of Christmas Past and Present . . . oops, I mean the Fates, of course . . . although one has to wonder if the occasion sparked any poignant memories of her own encounter with the Fates earlier that season ("Remember Nothing"). Peter Vere Jones, who plays the Scrooge-like king, would later appear as Zeus, king of the gods, in "Judgment Day," an episode of *Hercules* guest-starring both Xena and Gabrielle.

As for Santa Claus—that is, Senticles—his toymaking skills seem definitely ahead of the times in that his workshop contains both talking dolls and hula hoops. Gabby gives the latter a puzzled look, unaware that she would shortly see the same anachronistic plaything put to use in "Here She Comes . . . Miss Amphipolis."

For a while there, it looks as if Gabrielle might actually get a steed of her own, in the ungainly form of a donkey named Tobias, but—wouldn't you know it?—she ultimately donates Tobias to a strangely familiar Madonna and child. (Note: A companion episode of *Hercules*, "A Star to Guide Them," originally airing the same week as this show, cast Iolaus as one of the three Wise Men, indirectly placing the Nativity within the Xenaverse.)

Much of the music in this episode, including the children's choir singing that well-known traditional carol, "Solstice Night," can be found on Volume 2 of the *Xena* sound-track albums.

Let's see, we've done Halloween and Christmas now. Anyone up for an April Fool's episode? Guest-starring Joxer, of course. Or how about the Fourth of July? Xena could teach Betsy Ross how to sew . . .

Reality Check

Historians estimate that the baby Jesus would have been in need of Gabrielle's donkey around 4 B.C. Three centuries later, around 325 A.D., Nicholas of Myra was an early Christian bishop, residing in what is now Turkey, who would eventually be canonized as Saint Nicholas. Renowned for his generosity, he established a feast day that (December 6, not that far from the winter solstice) became an occasion for gift-giving and rejoicing and eventually merged with the celebrations of Christ's birth on December 25. His distinctive red garments, a fashion choice shared by Senticles, derived from the color of bishops' robes in the Middle Ages. Another fifteen centuries later, in the early nineteenth century, Dutch settlers in the New World brought with them the legend of Saint Nicholas, whom they affectionately called Sinterklaas, or, as he was later known, Santa Claus. Finally, in 1822, Clement Clarke Moore wrote "A Visit from St. Nicholas," which firmly established many of the attributes, from the portly girth to the descents down the chimney, that our modern Santa Claus shares with Senticles of ancient Greece. A remarkable coincidence, that.

A Christmas Carol, by Charles Dickens, first published in 1843, featured a holiday-hating miser much like King Silvas. Curiously, Gabrielle says of the king that he "makes Midas look like Lady Bountiful," an odd expression given that Lady Bountiful was a character in George Farquhar's comic play, *The Beaux' Stratagem*, which would not be written until 1707 A.D., a good deal after the reign of either Silvas or Midas.

Rating: ⵣⵣⵣⵣ

The Xena Scrolls

STORY BY ROBERT SIDNEY MELLETE
WRITTEN BY ADAM ARMUS & NORA KAY FOSTER
DIRECTED BY CHARLIE HASKELL

*It has the power to turn myth into history, history
into myth.*   —Dr. Janice Covington, archaeologist

What Happens
In 1940s Macedonia, if adventure has a name it must be . . .
Janice Covington? Two oddly familiar archaeologists, plus an
equally familiar jerk, excavate a hidden tomb that may hide
the secrets of a legendary Warrior Princess.

Remarks
Myth into history and history into myth, huh? Boy, truer
words have ne'er been spoken.

"The Xena Scrolls"—an elaborate spoof of *Raiders of
the Lost Ark* with Renee O'Connor cast as the Indiana Jones
character—succeeds in turning the inevitable clip show into
a special event, making this ep even more enjoyable than
Gabby's stint at the Academy in Athens. Of course, it helps
that Lucy Lawless sticks around this time, even if she doesn't
get to play Xena until the very end.

It's a shame that Lawless has vetoed any idea of playing
Wonder Woman in the future, since as Melinda "Mel" Pappas,
sidekick to the swashbuckling Janice Covington, with her features disguised behind a pair of horn-rimmed glasses, she's a
dead ringer for Diana Prince, WW's old alter ego, albeit with
a Southern-fried accent. In reality, of course, Mel turns out to
be the descendant and/or reincarnation of the Warrior Princess herself.

Not that this is obvious to everyone. Probably the funniest
bit has Covington, played by O'Connor, convinced that
she's the true descendant of Xena, then Callisto, before finally

realizing the awful truth—that her real ancestor was that "ir-ritating blonde." Also along for the ride is Ted Raimi, doing a shameless Inspector Clouseau impression as a self-important French officer of dubious authenticity.

Many fans cite this episode as proof positive that Xena and Gabrielle and, yeah, even Joxer will someday have children who will survive long enough to produce offspring of their own, but that may be too literal an interpretation of what is basically an hour-long joke. It strikes me as unlikely that a one-shot spoof like this episode is going to have that much impact on the future course of the series. (Granted, it's highly doubt-ful that Janice Covington is descended from Gabrielle's up-coming demon baby.)

Speaking of bloodlines, though, the ever-popular Ares paternity theory picks up some more support here. Not only do the Xena Scrolls refer to the "great bond" between the War-rior Princess and the God of War, but Ares even tells Xena, re-born in the body of Melinda, "I'm in your blood." Okay, he could be speaking metaphorically, but how come only a de-scendant of Xena can free Ares from his prison? Maybe be-cause she's also a descendant of Ares? Sounds right to me.

Janice and Mel have not been seen on television since, but they have continued their adventures together in plenty of the fan-written fiction to be found on the Internet.

For the record, "The Xena Scrolls" contains flashbacks to "Callisto," "Mortal Beloved," "Altared States," "Hooves and Harlots," "Ties That Bind," "The Reckoning," and "Is There a Doctor in the House?" plus what looks like a couple of old Mexican monster movies that were most likely filmed *after* 1942.

The clever epilogue, revealing the "true" story behind the genesis of the TV series, offers a brief cameo by Rob Tapert, executive producer of *Xena* and future husband of Lucy Law-less. Tapert would later be played by Bruce (Autolycus) Camp-bell in "Yes, Virginia, There Is a Hercules."

"The Xena Scrolls" remains the only episode to *end* with

The Big Time at Last

"32, Across. *Xena: Warrior Princess* star" (Crossword
puzzle, *TV Guide,* March 1, 1997)

---

the opening credit sequence, beating *Seinfeld*'s celebrated
"backward" episode by at least a year.

Reality Check

That it's an artifact called "The Eye of Hephaestus" that
holds Ares in his eternal prison is interesting when you recall
that Ares is famous in mythology for his illicit love affair with
Aphrodite, the wife of the god of the forge. Possibly the two
gods had a falling-out in the Xenaverse as well. (The Eye itself
can be glimpsed on the wall of Ares' temple in "Armageddon
Now.")

But the Free French Army in control of Macedonia in 1942?
Sacre bleu! More likely, Covington's dig site in Macedonia
would have been occupied, depending on its location, by
German, Italian, or Bulgarian forces.

The Xena Scrolls remain unrecognized by contemporary
historians.

Rating: ⋊⋊⋊

Here She Comes . . . Miss Amphipolis

WRITTEN BY CHRIS MANHEIM
DIRECTED BY MARINA SARGENTI

Honey, I'm no princess, I'm a queen!
—Miss Artiphys, clad in Xena's armor

What Happens

Summoned by Salmoneus, ever the entrepreneur, Xena reluctantly goes undercover at the Miss Known World beauty pageant in order to stop an unknown saboteur from disrupting the pageant—and starting a war. Disguised as the blond "Miss Amphipolis," Xena snoops around backstage, eventually discovering that each of the other leading contenders has her own reasons for wanting to win the crown, and that one of them, Miss Artiphys (Artifice?), isn't even a woman.

Remarks

Short on action, but long on humor, "Here She Comes . . ." is an enjoyable comedy episode with many funny bits, beginning with the very name of the pageant: Miss Known World? Possibly the most memorable moment comes when the triumphant Miss Artiphys plants a climactic smooch on Xena's lips while a surprised Gabrielle, who still thinks he is a she, looks on in bewilderment.

Despite the emphasis on laughs, Xena still manages to chase off a gang of hired thugs by pelting them with clamshells and later slices an arrow in half with her chakram. Gabrielle, posing as "the Marquessa," Miss Amphipolis's aristocratic sponsor, is content to employ an outrageous quasi-European accent that occasionally makes her sound like the villainous Natasha from the old *Rocky and Bullwinkle* cartoons.

Xena's creators ingeniously manage to have their cheesecake and eat it too, presenting a parade of underdressed actresses while ultimately delivering a message of female empowerment and self-esteem at the end, when the best beauty queen turns out to be a man, played by Karen Dios, alias Geoff Gann, a noted drag queen, gay rights activist, and porn star. It is perhaps no coincidence that his/her talent exhibition involved swirling rainbow banners, a recognized symbol of Gay Pride. This is also the first episode to be directed by a woman, which may serve to inoculate it against charges of sexism from the more serious-minded segments of the audience.

Lucy Lawless herself enjoyed feigning "dumb and blond" for a change, telling *TV Guide*, "As I pivot at the end, I give a little flick of my tush, and you get to see right up Xena's skirts. It was a happy accident, and the angle was good, so I didn't mind." Rob Tapert, on the other hand, was less happy with the episode, regarding it as one of their weaker shows.

The biggest mystery, of course, is why Lucy Lawless, who seldom misses an opportunity to show off her singing voice, makes a point of *not* singing during the talent competition. Instead, it is Robert Trebor as Salmoneus, returning to the world of Xena for the first time since "The Greater Good," who gets to warble not once but twice during the episode. For the record, his big numbers are "A Woman Is a Natural Thing" and the title tune, featuring such unforgettable lyrics as "A beauty so mythic/her figure's terrific/She's Miss Known World!"

The Hestian virgins, mentioned here in a throwaway line, would later play a larger role in both "A Comedy of Eros" and "Warrior . . . Priestess . . . Tramp."

Reality Check
The Miss America pageant debuted in Atlantic City, U.S.A., in 1921, although Greek myths tell of a beauty competition between the goddesses Athena, Aphrodite, and Hera·that indirectly led to the Trojan War. (When *Hercules* did their version of that divine contest, Hera was replaced with Artemis, presumably because, from Herc's point of view, Hera is strictly

a villainess.) It is doubtful whether actual Greek maidens ever practiced with hula hoops or took up snake charming.

Rating: ⟑⟑

Destiny

STORY BY ROBERT TAPERT
WRITTEN BY R. J. STEWART & STEVEN L. SEARS
DIRECTED BY ROBERT TAPERT

A new Xena is born—with a new purpose: death.
—Xena

What Happens

While protecting a band of villagers from a tribe of crazed savages, Xena get smashed into a tree by a swinging log. Mortally wounded, she slips back in her memory to a time ten winters ago when she was a pirate queen, bedecked in bangles and finery. She takes hostage an arrogant young Roman nobleman, Julius Caesar, who claims his destiny is to rule the world. She also encounters M'Lila, a mysterious female stowaway who fights with a skill that Xena has never before seen. Meanwhile, back in Xena's present, a desperate Gabrielle delivers her dying friend to a reclusive Asian healer. But she's too late, and Xena's life passes away . . .

Remarks

At last, the Secret Origin of Xena, or at least parts of it. "Destiny" reveals the source of Xena's astounding fighting skills as well as the turning point that irrevocably launched her on her career of evil—until Hercules reformed her, of course. Prior to Caesar's betrayal, she had been merely terrorizing neighboring kingdoms to protect her native Amphipolis. After M'Lila's tragic death, she apparently got really nasty. As co-writer Sears put it, "The thing that was so blatantly missing from what we set up was that we set up the peasant girl and when she turned back from evil, but we never said exactly when she *became* evil. The distinction is there's a difference between being George Patton and Josef Stalin, and there was a moment when that had to have happened."

Many mysteries remain, like who exactly was M'Lila and where did she learn all that incredible stuff? Because M'Lila only speaks un-subtitled Gaelic, except during a brief hallucination near the end of the episode, we can only wonder what her story was before she snuck onto Xena's pirate ship. I mean, a Gaelic-speaking Egyptian slave? What's that all about? Also, what is the significance of the fact that the child Xena rescues right before being struck by the log wears an amulet not unlike one worn by M'Lila ten years before? (It looks like some sort of Celtic design.)

For that matter, who in the world were the so-called Children of the Sun and what was a bunch of headhunters or cannibals or whatever they were doing running around in ancient Greece? And what's a Chinese healer doing on Mount Nessus? Sadly but perhaps understandingly, Gabrielle is so distracted by Xena's imminent demise that she never bothers to ask about any of this.

Jaw-dropping moment: a surreal-but-spectacular visual in which the crucified Xena tumbles through the afterlife while visions from her life float like bubbles in the air. The Last Temptation of Xena?

One assumes that this incident with Caesar takes place after Xena and Goliath battled Gareth together, also ten years ago ("Giant Killer"), but that can't be stated with certainty. Still, as we would subsequently learn in "The Debt," a crippled Xena traveled to China shortly after her crucifixion, so it's hard to imagine that she squeezed in a war against a giant along the way.

The cliffhanger ending, which was revised at the last minute to accommodate Lucy Lawless's equine accident, leads into an ongoing story that continues in "The Quest" and

"Necessary Evil." In the original script, now on sale, Xena's spirit is drawn back to her body just in time for a teary embrace with Gabrielle. Julius Caesar, who here enters the Xenaverse as possibly her most treacherous lover, would appear next in "The Deliverer." Actor Karl Urban, who plays Caesar, had previously appeared as Maell in "Altared States" and would return as Cupid in "For Him the Bell Tolls" and "A Comedy of Eros." The healer Niklio is played by Nathaniel Lees, who also played the corrupt mystic back in "Dreamworker."

Joseph LoDuca's score for this episode earned an Emmy nomination, a first for the series.

A flashback to the torching of Cirra gives us our first glimpse of Callisto as a child, played by a young actress who looks convincingly like Hudson Leick. An alternate-history version of the same incident would be seen in "Armageddon Now II."

The clips at the end, as Xena lay dying, come from "Is There a Doctor in the House?" and "The Greater Good," among other episodes.

Reality Check

Believe it or not, this episode is loosely based on an actual incident in the life of the young Julius Caesar in which he captured and crucified a band of pirates who had previously held him hostage (minus an avenging Warrior Princess or an Egyptian stowaway). Caesar eventually became the first emperor of Rome in the first century B.C. Late in life, he was also romantically linked with Cleopatra, last queen of Egypt (who was to enter the Xenaverse the next year in "King of Assassins"). History records that he was ultimately assassinated in 44 B.C. by his Roman contemporaries, including Brutus, who makes a brief appearance here.

Aside from that shamelessly anachronistic flash-forward to Spartacus in "Athens City Academy," the Roman era had not really been shoehorned into the Xenaverse before now, but with the introduction of Julius Caesar into the saga, a rubbery time line has just been stretched significantly (some might say egregiously) further than before. According to Xena lore, this encounter with the young Caesar took place nine years before the Fall of Troy ("Beware of Greeks Bearing Gifts," last season); in the real world as we know it, at least eleven centuries transpired between the Trojan War and Caesar's early campaigns in Gaul, and the Trojans definitely came first.

One has to wonder why, if the show's creators needed an arrogant young soldier destined to conquer the world, they didn't just use Alexander the Great instead? Alexander (356–323 B.C.) would have fit more easily into the show's loosely Grecian milieu and chronology—assuming, that is, that anyone is still worrying about such things.

Rating: ⅄⅄⅄⅄

The Quest

STORY BY CHRIS MANHEIM, STEVEN L. SEARS, AND R. J. STEWART
WRITTEN BY STEVEN L. SEARS
DIRECTED BY MICHAEL LEVINE

What would a dead woman want with me?
—Autolycus

What Happens

Xena is dead—or is she? As a grieving Gabrielle rejoins her Amazon sisters and prepares for Xena's funeral, the King of Thieves finds his body possessed by a singularly stubborn spirit. Meanwhile, an Amazon power struggle pits Gabrielle against the ruthless and ambitious Velasca.

Remarks

Written to accommodate Lucy Lawless's injuries, "The Quest" finds Xena's bodiless spirit possessing Autolycus while

Gabrielle copes with life without Xena. Bruce Campbell, whose experience with possessed limbs dates back to the *Evil Dead* flicks, manages to save Xena's body from cremation with a lot of prompting by the voice of Lawless. (I guess she knew better than to possess the body of Joxer.) Autolycus, whom Xena and Gabby met during "Royal Couple" would return again next season in "King of Assassins."

Just to add to the fun, Michael Hurst shows up for a brief appearance as Iolaus. Attentive viewers will recall that Gabrielle considered turning to Iolaus the *last* time Xena died, back in "The Greater Good." Where Gabby came up with Xena's very impressive sarcophagus is left unexplained. Perhaps Niklio also runs a funeral parlor?

The Amazon saga, begun in "Hooves and Harlots," continues as Gabby becomes Amazon Queen, over the violent objections of a homicidal female warrior named Velasca, the adopted daughter of the late Queen Melosa, recently killed by Velasca in a battle to the death. (Ephiny, returning to *Xena* after her harrowing delivery in the Temple of Asclepius, implies that the contest was less than fair, but we don't hear any details.)

Velasca is portrayed with Callisto-like intensity by Melinda Clarke, who at one time was considered for the part of Xena. Clarke has also played a zombie in *Return of the Living Dead III* and an assassin in *Spawn*. Velasca's story would continue in the very next episode.

The episode entered subtext heaven with The Kiss. Xena smooches Gabrielle for the first time since Gabby's wedding, albeit while occupying the body of Autolycus. No doubt there was much rejoicing at Meow Mix and elsewhere. Earlier in the episode, Gabrielle kisses Xena's chakram, as did Callisto in her first appearance. Decoding any symbolism here is left as an exercise for the reader.

It's highly convenient that the hidden "Hall of Ambrosia" seems to be less than a day's ride from the Amazon settlement, but in a plot this wacky it seems churlish to object. One has to wonder, though—how much of that orange Jell-O stuff have the gods left hidden here and there? More important, if the food of the gods can heal Velasca's mortal wounds (as seen in the next episode) and even bring Xena back to life, why didn't Xena or Gabrielle think to give some to Petracles, back in "A Fistful of Dinars," when he bled to death only a few feet away from a generous helping of ambrosia? I guess Xena didn't come to trust him *that* much.

Reality Check

The Dagger of Helios, the key to the Hall of Ambrosia, refers to Helios, a sun god who was also the son of Hyperion and Theia, two of the Titans Xena encountered in "The Titans." Helios was sometimes equated with both Apollo and Hyperion and worshiped primarily in Rhodes.

The Amazons, like almost everyone else in the Xenaverse, have crossbows as well.

Rating: ⲣⲣⲣ

A Necessary Evil

WRITTEN BY PAUL ROBERT COYLE
DIRECTED BY MARK BEESLEY

Does an Amazon Queen beat a Warrior Princess?
—Gabrielle

What Happens

To defeat Velasca, now imbued with godlike power and intent upon Gabrielle's death, Xena resorts to the rather drastic expedient of liberating Callisto. But who's more dangerous, the crazed Amazon—or Xena's unlikely ally?

Remarks

In "Surprise," a *Hercules* episode that aired one week before, Callisto was brought back to life by Hera, then achieved immortality by eating fruit from the Tree of Life, only to be trapped underground by Hercules—until Xena comes to free her.

Hang on. Let's think about this for a second. "A Necessary Evil" picks up more or less where "The Quest" left off. Last week Iolaus had not heard about Xena's death until he ran into Gabrielle; then he hurried off to tell Hercules. Now Xena knows exactly what Callisto and Hercules were up to *while* she was dead. Either Hercules dropped by the Amazon village for an instant visit and left just before Velasca came back or Xena's spirit was doing more than merely possessing Autolycus. (Hmm, maybe she tried to possess Herc first, only to discover that he was too busy coping with Callisto.)

You have to feel sorry for Iolaus, though; he's out there spreading the word about Xena's tragic demise, only to be proved wrong in a matter of days. Boy, he must feel stupid. Let's just hope the news didn't make it to Amphipolis before Cyrene found out that her daughter was alive again.

And speaking of resurrections, no wonder Xena seldom speaks well of the gods. This is the *second* time one of those meddling Olympians has released Calypso from Tartarus. First Ares, now Hera . . . doesn't Hades have anything to say about this? What's the good of killing Callisto, Xena must be wondering, if she won't stay dead?

A friend of mine pointed out the similarities between this adventure and the original *Star Trek* episode, "Where No Man Has Gone Before," in which a crewman is driven insane by godhood, denoted by his shiny white eyes, and starts throwing energy blasts around until Captain Kirk pits another newborn god, with the same weirdo eyes, against the first one, resulting in their mutual destruction as they are buried beneath an avalanche of falling boulders. Here, on the other hand, Velasca achieves godhood, and shiny white eyes, and starts throwing energy blasts around until Xena pits the newborn goddess Callisto, now equipped with (yep) white contact lenses, against Velasca, resulting in their mutual defeat, as they are buried alive beneath a river of flowing lava. Hmmm.

Then again, Xena never worried about the Prime Directive.

Coyle draws a careful distinction between an "immortal," which is what Callisto became by eating from the Tree of Life, and a "god," which requires a taste of orange Jell-O . . . that is, ambrosia. An immortal can simply not be killed, whereas a god can perform all sorts of nifty special effects, including spinning like the Tasmanian Devil in Warner Bros. cartoons.

Callisto, who last afflicted our heroines in "Intimate Stranger," still excels at stirring up painful emotions, as when she forces Xena to make a public apology for the destruction of Cirra, then taunts Gabrielle about the death of Perdicas. The Warrior Queen is almost sympathetic for a moment or two, as she recalls the death of her family, but she promptly reverts to sadistic-torturer mode.

Also returning, besides Callisto and Velasca, is Ephiny, who becomes de facto Amazon Queen in Gabrielle's absence. Ephiny would pop up briefly, along with her Centaur son, Xenan, in a Hercules episode titled "Prodigal Sister," before running into Xena again in "Maternal Instincts."

Callisto also returns, still a goddess but now curiously lacking the telltale white eyes, in the same episode, but first she and Velasca both escape from the lava flow in *Xena VR*, a "virtual reality" computer game in which Hera frees both Callisto and Velasca and sends them after Xena. Successful completion of the game, which also involves retrieving yet more ambrosia to save a dying Gabrielle, returns the two villainesses to the same lava pit, where Callisto remains until next season. In theory, the game can be accessed via the official Xena web site at *www.mca.com/tv/xena*.

Although more dramatic than humorous, "A Necessary Evil" does contain a priceless Xena moment early on, as the Warrior Princess casually corrects a dislocated shoulder by slamming herself into the wall of a cave, then proceeds as if nothing eventful had occurred.

One question: After Xena saves Gabrielle from falling to her doom by bungee-jumping off the side of a cliff (much as she did in "A Fistful of Dinars"), how in Zeus' name did they get back up to solid ground again?

Reality Check

Flush with divinity, Velasca takes time out to blow up a Temple of Artemis and proclaim herself the "god of Chaos." Velasca, god of chaos, cannot be found in Bulfinch, and neither can the great goddess Callisto.

Rating: ᚴᚴᚴ

A Day in the Life

WRITTEN BY R. J. STEWART
DIRECTED BY MICHAEL HURST

Your flying parchment is stuck in a tree. —Gabrielle

What Happens

From breakfast to bedtime, Xena and Gabrielle manage to save two villages from, respectively, a rampaging warlord and the biggest giant in the world, while still finding time to bicker, fish, play Twenty Questions, and take a refreshing bath. Xena tricks the giant, Gareth, into destroying the army of the evil Zagreus, then electrocutes Gareth by calling down a lightning bolt via the world's first kite. She also copes with an unwanted admirer and his jealous girlfriend.

Remarks

A typical day perhaps, but an atypical and thoroughly delightful episode. It speaks well for the show's confidence in itself, and its willingness to take chances and have fun, that an experiment like this can make it onto the air and be greeted with enthusiasm by the vast majority of fans. From the *Frasier*-style chapter titles (written in what looks to be real Greek) to the shameless clowning of Xena's attempts to launch her "flying parchment," this episode, directed by "Iolaus" himself, has enough great moments to enshrine it as an instant classic, which seems to have been exactly what everyone had in mind; in fact, page 5 of the script for "A Day in the Life" explicitly identifies it as "a very special episode of 'Xena: Warrior Princess.' "

Sometimes you've got to aim high to hit the mark, I guess.

As mentioned before, Xena's big battle with Gareth was originally filmed as the conclusion to "Giant Killer" but ended up being reserved for future use after that episode ran long. The giant footage and Xena's ultimate vengeance on behalf of the late Goliath blend seamlessly into this storyline, although it is kind of convenient that another giant burial ground happened to be located nearby.

New facets of the Xena–Gabrielle relationship are revealed here, including various forms of recreation. Most surprising, perhaps, are Gabrielle's playful sneak attacks on Xena, reminiscent of the way Inspector Clouseau's Asian manservant used to ambush him in the old Pink Panther movies. Frankly, surprising a Warrior Princess strikes me as a dangerous hobby; Gabrielle must be depending a lot (or not enough) on Xena's razor-sharp reflexes. Twenty Questions sounds a lot safer. The correct answer, by the way, to their guessing game is Theodorus (from "Intimate Stranger"), although the nitpicker in me feels compelled to point out that neither Xena nor Gabrielle was present when Callisto killed Theodorus. Perhaps they heard about it later from one of his surviving

---

"Who do we think we are today, Xena and Gabrielle?" —The Widow Twanky to "Autolyca" and "Salmonella" as they share a bubble bath in the *Hercules* episode "Men in Pink."

comrades? Xena and Gabby would be seen playing the game again in "The Dirty Half Dozen."

Needless to say, this episode provides a feast for subtext fans, including one surprising slip of the tongue. Listen carefully when a love-struck peasant asks Gabrielle if Xena would ever consider marrying and settling down. Gabby says no, *"she likes what I do,"* then corrects herself: "She likes what *she* does." For the record, this little slip does not appear in the published script. An ad-lib, or simply plausible deniability?

And then, of course, there's the bath scene, where our heroines scrub each other's back and hunt for the soap amid gallons of heated water. Let us not forget that in the Xenaverse a hot bath is almost always a prelude to romance.

Not to mention the brief, chaste kiss Gabby gives Xena just before they turn in for the night . . .

Perhaps the oddest mystery of this very special episode, however, is why its closing disclaimer ("No slippery eels were harmed during the production of this motion picture despite their reputation as a fine delicacy in some cultures of the known world") is almost identical to a similar disclaimer, also involving endangered eels, that once appeared on an episode of *Frasier*? ("The Innkeepers," to be exact.) A coincidence, or evidence of a secret synchronicity beyond our ken?

Reality Check

Xena's electrifying experiment, involving a kite, an iron belt buckle, and lightning, anticipates a similar experiment conducted by Benjamin Franklin in 1752 A.D., more than two millennia later.

Kite flying itself was first invented in China, perhaps as early as the fourth century B.C., and was subsequently introduced to Europe by Marco Polo, some sixteen centuries later. Since future episodes would reveal that Xena spent a portion of her villainous past in imperial China ("The Debt," Parts 1 and 2) it seems likely that the Warrior Princess may have picked up the basic concept in her travels.

Rating: ⳤⳤⳤ

For Him the Bell Tolls

WRITTEN BY ADAM ARMUS & NORA KAY FOSTER
DIRECTED BY JOSH BECKER

I have an overwhelming sense of groddiness.
—Aphrodite

What Happens

While Xena answers an urgent summons, Gabrielle is joined by Joxer, who becomes a pawn in a plot by the goddess Aphrodite to break up yet another impending royal marriage. Aphrodite places a spell on Joxer that causes him to become a dashing, swashbuckling hero every other time he hears a bell ring. A subsequent chime transforms him back into his usual bumbling self.

Remarks

A sidekicks-only adventure, with Xena appearing only in the prologue and epilogue, that kept the show on track during Lucy Lawless's recuperation from her accident. As the closing disclaimer divulges, the plot pays unmistakable homage to the classic 1956 movie comedy, *The Court Jester,* starring Danny Kaye as an incompetent swashbuckler under a similar hypnotic spell. One line of dialogue, involving "a vase from Thrace," is clearly a deliberate echo of the famous "flagon with a dragon" routine from the Kaye film.

On its own terms, this is an entertaining farce that largely makes up for its Xena-lessness by providing plenty of comic moments for both Gabrielle and Joxer. Poor Gabby ends up torn between disbelief and disgust as she is forced to play both chaperone and guardian angel to Joxer and the love-crazed princess, except for one terrifying moment when she briefly succumbs to the new Joxer's charms, only to snap out of it an instant later. "That was scary!" she comments, blissfully unaware that she would soon fall for Joxer more emphatically in "A Comedy of Eros."

Even though she claims here to be "just an over-achieving sidekick," it's clear that Gabby has picked up a few tricks from hanging out with Xena; in the big climax, she saves Joxer from being beheaded by throwing a stone with Xena-like accuracy, causing it to ricochet like a chakram on its way to its target. Of course, she has to spit on it first.

She also has a religious experience of sorts when she encounters both Aphrodite and her son, Cupid, for the first time. Her openmouthed awe at beholding a goddess in the flesh quickly gives way to disillusionment when she is confronted with Aphrodite's petty and self-centered personality. Aphrodite, in turn, treats the young and innocent Gabrielle with open condescension. Alexandra Tydings, who plays the goddess as a sort of celestial Valley Girl, had previously appeared in several episodes of *Hercules* before making her *Xena* debut here. Cupid and Joxer would be reunited with Xena and Gabrielle in the second-season finale "A Comedy of Eros." Karl Urban, portraying Cupid as a winged surfer dude, had previously appeared as Mael in "Altared States" and as Caesar in "Destiny." His new look includes a bad dye job on his hair that makes him look vaguely like Madonna in *Who's That Girl?*

Listen carefully to the sound track of this episode and you will hear an orchestral rendition of Joxer's self-congratulatory theme song, "Joxer the Mighty," playing during his most impressive action scenes. This choral version can be found on Volume 2 of the *Xena* sound-track albums. For complete lyrics to the various different versions of the song, try writing the Ted Raimi International Fan Club, at TRIFC, c/o Lana Andrews, 555 Surby Avenue, Battle Creek, MI 49015. (Elsewhere in the episode, you can also hear the sound of bowling pins tumbling when he sends a group of soldiers flying.) This insidiously catchy song would haunt the series for many episodes to come.

As for Xena, "off being a hero," the King Lias she rides forth to see is presumably the same weary monarch from "Warrior . . . Princess" and "Warrior . . . Princess . . . Tramp," leaving one to wonder exactly what sort of trouble Xena's look-alikes, Diana and Meg, have gotten into now. Meanwhile, this makes three royal marriages that either Xena or Gabrielle has managed to rescue. (See "The Path Not Taken" and "Warrior . . . Princess.")

Finally, the very concept of this episode would seem to demonstrate once and for all why Gabrielle needs a horse of her own, just to keep up with Xena and Argo. C'mon, folks—even Tonto had Scout.

Reality Check

As usual, the precise locale of this adventure is hard to pin down. The warring kingdoms have a vaguely Indian look to them (lots of turbans and saris) but also contain prominent temples to the Greek goddess Aphrodite. According to the *Iliad*, Sarpedon was a demigod who died in the Trojan War—which, according to the time line of the Xenaverse, concluded a year before this episode, as seen in "Beware of Greeks Bearing Gifts." It seems safe to assume that the lovesick prince here is not intended to be the same character.

Rating: ⅄⅄

Hercules: The Legendary Journeys: Judgment Day

WRITTEN BY ROBERT BIELAK
DIRECTED BY GUS TRIKONIS

Did you say Hercules got married?   —Xena

What Happens

Xena and Gabrielle come to Hercules' aid after he is framed for the murder of his new bride. Along with Iolaus, they struggle to save Herc from a lynch mob and expose the real killers: Ares and his giggling sidekick, Strife.

Remarks

Airing the same week as "For Him the Bell Tolls," this episode marks Gabrielle's first appearance on *Hercules* and the first Hercules/Xena reunion since "Prometheus" a season ago. Our heroines drop by their brother series to take part in the conclusion of a three-part story line involving Herc's ill-fated marriage to a woman known as Serena (played by Kevin Sorbo's future wife).

Although the emphasis is on Hercules, there's plenty for *Xena* fans here, beginning with Ares' nostalgic reminiscences about the infamous Battle of Corinth, apparently a tremendous slaughter committed by the Warrior Princess back in the bad old days. Despite her past attraction to Hercules, Xena takes his marriage in stride, stating, "We're long past the time we could have been together," while Gabrielle and Iolaus get a chance to bond some more.

Xena's own relationship with Iolaus remains somewhat intriguingly testy; she makes a point of insisting that she, unlike Iolaus, could put Herc out of his misery if necessary. "You haven't got the stomach for it," she sneers, perhaps recalling the way he let her down by refusing to kill Hercules way back when. Later, when Xena (apparently) stabs Iolaus to death, is it just my imagination or is she enjoying the act a little too much? Don't believe me? Take a good look at her bloodthirsty grin as she runs him through, and you'll see what I mean.

Xena Invades Pop Culture . . .
"Steve Harvey: Steve thinks his manhood is in question after Regina (Wendy Raquel Robinson), a.k.a. 'Xena the Warrior Principal,' beats the stuffing out of a too-fresh chicken mascot at a basketball game." (*TV Guide,* November 12, 1997

Naturally, the whole thing, including Hercules' apparent death at the hands of Iolaus, is a scam, intended to flush out the real culprits: Strife and Ares. The emphasis switches to Xena briefly as the God of War tries again to tempt her back to the dark side, offering to revive Hercules in exchange; the obvious implication, that a bad Xena is worth more to Ares than a dead Hercules, is a provocative one, adding more weight to the theory that Ares may be more than just Xena's former mentor. (It is unclear, however, whether Ares had this deal in mind the whole time or if he was simply improvising in response to Xena's appearance on the scene.)

Peter Vere Jones, who played the miserly king in "A Solstice Carol," now turns up as Zeus, king of the gods, to straighten everything out, although Herc's wife remains deceased. Xena sings her trademark funeral dirge, previously sung over Marcus and Perdicas, at Serena's lonely last rites.

Xena and Gabrielle would return (sort of) to Herc's life next season in "Stranger in a Strange World" and "Armageddon Now II."

Reality Check

In the myths, Hercules really did kill a wife in a fit of madness; the Xenaverse gets Herc off the hook by pinning the blame for the actual murder on Strife, urged on by Ares. Strife was the son of Discord (to be seen in "The Deliverer"), making him either the nephew or the son of Ares, depending on which account you choose to go by. The Ares of the Xenaverse tends to treat Strife as an idiot nephew, which is good enough for me.

Rating: ХХ

The Execution

WRITTEN BY ROBERT COLE
DIRECTED BY GRAHAM MAXWELL

You're so good!   —Meleager to Xena

What Happens

When Meleager the Mighty is found guilty of murder and condemned to death, Gabrielle ends up on the wrong side of the law, placing Xena in a difficult position.

Remarks

As I watched Xena, in the opening scene of this episode, race up the side of a wall to get a running start for a spectacular flip, it finally dawned on me that the true precursor of Xena-style acrobatics is neither Hong Kong cinema nor Emma Peel, but the "Make 'Em Laugh" routine in *Singin' in the Rain*. Hmm. Maybe the Donald O'Connor character was actually a descendant of the Warrior Princess, much like Melinda Pappas?

Anyway, "The Execution" marks the return of Meleager from "The Prodigal" and is most notable for the conflict that arises between our heroines over just what to do with the fresh-off-the-wagon warrior, who may or may not have murdered someone in a drunken haze. Xena looks genuinely surprised when a staff-wielding Gabrielle steps between her and the fugitive Meleager—not that Gabby's efforts delay the Warrior Princess more than a second or two. And let it never be said that Xena doesn't enjoy her work; even with all the angst involved, look at the grin on her face and the gleam in her eye as she pits her skills against Meleager. As with her mock killing of Iolaus in "Judgment Day," she seems to be having rather more fun than might seem appropriate under the circumstances.

Argo gets to show off a bit, too, at one point using a jury-rigged seesaw to send Xena flying through the air.

What If They Paid in Dinars?

"Only 9 percent [of Americans] would be willing to pay to follow the exploits of *Xena: Warrior Princess*." (*TV Guide,* February 7–13, 1998)

In general, though, a fairly low-key episode, although Gabrielle's heartfelt declaration that "friends don't lie" and Xena's warning not to put people on pedestals seem more significant after next season's traumatic Rift.

Reality Check

Not a lot of history or mythology here, but the old woman knitting in front of the gallows, impatient for the execution, is a nod to Charles Dickens's *A Tale of Two Cities* (1859).

Rating: ⵣⵣ

Blind Faith

WRITTEN BY ADAM ARMUS & NORA KAY FOSTER
DIRECTED BY JOSH BECKER

Leather, eh? Bold choice.   —Vidalus to Xena

What Happens

After Gabrielle is abducted and sold into captivity by a would-be warlord named Palaemon, Xena is accidentally blinded by a bottle of sumac oil. Forcing Palaemon to act as her reluctant seeing-eye dog, she drags him along on her quest to rescue Gabrielle, who is being groomed to marry a king.

Remarks

What goes around comes around. Two years before, Lucy Lawless as Lyla in "As Darkness Falls" slipped Hercules a poison that rendered him temporarily blind. Now Lawless is the one acting blindness, which barely slows the Warrior Princess down.

"Blind Faith" is an enjoyable adventure that benefits from some nice chemistry between Xena and Palaemon, who turns out to be a decent sort after all, not to mention a useful guide for our sightless heroine. At first, he's overly enamored with Xena's bloodthirsty past, gushing about a slaughter in Corinth and another incident in which Xena apparently set some oil reserves on fire, creating an inferno that could be heard even in distant Athens, and comparing himself to both Draco and Callisto, until Xena sets him straight with her customary tact and diplomacy (i.e., she knocks him around some). In the end, he even gets a sidekick of his own, in the form of the apparently gay Vidalus, as he sets forth to follow Xena's heroic example.

In a neatly self-referential touch, Palaemon becomes the first person to beat our heroine's infamous pinch interrogations, by the simple but torturous expedient of calling her bluff. Even with Gabby's life at stake, you can hardly blame him for bragging about it.

But poor Gabrielle! What's with her and weddings, anyway? She almost becomes the bride of Morpheus, Perdicas is murdered on their honeymoon, now she's made to marry a dead king—and nearly sent to a fiery death on what fortuitously turns out to be history's slowest-moving conveyor belt. Even Gabrielle comments on her miserable luck: "All the men I get serious about seem to wind up dead."

Briefly hailed as the queen of this unnamed city-state, Gabby would become a queen for real in "The Quest," although at least she wouldn't have to marry anyone that time. Vidalus's comic efforts to convert our humble bard into a suitably ladylike queen recall *My Fair Lady* (1964), which leads me to wonder when the original Pygmalion is going to show up.

Judging from the paintings and sculptures that adorn the future queen's chambers, depicting Gabrielle's illustrious predecessors, it looks like the Xenaverse might actually hold some Gabby look-alikes after all.

Reality Check

The "wine of Dionysus" utilized during the marriage rite is presumably a less potent vintage than the brew quaffed by the Bacchae in "Girls Just Wanna Have Fun."

As for the notion that sumac-induced blindness can be cured by a mixture of palm oil and Egyptian senna, all I can say is, Kids, don't try this at home.

Rating: ⵣⵣⵣ

Ulysses

WRITTEN BY R. J. STEWART
DIRECTED BY MICHAEL LEVINE

Xena, would you mind knocking me unconscious?
—A seasick Gabrielle

What Happens

Xena does *The Odyssey* as our heroines run into Ulysses, long-missing king of Ithaca. Ulysses is on his way home from ten long years at the Trojan War, but Poseidon, God of the Seas, has vowed that Ulysses will never again see his homeland or his wife, Penelope. While Gabrielle copes (badly) with seasickness, romance blossoms between Xena and Ulysses.

Remarks

At last, Xena confronts Poseidon—as in that tantalizing scene in the opening credits. Although most of the clips in the credits sequence come from actual first-season episodes,

Xena's spectacular encounter with a towering, computer-generated sea god remained elusive and unexplained until now. In fact, that scene was dreamed up by producer Rob Tapert at the last minute, when it was felt that the credits needed more special effects.

The portrayal of Poseidon as a gigantic, Harryhausen-esque, animated figure is impressive, although markedly different from the way the other Greek gods normally appear on both *Hercules* and *Xena*, where they are portrayed by human-size actors in costume. Not even Zeus makes such flashy entrances, so we are left to assume that Poseidon is a blowhard with an ego larger than Mount Olympus.

"Ulysses" aired about the same time as a much-hyped NBC miniseries version of *The Odyssey*, which may have influenced the show's creators to dip into Homer once more. (One wonders whether Gabby eventually passed the story on to her friend from the "Athens City Academy of the Performing Bards.") A nice nod to series continuity has Xena and Ulysses acknowledging that they fought on opposite sides of the Trojan War before agreeing to let bygones be bygones. The character of Ulysses did not actually appear in "Beware of Greeks Bearing Gifts," but he would have borne some responsibility for the wooden horse that brought Troy down.

Sadly, there was not enough time in a one-hour episode to squeeze in all or even most of the entire Greek epic; the blinding of the cyclops, for instance, occurs offstage. Still, Xena does manage to co-opt two of the saga's big scenes, outsinging the dreaded Sirens (portrayed here as the original girl group à la the Supremes) to lure Ulysses back from a watery grave and sneaking under a table to give him a hidden assist when he has to string his legendarily unbendable bow. As is so often the case, history and literature have little idea how much they owe to the Warrior Princess of Amphipolis.

With the emphasis on Xena and Ulysses, Gabrielle doesn't have much to do except vomit over the rail of the ship, although she does have a whole comedy number in which she poses as a gypsy dancing girl, complete with phony,

Esmeralda-style curls, to distract the pirates. She and Xena even find time for a heart-to-heart that explicitly echoes the conversation they had in "Return of Callisto," when Xena gave Gabrielle her blessing to marry Perdicas. Gabrielle returns the favor here by wishing the best for Ulysses and Xena, no matter what.

Xena looks positively appalled, though, when Ulysses first suggests ditching his long-suffering bride to go adventuring with our Warrior Princess. It's probably just as well that she turns him down; if Homer's version is to be believed, Ulysses was hardly the most faithful of sweethearts. On his way back to Ithaca, the mythological hero loved and left a number of women, including such mythological sorceresses as Circe and Calypso. (No, not Callisto—*Calypso.*)

Actor John D'Aquino (Ulysses) had previously appeared on *seaQuest DSV*, *Quantum Leap*, and even an episode of *Seinfeld*. He's handsome enough, but seems a bit young and lacking in *gravitas* for such an epic hero. Amazingly, he and Xena manage to fall for each other despite the conspicuous absence of a single hot tub (which would have been a bit hard to pull off at sea, I guess). Then again, they do have a few things in common: Ulysses' faithful dog is named Argos, which is awfully close to Xena's beloved equine, Argo. And they've both blinded a cyclops or two.

Xena and Gabrielle would go to sea again this season, facing both Poseidon and *mal de mer*, in "Ancient Mariner." Counting the extended pirate flashback in "Destiny," Xena spent three episodes on the waves in one year alone.

Reality Check

Ulysses, known as Odysseus to the Greeks, was the hero of *The Odyssey*, an epic poem by Homer that dates back to approximately 900 B.C. Xena's Ulysses had it easier than Homer's hero, whose voyage home took a full ten years; given that in the Xenaverse, the Trojan War wrapped up the previous season, this Ulysses got back to Ithaca in record time. Many of the incidents in this episode are derived from the original poems:

the Sirens, Poseidon's wrath, the battle with the suitors. Conspicuously missing from the *Xena* version is Ulysses' son, Telemachus, a youth who Homer says helped his father slay the unruly suitors. Too bad. He would have given Gabrielle someone to talk to. (Telemachus, along with both Penelope and Circe, run into Xena in Ru Emerson's novel *The Empty Throne*, in which the Warrior Princess defends Ithaca while its king is away.)

Rating: ⟨⟨

The Price

WRITTEN BY STEVEN L. SEARS
DIRECTED BY OLEY SASSONE

We're going to kill them all! —Xena

What Happens
Xena takes command of a military outpost under siege by the relentless and implacable Horde and begins to revert to the bloodthirsty Xena of old, much to the dismay of Gabrielle. But a harder, meaner Xena may be their only hope for survival.

Remarks
Inspired by the 1964 movie *Zulu*, "The Price" is easily the scariest episode to date. From the moment the first dying body lurches onto the shore, abruptly terminating an idyllic afternoon of fishing, the episode grows steadily grimmer and more intense. "Things are going to get worse," Xena warns Gabrielle early on, and she's not kidding. The gripping canoe chase that follows is reminiscent of the excellent 1992 movie version of *The Last of the Mohicans*, while the Warrior Princess's takeover of the doomed garrison offers a fascinat-

ing look at the ruthless but effective military commander she once was and the loyalty she could inspire in her troops.

Wearing a bloodstained apron like her own bleeding sensibilities, Gabrielle proves she was paying attention in "Is There a Doctor in the House?" by setting up a combat hospital with little or no assistance from anyone else, including her best friend. Meanwhile, Xena puts even the dead bodies to work— just as she would, in a different fashion, in "The Debt."

In retrospect, "The Price" can be viewed as a thematic prequel to next season's Rift saga, which also would use harsh life-or-death decisions to test the limits of our heroines' friendship. Much of the Rift would be directed by Sassone, making his *Xena* debut here after previously directing a famously low-budget movie adaptation of *The Fantastic Four* comic book. That film was never officially released, but bootleg videos still turn up at science fiction conventions and some video stores (although you didn't hear that from me). After watching "The Price," I'm tempted to take a peek at it someday.

The roll call of Xena's former enemies grows longer as we learn that her original army barely survived an encounter with the Horde many years ago. What with the old Xena's wars against the Centaurs, the Bacchae, and now the Horde, one wonders when she had time to raid all those peasant villages.

In a rare quiet moment amid the carnage, listen as Xena almost tells Gabrielle she loves her, then wimps out and simply praises Gabby's compassion instead: "You don't know how much I love . . . that."

As for the frightening and mysterious Horde, Xena warns us that they'll be back, but there's been no sign of them since.

Reality Check

Okay, I'm stumped. Who in what passes for history in the Xenaverse are the Horde supposed to be? Zulus? Apaches? Picts? Klingons? Not even Xena knows where they're from. She implies at one point that they come from the west, but how far west are we talking about? With their bones and furs and garish war paint, they don't look like Italians to me.

Maybe I've been spoiled by too much *Star Trek*, but sometimes when Xena says "Horde," I hear "Borg." Certainly the Horde seems to be just as inexorable as those creepiest of twenty-fourth-century alien conquerors.

Rating: ⟨⟨⟨⟨

Lost Mariner

WRITTEN BY STEVEN L. SEARS
DIRECTED BY GARTH MAXWELL

Athena knew what she was doing. You just have to have faith. —Xena to Cecrops

What Happens

Our heroines become unwilling passengers on a cursed ship captained by the ageless and undying Cecrops. To free Cecrops and his crew of the damned, Xena must brave both the wrath of Poseidon and the fury of Charybdis to fulfill an ancient prophecy by the goddess Athena.

Remarks

The big surprise of "Lost Mariner" is that neither Xena nor Gabrielle ends up falling for Cecrops, even though he's much more appealing than either Ulysses or Perdicas. Actor Tony Todd, who plays the immortal ship captain, had previously played a wide variety of characters on the *Star Trek* shows— *The Next Generation, Deep Space Nine, Voyager—The X-Files*, and *Hercules*, as well as a cursed ghost in two *Candyman* horror movies. The character was popular enough with *Xena* fans for rumors to spread on the Net that Cecrops would return in the third season, possibly as a love interest for either Xena or Gabrielle, although this turned out not to be the case.

Xena's faith in Athena, as cited above, is surprising, given that until now the Warrior Princess has seldom had a kind word for any of the gods; she even snarled at a priest's faith in the god of healing back in the first season. One wonders whether Xena has had any personal experience with the goddess of wisdom in the past.

Xena in Pop Culture . . .

"Move over, Xena: Wonder Woman could be coming back to TV to reclaim her title as the small screen's sexiest superheroine." (*New York Post,* December 12, 1997.)

Memo to our heroines: After pissing Poseidon off twice in three episodes, stay off the water for a while! Despite his bluster, however, he must have a short attention span; Xena would sail to both Britannia and China next season without encountering any grief from Poseidon.

Although confined to the Ship of Coots for most of the episode, Xena manages a few nifty stunts near the beginning as she eludes a pack of scurvy pirates by skipping her chakram off the surface of the sea and making her most spectacular leap ever—over what looks like hundreds of feet of briny ocean. As for Gabrielle, reduced to eating raw squid and fending off geriatric admirers . . . well, she copes with *mal de mer* slightly better than she did in "Ulysses," thanks to a little pressure-point medicine from Xena, but it's still not exactly her finest hour.

Cecrops may have been confined to his ship for three hundred years, but he's obviously been keeping up with current events. At one point, he compares Xena to Lord Sinteres, the warrior-philosopher she dispatched back in "Royal Couple" (also written by Sears). But who is this "Mordechai" who has supposedly placed a price on Xena's head? Did we miss something?

Reality Check

Just as "Girls Just Wanna Have Fun" merged the historical Bacchae with Victorian vampire lore, "Lost Mariner" blends the Greek tale of Cecrops with a much later legend, that of the Flying Dutchman. The story of how Cecrops selected Athena over Poseidon when it came time to choose his city's patron god goes pretty much as Gabrielle recalls it here, except that the mythological Cecrops was half man and half serpent.

The Flying Dutchman was a late-medieval legend about an arrogant sea captain who was cursed by God (as opposed to by Poseidon), and doomed to sail the seas until the Day of Judgment. Unlike Cecrops's, this captain's curse had no loopholes nor was there any Warrior Princess to help him escape his doom.

Charybdis was a gigantic whirlpool and/or sea monster created by Zeus, which challenged both the Argonauts and Ulysses on their respective voyages. Traditionally located in the Strait of Messina, between Sicily and Italy, it is usually paired with another maritime menace, a cliff-dwelling sea monster named Scylla; I guess *Xena* lacked the time (or the special effects budget) to include Scylla, too.

Cecrops's claim that he had been cursed for three hundred years, ever since the founding of Athens, gives us another historical touchstone; legend holds that Cecrops was the first king of Attica, who founded the city of Athens sometime between 2000 and 1500 B.C., while the historical record suggests that Athens dates back to at least the twelfth century B.C.

Athena, the Greek goddess of wisdom, was portrayed as a scantily clad beach babe (wearing glasses!) in her single appearance in the Xenaverse, a brief cameo in "The Apple" on *Hercules*. One hopes that the character will get a less silly interpretation if and when she ever shows her face on *Xena*.

Finally, Cecrops is called "Rama" by an apparently Hindu crew member. Although the name is unfamiliar to both Cecrops and Xena, Rama is a major hero in Hindu mythology, often considered an incarnation of Vishnu. The epic poem *The Ramayana*, which tells his story, dates back to around 500 B.C., although pantheistic religion in India is considerably older, roughly coincident with classical paganism in Greece. (Just to clarify, Cecrops is clearly not meant to be Rama himself, but this reference gives some grounding to alternative faiths in the Xenaverse . . . boy, doesn't that sound like a future thesis title!)

Rating: ⳤⳤⳤ

A Comedy of Eros

WRITTEN BY CHRIS MANHEIM
DIRECTED BY CHARLES SIEBERT

Round up those virgins!   —Draco

What Happens

Cupid's infant son, Bliss, steals his father's bow and arrows and slips away to have a little fun on his own. Soon unrequited love is breaking out all over, including men for men, men for cows, young maidens for old men, and even a Warrior Princess for one of her oldest foes. Thanks to the invisible cherub's bowmanship, Xena develops a massive crush on Draco, who lusts after Gabrielle, who becomes Joxer's number one fan.

Remarks

The second season ends on a comic note (for all but Joxer) with this romantic roundelay, which actually owes more to *A Midsummer Night's Dream* than to *A Comedy of Errors*, although one could scarcely expect a writer to pass up a pun like that, Eros being the original Greek name for Cupid. For once, Xena wants to make love, not war, and ends up inflicting a little bit of both on an understandably suspicious Draco, who gives a return performance here, after his debut way back in "Sins of the Past." Intent on abducting the virginal worshipers of Hestia, he no doubt remembers the seductive tricks Xena used to pull in her bad old days, as seen in "The Warrior Princess." And are we surprised that, in the grand tradition of *Xena* seduction scenes, she drops in on him during a private bath?

Besides being a lot of fun, "A Comedy of Eros" is also a sort of sequel to "For Him the Bell Tolls," with Joxer again the temporary beneficiary of a supernatural love charm. Gabrielle calls him "Pookie" and even joins in a spirited rendition of "Joxer the Mighty," until she comes to her senses. As in "Bell," it falls upon Xena to offer a bit of sympathy to the dejected Joxer at the end of the episode, while Gabby remains oblivious to the poor sap's true feelings . . . at least for now.

The sound effects team has a ball on this episode. Check out the sound of rubber being snapped as Gabby tugs on Joxer's ear with her teeth, not to mention the childish giggles of the floating baby cherub, a laugh-provoking special effect in his own right who looks more like the conventional Valentine's Day conception of Cupid than like his surfer dude father (Karl Urban, popping up for the third time this season).

Subtext seekers are further tantalized by a slow-motion bait-and-switch routine in which, for a few provocative moments, it looks as if Bliss's archery is about to set Gabrielle's heart afire for Xena—until Joxer accidentally steps between them. So near and yet so far . . .

Amazon fans should note that Gabrielle dons her Amazon princess regalia for the climax. I guess she carries it with her everywhere. Draco has apparently been keeping tabs on Xena, casually referring to the "mind games" she played on Zagreus ("A Day in the Life").

Reality Check

Hestia, known as Vesta to the Romans, was the Olympian goddess of hearth and home. She was also sister to Zeus, father of Aphrodite, which makes her (according to most mythological accounts) Cupid's aunt. Her temple in Rome was indeed attended by untouched maidens, better and more accurately known as the "vestal virgins." She does seem to be a homebody; to date, she has yet to manifest herself on *Xena*, although the Hestian virgins were the subject of a funny one-liner in "Here She Comes . . . Miss Amphipolis" and Anteus's wife pleaded for Hestia's aid in "Altared States."

(What's with these goddesses, anyway? Hera and Aphrodite get all bent out of shape if anyone even scratches their temples, yet Artemis let Velasca blow one of her temples to smithereens in "A Necessary Evil" while Hestia doesn't lift a finger when Draco tries to sell her virgins to slavers. The ways of the gods really are mysterious sometimes.)

Rating: ⵣⵣⵣ

Year 3 a.x.

The third season began with the show already a bona fide media sensation. The highest-rated drama in syndication, *Xena* had become almost as unstoppable as its eponymous heroine, while its star achieved new heights of celebrity. It seemed you couldn't pick up a magazine or turn on a TV talk show without seeing Lucy Lawless or a reference to the show. (See "The Lucy Lawless List of Lists.") As the first new episode debuted in October 1997, Lawless was starring (and singing) at the Eugene O'Neill Theatre on Broadway as unrepentant bad girl Rizzo in the musical *Greece*—oops, I mean *Grease*—eliciting cheers and applause when, night after night, she emitted Xena's fearsome battle cry during the big dance contest at Rydell High. Besides appearing on such shows as *The Rosie O'Donnell Show* and *Late Night with Conan O'Brien*, she still found time to attend New York's first official *Xena* convention at the Marriott Marquis Hotel in Manhattan's Times Square on Sunday, September 28. (Okay, the event was officially billed as a combined *Hercules/Xena* convention, but it was a real *Xena* crowd that showed up, greeting plugs for *Hercules* with polite applause while reserving their most enthusiastic whoops for Lawless herself.) A weekend later, Renee O'Connor, Hudson Leick, Robert Trebor, and Ted Raimi all trooped out to Valley Forge, Pennsylvania, for yet another convention. Fans at both events were tantalized by clips from upcoming episodes, including "The Furies," "Been There, Done That," and "Warrior . . . Priestess . . . Tramp." Elsewhere, producer Rob Tapert promised that "season three will be a slight continuation of last season but with fewer comedies and the darker shows being really dark."

But could the new season possibly live up to the fans' expectations? The gods (or at least the Internet) were buzzing with rumors about an event ominously referred to as "the Rift." Could it be true? Would the powers that be actually tear apart the unbreakable bond uniting Xena and Gabrielle?

The world held its breath . . .

The Lucy Lawless List of Lists

. Like I said, Lucy Lawless was a genuine media darling as the third season began, appearing again and again on the hot lists of both mainstream and genre magazines:

1. "The 50 Most Beautiful People in the World" (*People*, May 12, 1997)

2. "TV's 40 Most Fascinating Stars of '97" (*People*, September 1, 1997)

3. "The 25 Most Intriguing Women in Science Fiction" (*Sci-Fi Universe*, September, 1997)

4. "1997 Performers of the Year" (*TV Guide*, November 20, 1997)

5. "TV's Top 20 Sexy Stars" (*TV Guide*, December 22, 1997)

6. "The 25 Most Intriguing People of the Year" (*People*, December 29, 1997)

7. "The Top 10 Warlords of 500 B.C." (*Athens News & World Report*, Ides of March/-500)

(Okay, I made that last one up, but it's still impressive.)

The Furies

WRITTEN BY R. J. STEWART
DIRECTED BY GILBERT SHILTON

I'm a lunatic with lethal combat skills. —Xena

What Happens

Ares persuades the Furies to afflict Xena with madness and persecution for having failed to avenge the death of her father. In the temple of the Furies, however, a crazed and occasionally goofy Warrior Princess convinces them that her true father is someone else.

Remarks

And Hercules thinks he has family problems! The big question here, of course, is who is Xena's father, anyway? Is Ares really Xena's dad, or was she just pulling a fast one on the Furies? Xena says it doesn't matter, but the evidence is provocative. She puts on a pretty impressive display of demigoddesshood at the climax of this tale, defeating the God of War in a fair fight, but I suppose it could be argued that her temporary insanity gave her the extra edge she needed to hold her own against a god. On the other hand, Ares' alleged paternity, hinted at as far back as "Ties That Bind," would certainly explain his relentless interest in turning Xena to his side—not to mention her near-supernatural abilities. Even Alecto remarks on Ares' "obsession" with Xena, while we have previously seen (in "The Xena Scrolls") that the love/hate relationship between Xena and Ares will extend even unto the twentieth century.

In the final scene, Xena mourns the loss of her mortal father, apparently killed by Cyrene when Xena was only seven years old (to stop him from sacrificing Xena to Ares), but is she regretting the fact of his death or the loss of her belief that he actually was her father? Curiously, his name, previously revealed as Atrius, is never mentioned in this episode. The possibility that Ares might be Xena's genuine parent adds an ickily incestuous flavor to some of their previous scenes together, including his carnal coupling with Callisto while she occupied Xena's body in "Intimate Stranger." (Let's see, if Xena is Ares' daughter, that makes Hercules her uncle, Aphrodite her aunt, Cupid her cousin, and Zeus her grandpa. This could get sticky.)

Xena in Pop Culture . . .

"The popularity of Buffy and her spiritual sisters—Xena, Captain Janeway on 'Star Trek: Voyager' and Dana Scully on 'The X-Files'—suggests that fantasy television can tell stories about women that reality-based shows won't." (Adam Rogers, *Newsweek*, March 2, 1998)

According to Lawless, "We decided it was not good for the character to be a demigod, in spite of all the amazing things she does. The strength of the character is her mortality, and that's what people relate to."

Still . . . a murdered husband, attempted matricide, hints of incest and adultery. Geez, what is this supposed to be, a Greek tragedy?

Oh, yeah, that's right.

Anyway, the third season definitely gets off to a dramatic, occasionally tangled start with at least a couple of indisputable revelations about Xena's childhood. One has to wonder how her surviving brother will react when and if he hears the news.

It's not all doom and gloom, though, especially in the opening scenes, when Psycho Xena's wacky antics provide some utter hilarity. Riding backward on Argo or anticipating the dreaded fighting style of the Three Stooges, Lucy Lawless seems to be having a ball playing a total loon (although a vocal contingent of fans was turned off by the heavy dose of slapstick in an otherwise dramatic episode). Her ultimate battle with Ares, high atop a row of mounted flagpoles, is an exhilarating one, with Xena even more manic and hyperactive than usual.

In her madness, she also confronts hallucinations of some of her most deadly foes, including Bacchus, Callisto, and the skeletal dryads from "Girls Just Wanna Have Fun." She proves as well that even a crazy Xena can easily clobber a bevy of bounty hunters, skipping her usual battle cry in favor of an enthusiastic cock-a-doodle-doo. It does seem kind of odd, though, that Gabrielle is so agitated about this price that the Furies' high priest has placed on Xena's head. So what else is new? Xena has been a target for bounty hunters at least as recently as "Lost Mariner." One suspects that half the warlords in the Xenaverse would gladly pay to see her dead; why, even her deceased body was worth a pile of dinars in "The Quest."

Gabrielle doesn't have a lot to do in this episode besides look concerned (and, okay, talk a naked Xena out of torching an innocent village), but we do see a few carefree moments between the two before the Furies' whammy takes effect, during which we learn that Xena doesn't like to gamble (except with her life), cooks an unappetizing breakfast, and really likes those "little dumplings with the red stuff inside," apparently a specialty of Gabrielle's.

The first airings of this episode ended with a public service announcement in which Lucy Lawless stepped out of character to address the problem of domestic violence and recommend the National Domestic Violence Hotline.

Reality Check

According to Greek mythology, the Furies—Alecto, Tisiphone, and Megaera—indeed punished those who defied their harsh codes of justice. Most accounts portrayed them as serpent-tressed terrors who dwelt in Tartarus, whereas these Furies seem to be moonlighting as exotic dancers. They were also known as the Erinyes or the Eumenides. Alecto should not be confused with Electra, who was Orestes' sister (unseen in this episode).

The story of Orestes, who was tormented by the Furies under similar circumstances, is often cited in this episode, and Gabrielle eventually finds him in an asylum, still insane despite his having killed his mother, Clytemnestra, to avenge her murder of his father, Agamemnon. This conforms more or less to the standard mythological account, except that Orestes drew the wrath of the Furies for killing his mother, not for *not* killing her, which seems to be the problem in Xena's case. It was instead the Oracle of Delphi that required his mother's death of Orestes. Rather than ending up in an asylum, he was eventually pardoned by the goddess Athena. (Apparently, Ares expected Xena to remain insane after sacrificing Cyrene, but it's all a bit confusing.)

As usual, time in the Xenaverse seems to flow differently than elsewhere. Mythology claims that Orestes avenged his father's death at least seven years after the Fall of Troy, which we all know took place just two years prior to this episode.

Xena, in her madness, also manages to paraphrase a bit of
Shakespeare's *King Lear* ("As flies to wanton boys, are we to
the gods/They kill us for their sport")—not bad, considering
that the play wouldn't be written for another two thousand
years!

Rating: ⵣⵣⵣ

Been There, Done That

WRITTEN BY HILARY J. BADER
DIRECTED BY ANDREW MERRIFIELD

*Frankly, I was expecting Hercules . . . or at least
Sinbad.*   —A helpless villager

What Happens

A rooster awakens Xena and Gabrielle one morning, and
they are joined shortly thereafter by an ebullient Joxer. As they
make their way through an unnamed village, Joxer is accidentally killed when he wanders into a duel between members of
two feuding houses. Xena mourns her comrade's loss, until
she wakes to find the same day starting again. Convinced that
she is somehow destined to change things for the better, Xena
keeps trying to straighten out all the conflicts in the feud-torn
hamlet, but things keep going tragically awry. Argo dies, or
Gabrielle dies, or Xena dies, or the damn rooster dies . . .

Remarks

Groundhog Day comes to ancient Greece as Xena finds
that tomorrow is not necessarily another day. The body count
is appalling as utter carnage breaks out in what appears to be
the grumpiest village in the Xenaverse, but it's all in good fun,
and a welcome change of pace after the intense dramatics of
the previous episode. "Been There, Done That" is an inge-

nious farce that is often laugh-out-loud funny, never more so than when a thoroughly fed-up Warrior Princess uses her chakram to turn that annoying rooster into an explosion of feathers. Or when an even more frustrated Xena casually murders Joxer and then goes back to sleep!

Speaking of which, this episode probably sets an all-time record for Joxer abuse. In a single one-hour show, he is hit on the noggin with an iron horseshoe, splattered with egg yolk, stabbed through the heart with a rapier (demonstrating once and for all just how ineffective that hubcap thingie on his chest is), subjected to noogies from Xena, has the same horseshoe dropped on his foot, smacks himself in the face with the horseshoe, gets his chest pinched by Gabrielle, faints dead away, is conked on the head by the horseshoe again, has his face shoved into raw eggs, is knocked to the ground by Xena, kicked and beaten during a "group hug," killed by a volley of arrows, killed by a well-thrown chakram, sent spinning like a top, knocked to the ground again, brained by a mace, slammed by a swinging barn door, and (finally) hit by a mallet. In short, there's plenty here for Joxer lovers and Joxer haters alike.

And is it just me, or does Xena look a bit more broken up by Argo's temporary demise than by Joxer's? Poor Argo, this is the second time she's almost been killed by a vengeful foe of her warrior mistress. (Remember Callisto-as-Xena in "Intimate Stranger"?) At least this time she didn't pick up any scars.

Only Xena retains any recall of what occurred before each day's renewal, and Gabrielle and Joxer and even Argo look more than a little baffled by her increasingly odd behavior. Given that she recovered from insanity only the episode before, their looks of concern come off as even more heartfelt than they might have been otherwise.

If the structure of this adventure seems much like an interactive computer game, with an infinite number of resets but only one correct solution, it may not be a coincidence. The screenwriter, Hilary J. Bader, had previously authored two successful CD-ROM games, *Star Trek: Klingon* and *Star Trek: Borg*. (Thanks to Kim Kindya of Simon & Schuster Interactive for this particular insight.) And just as in any good computer game, a grisly (if fortuitously short-lived) death lurks around every corner.

Meanwhile, subtext fans can take comfort in the way Xena and Gabrielle drift asleep in each other's arms after Joxer's funeral. And just who gave Xena the hickey that Joxer spots the next morning?

Xena also gets a chance to reprise (briefly) her song of lament, heard previously in "The Path Not Taken," and other tragic episodes as she keens over Joxer's funeral pyre. And check out her colorful new epithet: "Son of a Bacchae!" For those counting, Xena's efforts to reunite a doomed couple now makes *four* royal marriages preserved by our heroines. And now that I think of it, they also reunited the king in "A Solstice Carol" with his estranged wife. Perhaps their true calling is not fighting evil at all, but couples' counseling?

We also learn that Joxer is fluent in pig Latin: "Ix-nay on the ove-lay alk-tay!"

For the record, Xena wakes thirteen times, counting the last time.

Reality Check

Although the actual location of this episode is never specified, it bears a marked resemblance to the Verona of Shakespeare's *Romeo and Juliet*, right down to the star-crossed lovers with suicidal tendencies. The rival houses here are called Manos and Lycos, not Montague and Capulet, but as Juliet herself once asked, "What's in a name?"

Rating: ⚡⚡⚡⚡

The Dirty Half Dozen

WRITTEN BY STEVEN L. SEARS
DIRECTED BY RICK JACOBSON

I don't think I've ever been a part of a true disaster before.

—Gabrielle

What Happens

When Ares provides Agathon, yet another ambitious warlord, with the unbreakable metal of Hephaestus, Xena recruits a gang of cutthroats to raid Agathon's fortress and destroy the metal before the warlord can lead his invulnerable troops to conquer the world. Xena's new team includes a thief, an assassin, a swaggering gladiator, and a man-hating, knife-throwing female slaver, all of whom are former protégés of the Warrior Princess and all of whom trust each other about as much as they trust Xena, which is not very much at all.

Remarks

While not quite the disaster that Gabrielle envisioned, this episode was a bit of a disappointment after the dramatic and comedic highlights of the previous two. A relatively (by *Xena* standards) straightforward, run-around-and-save-the-world, action-adventure yarn, it suffers by comparison to both "The Furies" and "Been There, Done That." Oh, well, I suppose they have to do a routine show now and then, if only so we can truly appreciate the more unconventional episodes.

Taken on its own terms, this adventure has its moments, like an all-night Mexican standoff between the newly assembled cutthroats that lasts until all involved are practically (and, in one case, literally) asleep on their feet—although Agathon's supposedly indestructible warriors, clad in their spiky steel armor, prove considerably less formidable than they're made out to be. These would-be terminators can slaughter six thousand Athenian soldiers (offstage) but are repelled with surprising ease by Xena's scruffy band of riffraff. Even Gabrielle's wooden staff, which conspicuously *doesn't* break against the super-armor, is enough to keep the bad guys at bay, which makes you wonder whether the aforementioned Athenian infantry had really been eating their Wheaties. Agathon himself comes off as yet another heavy-metal warlord with more attitude than personality; it's not at all clear what exactly Ares sees in him, even though Agathon does have a chakram-like throwing weapon of his own. (This episode implies, more than once, that Xena's round killing thing is made of some similarly supernatural material; certainly, the chakram makes mincemeat of Agathon's supermetal in the climactic showdown.)

Xena is in her element, of course, killing mercenaries with bloodthirsty abandon while keeping her uneasy allies in line through sheer intimidation, not to mention adept manipulation. As usual, her battle-hardened former associates have no idea why she keeps Gabrielle around, at least not until the perky bard proves herself in combat. (And why doesn't that staff break, anyway? For Zeus's sake, Xena's sword does!)

On a more serious level, Xena is forced to confront her guilty past once again, especially since she claims to have turned all four of her recruits into the callous killers they are today, provoking much sincere (and slightly mushy) conversation between Xena and Gabrielle about their effect upon each other.

Ares reappears for the first time since the gut-wrenching events of "The Furies," but, curiously, neither he nor Xena shows any interest in discussing matters of parentage or mutual recrimination. That would have to wait until next week, in "The Deliverer," which finds Ares once again toying with the notion of bestowing the metal of Hephaestus on deserving warlords. (See the "Remarks" on that episode for some thorny questions of chronology.)

For continuity buffs, this episode is a feast of name-dropping, with references to Callisto, Perdicas, Autolycus, Thersites ("A Fistful of Dinars"), and even King Gregor ("Cradle of Hope"). In particular, knife lady learns the hard way just how touchy Gabrielle still is regarding her late, lamented husband. Xena and Gabrielle are also briefly seen playing a game of Twenty Questions, as in "A Day in the Life."

"Prometheus," two seasons before, demonstrated that the metal of Hephaestus, turned against itself, produced an effect that invariably destroyed its wielder. Given the way Xena and her allies eventually use Agathon's own weapons against his troops with no fatal consequences, I suppose we have to assume that this is a significantly different alloy—or that Hephaestus has finally worked that particular bug out of the process.

And where exactly does all this take place? Well, the Athenian army is near enough to be massacred, but the prison that Xena breaks most of her recruits out of is noticeably Egyptian in design, with mammoth Pharaonic sculptures adorning its walls. Egypt under the reign of the Ptolemies, perhaps? Xena sure gets around; next episode she makes it to Britannia.

Reality Check

According to mythology, Hephaestus had little reason to aid Ares, with whom Aphrodite carried on an adulterous affair, although it is unknown whether this scandal has yet occurred in the Xenaverse.

The exact nature of "the metal of Hephaestus" is never defined, but we should note that iron was in use in classical Greece as early as about 1000 B.C. Possibly this mysterious metal was some special alloy as yet unknown to the ancient world.

Traditionally, Agathon was not a maniacal warlord but a Greek poet mentioned in Plato's *Symposium*.

The Dirty Dozen (1967) is a classic adventure movie set during World War II, featuring a similar team of convicts and killers. As I recall, no ancient Greek deities figured in the plot.

Rating: ⚚⚚

The Deliverer

WRITTEN BY STEVEN L. SEARS
DIRECTED BY OLEY SASSONE

Still miffed about the insanity thing? Get over it.
                                        —Ares

What Happens

Learning that her old enemy Julius Caesar is at war with the warrior queen Boadicea, Xena travels to Britannia to join the fight. Along the way, Gabrielle befriends Khrafstar, a priest who preaches the glory of "the One God." While Boadicea and Xena prepare for their final battle against Caesar's Roman legions, Gabrielle joins Khrafstar at his temple—where she is tricked into killing a priestess in self-defense. Turns out that Khrafstar's god is a nasty entity named Dahak, who required the sacrifice of Gabrielle's blood innocence to enter our world. Too late, Xena arrives to bring down the temple, the ruins of which would someday be known as . . . Stonehenge.

Remarks

Oh, my. To say this episode was momentous is something of an understatement. When Xena's much-anticipated re-match with Caesar turns out to be largely peripheral to the real dramatic fireworks later on, you know that more is at stake than usual for our intrepid duo. The entire first half of "The Deliverer" turns out to be an elaborate exercise in misdirection, distracting the viewer from the shocking revelations sneaking up on Gabrielle. Xena pretty much ignores the entire "One God" subplot (despite a personal warning from Ares to destroy the temple) until hell has literally broken loose, and Khrafstar seems at first to be merely another in that long line of sensitive males whose primary job is to keep Gabrielle company while Xena wreaks havoc, as in "The Titans," "Altared States," "Giant Killer," and others.

Surprise! Khrafstar is anything but a nice guy, and neither is his god. Even the musical score plays along with the deception, providing Khrafstar's sermons with gentle melodies before erupting into *Omen*-style chanting during the horrific blood sacrifice sequence.

"The Deliverer" starts out as a sequel to "Destiny," but its true thematic precursor is "Dreamworker," also written by Sears. The followers of Dahak succeed where the priests of Morpheus failed—in bringing about the loss of Gabrielle's blood innocence for the sake of their god. That Gabrielle's first kill was more or less inevitable, given her association with Xena, makes it no less shocking. Gabrielle, who could not bring herself to take a life even after Callisto murdered her beloved husband, finally has blood on her hands, both literally and spiritually. Small wonder that she murmurs at the end, "Everything's changed. Everything," in what is almost a direct quote from Xena in "Dreamworker" two years before: "The moment you kill . . . everything changes. Everything."

Yes, Virginia, the Rift has begun.

Before Xena realizes that Khrafstar's god is "not the one god of the Israelites," the emphasis is on Caesar and Boadicea. Indeed, with warring Romans and Celts and (we think) early Christians, it almost feels as if Xena has wandered into an episode of *Roar*, a short-lived fantasy television series set in the Roman-occupied Ireland of 400 A.D. The usual Xena humor is largely absent as our heroine finds herself confronted with not one but two specters from her past.

More of the Warrior Princess's personal history is revealed as Xena confesses that "long ago" she and Boadicea were allies in Gaul. But the old, bad Xena betrayed Boadicea, stealing her army out from under her and ordering her killed. The other woman escaped to Britannia, however, and only reluctantly accepts Xena's aid here and now. Jennifer Ward-Lealand makes a vivid impression as the legendary British heroine, complete with fabled war chariot, even though her saga is dropped like a hot potato once the threat of Dahak kicks into high gear. One has to assume that Boadicea is not going to look kindly on Xena for abandoning her here, right on the verge of her big battle with Caesar's legions.

As for Caesar, once again played by Karl Urban, he appears to have changed not at all in the eleven years that have supposedly passed since "Destiny." The sight of Gabby crucified upon a hilltop eerily echoes Xena's similar ordeal, although, mercifully, help comes in time to keep Gabby's legs from being broken, as Xena's were. Xena achieves a measure of revenge against her old betrayer, snatching away his hostages before his eyes, but their reunion is limited to a few hostile stares and a single exchange of weapons, across an empty battlefield. A more satisfying confrontation between the two would have to wait until "When in Rome . . ." later in the season. (It's also possible that Xena and Caesar have run into each other at some other time since that unsuccessful crucifixion years ago; this episode does not explicitly state that this is their first meeting since "Destiny.")

Possibly the oddest, and least satisfying, aspect of this episode is that we are never told the outcome of the "one great battle" between the Romans and the Britons that is brewing even as Xena rushes off to save Gabrielle from the sinister cultists. Judging from history—always dangerous where *Xena* is concerned—it seems moderately safe to assume that Caesar's destiny did not come to an inglorious end beneath the wheels of Boadicea's chariot, even though he may well have been repelled for the time being. History tells us that both Caesar and Boadicea lost decisive battles in Britain, although they never actually fought each other, so the battle could conceivably have gone either way. (See Reality Check for the real scoop.)

Xena, by the way, must have gotten chatty one night when no one was looking: Gabrielle now seems quite familiar with Xena's history with Caesar, even though she was not privy to the fever-induced flashbacks in "Destiny." Perhaps Xena talked in her sleep during that long trek to Mount Nessus?

And that's not all Gabby has learned; an early scene makes it clear that she has mastered the seasickness cure that Xena taught her in "Lost Mariner," a trick she shares with Khrafstar before his true colors are revealed.

And speaking of Khrafstar, the self-proclaimed "Deliverer" of the title . . . while one can only admire the false sincerity with which he played a visionary man of peace, you have to wonder about that scheme of his. It worked, granted, but it seems a bit on the risky side. Did he actually plan to get captured by the Romans *twice*, and nearly executed in the process, or did he just have a heckuva lot of faith in his god?

Little is known of Dahak himself, also called the Dark One, except that even Ares and the other Olympians are reluctant to oppose him directly. He may be the dreaded god of mixed metaphors, though, since we are told at different points that he will "bring the winter of a thousand years" and "the cleansing fire of war." Make up your mind, folks!

Finally, the chronology of the third season is confused somewhat by a puzzling prologue in which Ares toys once again with an amazing new metal that he intends to provide to the worthy few. This sounds like a teaser for "The Dirty Half Dozen," which actually aired the week before, making one wonder at first whether these two episodes took place in reverse order. "Gabrielle's Hope," which picks up the story almost immediately after the events of "The Deliverer," pretty much kills that theory, though. Perhaps Ares plans to try out the supermetal on another warlord later on? (The prologue also contains a brief appearance by a brand-new immortal, Discord, who comes off as the God of War's bratty Goth kid sister. Her sole purpose in the plot seems to be to give Ares someone to talk to, although she would make subsequent appearances on *Hercules*.)

Actor Marton Csokas, who plays Khrafstar with deceptive humility, would return shortly as Xena's former lover Borias in both parts of "The Debt."

Director Oley Sassone, who previously tested Xena and Gabrielle's friendship in "The Price," would ultimately direct the majority of the Rift story line, including "The Debt" (both parts) and "The Bitter Suite."

Reality Check

Whew! Where to begin? History gets wrung through a wringer here, beginning with the climactic revelation that Xena created Stonehenge. In fact, the construction of Stonehenge is generally believed to have occurred between 2000 and 1500 B.C., predating even the Trojan War and making it the oldest event to be squeezed into the Xenaverse so far. I suppose one could rationalize that the construction of the temple of the One God occurred several centuries before it collapses into ruins here, but that assumes a much more advanced knowledge of architecture than is believed to have existed in the British Isles at that time.

At the other end of the time line we have Boadicea, a genuine British heroine who fought a losing war against the Roman occupation around 62 A.D., more than a hundred years after the death of Julius Caesar. Xena informs Gabrielle that Boadicea and her late husband, Prasutagus, began their war in Gaul and were forced to retreat to Britannia only after Xena stole their army, but conventional history suggests that this revolt against Roman rule began and ended in Britain. She eventually committed suicide by poison, hopefully not five minutes after the end of this episode! A monument to Boadicea, sculpted by Thomas Thornycroft in the 1850s, can still be found in London, near Big Ben. *Xena* fans may want to compare the statue to her portrayal in this episode.

Julius Caesar invaded Britain in 54 B.C. but never entirely subdued the island in his lifetime. His successors fought and defeated Boadicea a couple of generations later.

Dahak is a demon from Persian mythology, destined to be loosed upon the world at the end of time, and a fairly obscure figure these days. While it seems a bit odd that he would have worshipers in Celtic Britain, it is not strictly impossible; Eastern religious beliefs, most notably Mithraism, are known to have made their way to the British Isles by way of the Roman occupation.

Discord, also known as Eris, is the sister of Ares and the mother of Strife.

Rating: ⵣⵣⵣ

Gabrielle's Hope

WRITTEN BY R. J. STEWART
DIRECTED BY CHARLES SIEBERT AND ANDREW MERRIFIELD

Nice blade.   —Xena on the Sword in the Stone

What Happens

Shortly after the previous episode, Xena and Gabrielle's attempt to leave Britannia is foiled by angry peasants, sword-wielding knights, and a trio of creepy banshees. Eventually they discover that Gabrielle is pregnant with Dahak's child. But is the baby girl, who is born hours later in a stone fortress, innocent or inherently evil? The question divides first the Warriors of the Pierced Heart, a fraternal order of the knights, then Gabrielle and Xena themselves.

Remarks

Not wanting to beat a dead Celt, but isn't Xena even vaguely curious who won that big battle between Caesar and Boadicea? As I recall, history as we know it hung in the balance.

Oh, well. That nagging loose end aside, "Gabrielle's Hope" is a gripping sequel to "The Deliverer." Xena and Gabrielle's friendship has been tested before, as in "The Execution" and "The Price," but the intensity is heightened considerably when the life of Hope, Gabby's newborn daughter, is at stake. To make matters even more complicated, it's impossible to tell which woman is in the right. The burning question of who killed a knight in the castle remains unanswered, at least for now. Was it really Hope or was it some unknown party who came and went through one of the fortress's many secret

---

"It looks like they put my head on He-Man's body!"
—Lucy Lawless on the first Xena action figure (*Entertainment Weekly*, November 24, 1995)

---

passageways? The answer would not be revealed until "Maternal Instincts," several weeks later.

The show's creators deserve credit for not backing away from Xena's dark side and all its implications. When was the last time you saw a prime-time heroine determined to hack a little baby to death? Holy infanticide, Batgirl!

Gabby's solution of last resort, placing the baby in the river, echoes both "Cradle of Hope" from the first season and the Old Testament story of the infant Moses. Curiously, the episode of *Hercules* that aired the following week, "Two Men and a Baby," featured yet another child of destiny set afloat in a stream, leading one to wonder whether the waterways of the Xenaverse are positively overflowing with misplaced infants.

I was sure at first, by the way, that Gabrielle's baby was going to turn out to be Merlin, who was also supposedly sired by a demon, and my suspicions only grew stronger as Xena stumbled onto both the Knights of the Round Table and the

Sword in the Stone. Then the baby turned out to be a girl. Go figure.

If nothing else, Hope's birth, bringing new life into the world, helps Gabrielle overcome some of her guilt about murdering that priestess, whose name we learn here was Meridian; in geography, a meridian is a line of division, so it's probable that the priestess was so named because she marks a crucial transition in Gabrielle's life. Conspicuously, and perhaps just as symbolically, Xena is shown to be still bearing the physical scars she received from the Deliverer's claws last episode. The birth itself, in a stable under the baleful eye of an ominous-looking goat, plays as a demonic parody of the Nativity, complete with a solar eclipse and more *Omen*-esque chanting. Gabrielle may be unconvinced that her baby is evil, but the universe (and the director) are definitely pointing the other way.

Despite the extremely grim subject matter, the episode contains a surprising amount of humor, focusing on Gabby's prenatal cravings for "chicken gizzards fried in sheep lard" and other disgusting delicacies, Xena's verbal taunting of the banshees ("I'm going to slap these bitches silly"), and an absolutely priceless sight gag in which Xena casually pulls the Sword out of the Stone, looks it over, then shoves it back into the rock, completely oblivious to the aghast expressions of the flabbergasted knights.

The banshees themselves are portrayed as yet another unearthly trio of spooky females, not to be confused with the Fates ("Remember Nothing"), the Sirens ("Ulysses"), and the Furies. Xena and Gabrielle have some fun dialogue early on, comparing Britannia's resident spooks to the Grecian immortals they're more used to.

This episode also provides a showcase for Gabrielle's developing talents, both physical and verbal, as she escapes an angry mob with a Xena-like stunt, pole-vaulting out of a burning inn, then pushes her skills as a bard to their limits as she fabricates an elaborate and ultimately convincing lie to deceive Xena.

It's interesting to note that, over the course of the story, neither woman ever compares Hope to Solan, the baby Xena was forced to abandon. Granted, they are pretty busy with other things.

During the final chase across Britannia, Xena runs through some strangely familiar scenery. Isn't that the very same grassy-green cliff face where she poses in the credits every week? Funny, I never realized that wasn't in Greece.

A curiosity: The voice-over narration in the promos for this episode consistently refer to Gabrielle's offspring as "he." Does this reflect some confusion with the baby's demonic father, or was a female devil-baby considered insufficiently threatening?

Baby Hope returns—with a vengeance—in "Maternal Instincts."

Reality Check

I knew it! I've been waiting for the Xenaverse to claim the Arthurian mythos since the first season, despite (or, more likely, because) of the glaring historical inaccuracies.

The Knights of the Round Table and the Sword in the Stone are associated with the reign of King Arthur of Camelot. Although the stories of Camelot contain more myth than history, the historical Arthur is believed to have died in 537 B.C., close to five hundred years after the death of Boadicea. According to some legends, the first Round Table was brought to Britain by Joseph of Arimathea around the first century B.C., which brings these Warriors of the Pierced Heart rather closer to what we (extremely) loosely think of as Xena's era. As for that sword in the rock, one of the knights explains that the blade was placed in the stone by the last British king before the Romans came, roughly 54 B.C. In Arthurian legend, however, the Sword in the Stone is generally said to have appeared no more than a generation before Arthur's coronation, which places it several centuries later.

The Round Table viewed by Xena featured a large golden goblet in its center. The Holy Grail? The episode doesn't say, although Xena is bound to run into the Grail one of these days.

Banshees belong in Ireland, not Britain, and are usually portrayed as either crones or ghostly young women (as here). Their cries foretell a coming death, often of a relative or descendant, instead of the birth of a baby demon. More than one banshee signifies the death of someone very important. According to Xena, banshees cannot enter a residence until invited, but that's more of a vampire thing. As in "Girls Just Wanna Have Fun," traditional vampire lore is being overlaid with another myth. God only knows what will happen if Xena and Gabrielle ever make it to Transylvania. Vlad the Impaler, anyone?

Rating: ⵌⵌⵌ

Hercules: The Legendary Journeys: Stranger in a Strange World

WRITTEN BY PAUL ROBERT COYLE
DIRECTED BY MICHAEL LEVINE

There's a world of scheming going on behind those baby blues.　　　—The Sovereign on "Xena"

What Happens

Zeus is dying, and his thunderbolts open a gateway to another world where the gods and heroes we know are reflected by their polar opposites: "Hercules" is a murderous tyrant known as the Sovereign, "Ares" is the God of Love, "Aphrodite" is prim and modest, "Joxer" is a fearless rebel leader, and so on. When our Iolaus exchanges places with his twin, a cowardly jester, he eventually encounters the other world's "Xena": the Sovereign's conniving mistress who, between bouts of literally acrobatic foreplay with "Hercules," is behind the plot to poison Zeus with the blood of the Golden Hind, which she conceals in an amulet that oddly resembles a chakram.

Remarks

Airing the same week as the wrenching "Gabrielle's Hope," this exercise in utter goofiness really did seem to come from another world. Lawless looks like she's having a ball, playing a gleefully evil floozie in a Louise Brooks hairdo. For those who are counting, this now makes *seven* characters that Lawless has portrayed in various Herc and Xena adventures. There's more than a little Meg (from "Warrior . . . Princess . . . Tramp") in this comic characterization, although "Xena" has even fewer scruples. We can only wonder where she obtained her precious stash of hind's blood (which, according to past *Hercules* episodes, is the only poison that can kill a god) and shudder accordingly, but we get to see "Xena" pout to get her way with Hercules, switch the figures on a wedding cake, end up slathered with frosting after an all-out food fight with "Aphrodite," and, finally, throw a high-heeled shoe with lethal accuracy.

"Stranger in a Strange World" owes an obvious debt to the classic "Mirror, Mirror" episode of the original *Star Trek* television series (written by Jerome Bixby), right down to the satanic goatee affected by both the mirror Spock and Hercules. Advance publicity in *TV Guide* predicted that Lawless would play "a 1930s-style mobster moll," which was not entirely accurate, although there are echoes of Judy Holliday in the 1950 comedy film *Born Yesterday*. The closing twist, in which the evil regime's fearsome Executioner is unmasked as "Gabrielle," would have been more surprising had not the opening credits announced Renee O'Connor's involvement, but it's still a cute twist.

Still, cunning, wild-eyed, and murderous . . . this is supposed to be Xena's *opposite*? I suppose the existence of "Xena II" is the ultimate confirmation of the essential goodness at the heart of the real Warrior Princess—if you want to take it that seriously.

Reality Check
This episode bears no relationship whatsoever to reality.

Rating: ᛉᛉ

The Debt

WRITTEN BY R. J. STEWART
STORY BY ROBERT TAPERT AND R. J. STEWART
DIRECTED BY OLEY SASSONE

I hope I never disappoint you, Xena. —Gabrielle

What Happens
An emissary from the kingdom of Chin delivers a cryptic message to Xena that sets her on a lengthy journey to that distant realm. When she reveals to Gabrielle that she intends to kill someone at the end of the journey, Gabby is appalled. Xena explains (sort of) by recalling her days as a Mongol warrior, close to ten years before. Back in the present, Xena leaves Gabrielle behind and begins the final leg of her trip, but when she attempts to assassinate the Green Dragon, a shocking discovery awaits her . . .

Remarks
Xena is certainly wandering far afield from her usual Greco-Roman haunts this season. No sooner do our heroines return from the British Isles than they set off for the Far East, anticipating the journeys of Marco Polo by some seventeen centuries. Given the huge distances involved, it's only appropriate

that Xena spends the entire episode en route, arriving in China only in the climactic scenes.

The flashbacks provide the meat of the story, revealing aspects of Xena's past only hinted at before. Picking up shortly after Xena's crucifixion in "Destiny," roughly ten years prior to her present, "The Debt" shows us a lame, limping, almost feral Xena at her nastiest yet. This is a Xena still smarting from her betrayal and brutal treatment at the hands of Caesar, a Xena who thinks nothing of slaughtering a legion of Chinese soldiers, erecting a grisly wall of severed heads to display her handiwork. Even today's Xena, looking back at that period in her life, describes the Mongol Xena as "an animal living from one moment to another, driven by desire." Once again, the show's producers pull no punches depicting the Warrior Princess's shameful past; it's doubtful whether any previous TV heroine has ever had quite so many atrocities to atone for. Hell, she even kidnaps and terrorizes a small child.

I mean, can you imagine Wonder Woman mutilating the corpses of her victims? The Bionic Woman? Don't make me laugh. Major Kira on *Star Trek: Deep Space Nine* is supposedly a former terrorist with a fair amount of blood on her conscience, but her crimes have always been given a political rationale; she was a freedom fighter intent on liberating her planet from alien conquerors. Not quite the same thing, although it's worth noting that Xena started out defending her homeland, too.

Such idealistic motivations are far behind her by the time she first ends up on the sprawling plains north of the Great Wall of China. Although a good deal more bitter, however, the evil Xena here has clearly evolved from the pirate queen in "Destiny." Both seem overfond of bangles and dangerous, untrustworthy men. Xena's "shattered" legs come as a surprise after Niklio's healing efforts in "Destiny," but I guess trashing all those Roman soldiers while she had two broken legs might have undone some of the healer's hard work.

"The Debt" introduces us to two crucial figures in Xena's

life. The first is Borias, much discussed in "Orphan of War" but seen here for the first time. Actor Marton Csokas, who only two episodes ago played the treacherous Khrafstar, is unrecognizable here as a swarthy Mongol leader similar in style and appearance to the young Omar Sharif in *Lawrence of Arabia*. His eventual betrayal of Xena is all the more surprising when one remembers, as every Xenaphile surely does, that he would eventually become the father of her child, Solan, conceived much later on, during Xena's war with the Centaurs. Then again, he and Xena are shown to have a notably combative, if passionate, relationship (including sex on horseback!), which may foreshadow their final conflict during the those same Centaur Wars.

The other major character introduced here is Lao Ma, a mysterious Chinese courtesan with supernatural powers, who would become the second woman to play a crucial role in the development of the Warrior Princess, after M'Lila in "Destiny." Lao Ma is played by actress Jacqueline Kim, who had previously appeared as Sulu's daughter in the feature film *Star Trek Generations* and as an embattled emergency room physician in *Volcano*. We would learn much more about Lao Ma in Part 2 of "The Debt," but she makes a memorable impression here as a mystery woman who rescues our heroine despite Xena's earlier attempt to kill her. Subtext fans will savor the two women's life-saving kiss beneath the warm water of (what else?) yet another hot tub.

All of which brings us back to the present, as Xena sneaks into the imperial palace of the Green Dragon, to be confronted with a truly unexpected cliffhanger. Gabrielle in China, and responsible for Xena's capture by her enemies? The first time I saw this episode, I was momentarily convinced that Gabrielle's surprise appearance was some sort of flashback or hallucination, especially since that scene had been preceded by brief clips from past episodes (including "Return of Callisto," "Is There a Doctor in the House?" "The Price," and "The Greater Good") as Xena wrestled with her conscience just before she attempts to assassinate her target. Then it sank in that she was really there . . .

Okay, leaving aside the whole question of how Gabby got to China before Xena did (which would not be answered until "Forget Me Not" later this season) and when exactly she learned Chinese, what in the name of Zeus and all the other gods is our favorite bard up to? Granted, Gabrielle had been opposed to the whole assassination notion from scene one, but turning her best friend over to the Green Dragon seems a bit drastic. And since this comes so soon after her little white lie last episode, one could be forgiven for thinking that the precious relationship between Xena and her sidekick had been irreparably trashed.

Hellishly, we would have to wait a full week to find out what happened next. (Before moving on, though, we should take note of the way Xena dispatches a sword-juggling assassin with a single throw of her chakram, in yet another homage to *Raiders of the Lost Ark*.)

Reality Check
The Great Wall of China was not completed until 215 B.C., although early attempts to build walls against invaders began as early as 356 B.C. As we will see shortly in "The Debt II," this is a few centuries later than we would expect to find Lao Ma.

Rating: ꠰꠰꠰

The Debt II

WRITTEN BY R. J. STEWART
STORY BY ROBERT TAPERT AND R. J. STEWART
DIRECTED BY OLEY SASSONE

Scratch my nose, will you? —Xena to Gabrielle

What Happens

In the present, Xena is imprisoned and sentenced to death by the Green Dragon, over the strenuous protests of Gabrielle. Meanwhile, flashbacks continue the story of Xena's tutelage under Lao Ma, who heals her legs, reunites her with Borias, and attempts to teach her a measure of self-control. Ultimately, however, Xena is unable to conquer her lust for vengeance. Years later, she is finally able to tap into the mystical source of Lao Ma's abilities, and she uses them to escape her execution and bring down the Green Dragon.

Remarks

Xena discovers the power of the Force, but succumbs to the dark side once more as the saga concludes. The writers had to pull off a tricky balancing act here, in both the past and the present segments. In the flashbacks, Lao Ma had to have an impact on Xena but could not reform her entirely because she had to stay essentially evil until her encounter with Hercules many years later. Similarly, in the present, Xena cannot achieve true inner peace and tranquillity without radically altering the character and her series; ditto for permanently imbuing her with Lao Ma's telekinetic powers. Presumably Xena sacrificed those abilities, at least for the time being, when she gave in to her anger and killed the Green Dragon. She certainly didn't start levitating things right and left upon her return to Greece in the next episode.

Given that Lao Ma could theoretically have prevented her own execution the way Xena does here, we have to assume that she submitted to death voluntarily, perhaps unwilling to turn against her own tyrannical son. Apparently, the full application of her philosophy involves a lot more sacrifice than most of us might be willing to endure. We do learn, though, that it was Lao Ma who first christened Xena with the title "Warrior Princess," seeing a need for a more militant-type personality to preserve the peace in the more enlightened China that she hoped to bring about. Unfortunately, she underestimated the full extent of the darkness within both Xena and her own son.

Vicious as he is, Ming T'ien turns out to be another legacy of Xena's violent past. "You made me!" he declares, recalling the ways in which the old Xena terrorized him as a child and later murdered his father in cold blood. Parallels with Callisto are surely intended, especially since it is Callisto's death in the quicksand pit that Xena recalls right before trying to kill him at the end of the previous episode.

Not surprisingly, Gabrielle has plenty of second thoughts about her rash behavior last week. It seems she didn't quite realize how tyrannical the Green Dragon was when she interrupted Xena's mission of vengeance—kind of a curious oversight, given all the demons and warlords Xena has opposed over the last couple of years. You'd think she would give Xena the benefit of the doubt when it comes to identifying the bad guys; after all, this was hardly the first time Xena had tried to kill a heartless villain, even if she usually did them in the heat of battle rather then like a thief in the night. (Then again, as various commentators on-line have pointed out, Xena never does get around to finishing the story she starts to tell Gabby in Part 1.) In any event, one hopes our favorite bard will think twice before second-guessing Xena like this again.

The two women's reconciliation in a mucky pit of a dungeon comes as quite a relief, but an ominous ending warns us that we're hardly out of the woods yet. At first, Xena intends to leave the disgraced emperor alive, but when he taunts her, revealing that he personally killed Lao Ma, his own mother, she kills him with a polished hairpin that Lao Ma had given her years ago, then lies about it to Gabrielle.

In the space of three episodes, Gabrielle and Xena have each lied to the other at a crucial moment, and in strangely complementary ways. Gabrielle doesn't kill but says she does. Xena does kill but pretends she didn't. Ming T'ien's death, and Xena's deception, would literally come back to haunt her in "The Bitter Suite."

According to Judith Parker of the International Center for Xena Studies, the ankh-like symbol upon which both Xena and Lao Ma are crucified before their executions is the Chinese character for "wood." The significance of this eludes me, but then, I haven't studied under Lao Ma.

Reality Check

Conventional history gets a neat feminist twist as the enigmatic Lao Ma is revealed to be the true source of the ancient wisdom generally attributed to Lao-Tse (604–531 B.C.) author of *The Tao te Ching* and the founder of Taoism. According to *Xena*, the true author was Lao Ma, who wrote down her wisdom under her comatose husband's name, knowing that the words of a woman would not be taken seriously at that time in history. Little is known of the real Lao-Tse, although he is said to have lived during a period in which the Chinese Empire had broken apart into warring states and rival kingdoms, as seen in these two episodes.

In theory, though, Lao-Tse (or Lao Ma) predated the Great Wall by close to three hundred years.

Rating: ⵣⵣⵣ

King of Assassins

WRITTEN BY ADAM ARMUS & NORA KAY FOSTER
DIRECTED BY BRUCE CAMPBELL

I've been grabbed more times than the Golden Fleece.
—Gabrielle

What Happens

It's brother against brother ("Oh, brother!") as Joxer attempts to prevent his identical twin, Jet, from killing the Queen of the Nile. Fortunately, he has Gabby and Autolycus, and eventually Xena, on his side.

Remarks

More look-alikes, but at least Joxer is legitimately related to his twin(s), unlike Xena and her various doubles. At this point, multiple Gabrielles are pretty much inevitable . . . and, in fact, only two episodes away ("The Quill Is Mightier . . .").

But first, the King of Thieves meets Joxer the Mighty in this comic romp, which is not quite as Xena-less as "For Him the Bell Tolls" but close. More about Joxer's sociopathic family is revealed, including the fact that his theme song dates back to his mother, whose musical interests were previously discussed in "Girls Just Wanna Have Fun." Granted, Mom's version, "Joxer the Tidy," apparently had slightly different lyrics.

Meanwhile, Gabby gets stuck in a dungeon for at least the *fourth* time (see "The Path Not Taken," "The Black Wolf," and "Warrior . . . Princess . . . Tramp"), although she eventually gets to dress up in a cute Egyptian disguise. She also attempts a nerve pinch and a Xena-style discus throw, with considerably less success than she had in "Bell." Maybe she got out of practice on that long trip home from China.

The legendary Cleopatra, Queen of Egypt, enters the Xenaverse in the form of actress Gina Torres, who had previously played a swashbuckling female pirate in the *Hercules* episode

"Web of Desire" and who would later return as the casting director of Renaissance Pictures (!) in another Herc show, "Yes, Virginia, There Is a Hercules." Surprisingly, Cleopatra does not turn out to be an old acquaintance of Xena's, like Helen of Troy and Boadicea; the Warrior Princess and the Queen of the Nile basically pass like ships in the night here, although Cleo does invite Xena to visit her in Egypt sometime, which could get awkward, given Cleo's historical liaison with Julius Caesar (which doesn't seem to have happened yet).

This episode was actually directed by Bruce Campbell, so should we be surprised that Autolycus ends up in bed (or, more precisely, a tub) with Cleopatra herself? I don't think so.

Incidentally, the prison Xena visits in the beginning of the episode appears to be the same one she liberated the convicts from in "The Dirty Half Dozen." Curiously, the guards don't hold any grudges over that successful break-out. Gabrielle also refers to Xena's exploits in "Cradle of Hope," two seasons ago.

In a bit of obvious foreshadowing, Joxer and Jet allude to their even more embarrassing brother "Jace." At a convention in New York City, Ted Raimi hinted that Jace is actually Joxer's sister, or maybe a sister who used to be a brother . . .

Reality Check

As of this episode, Cleopatra is preparing to go to war to reclaim her rightful throne from Ptolemy. In fact, the historical Cleo had to contend with her ambitious brother, Ptolemy, one of the several Ptolemies who reigned over Egypt after Alexander the Great. Cleopatra ultimately came out on top and ruled until her death in 31 B.C., eleven years after the assassination of Julius Caesar, who was still alive and kicking in the Xenaverse.

Rating: ⚕⚕

Warrior . . . Priestess . . . Tramp

WRITTEN BY ADAM ARMUS & NORA KAY FOSTER
DIRECTED BY ROBERT GINTY

*Sometimes you have to take matters into your own
hands.*   —Xena to frustrated virgin

What Happens

How about that? Turns out that Leah, virgin priestess of
Hestia, is a dead ringer for both Xena and Meg, which comes
in handy (though a little confusing) when an unscrupulous
villain plots to murder a templeful of Hestian virgins.

Remarks

Okay, repeat after me: Lysia, Lyla, Xena, Diana, Meg, Callisto, Melinda, "Xena," Leah . . . yep, this now makes *nine*
characters Lucy Lawless has played in the Xenaverse. Someone give this woman a raise, then hit Ares with a *lot* of paternity suits.

***

Did You Say Chicks?!, an anthology of women warrior stories edited by fantasy author Esther Friesner, begins with a
lengthy ode to a certain actress: "Hail to thee, O Lucy Law-
less/*Xena* actress great and flawless . . ."

***

Anyway, it looks like that cushy job in King Lias's kitchen
didn't work out, as Meg is now the proud owner of a house of
ill repute—and mixed up in another assassination plot. The
bordello setting makes for plenty of racy humor, although it
probably helps if you find virgins inherently funny. The plot,
which is too complicated and a bit exhausting with all
the shuttling back and forth between the brothel and the temple, might have been easier to follow without the addi-

tional complication of a slightly gratuitous Joxer. An elaborate production number involving yet another variation on Joxer's theme song is fun, though, and probably served as a good trial run for the big musical episode coming up.

Despite Leah's telltale lisp, I admit I occasionally had trouble telling her and Meg apart. They're both pretty goofy, albeit in slightly different ways. Probably the best bit comes early on when Gabrielle, confronted with yet another Xena imposter, understandably runs through all the possibilities. Callisto? Diana? Meg?

Early reports have it that Lawless will expand her repertoire next season by taking on the role of Sappho. "Warrior . . . Poetess," anyone?

Reality Check
Since it's the world's oldest profession, it's none too surprising that prostitution is apparently thriving in the Xenaverse.

Rating: ХХ

The Quill Is Mightier . . .

WRITTEN BY HILARY J. BADER
DIRECTED BY ANDREW MERRIFIELD

Make someone else the hero for a change.
—Xena to Gabrielle

What Happens
At the urging of Ares, Aphrodite grants Gabrielle the ability to transform reality to whatever she writes on her scroll. But rewriting the world proves more complicated than anyone realized, especially since her scroll takes things very literally. The gods are humbled, Gabrielle is cloned, and Xena catches a *lot* of fish before the chaos is brought under control.

Remarks

Hilary Bader strikes again, with another ingenious puzzle/comedy in the hilarious tradition of "Been There, Done That." There's even another dead bird joke, reminiscent of the now-legendary murdered rooster in her last script.

Not much Xena, but in her place we get Ares, Aphrodite (for the first time this season), Joxer, and even Minya, Xena's number one fan from "A Day in the Life." The Warrior Princess herself shows up for a funny finale in which she puts seafood to even better use than she did in the unforgettable fish fight of "Altared States."

Despite all the wonders brought about by the enchanted scroll, perhaps the greatest miracle in this episode is that Gabrielle somehow manages to remain oblivious to Joxer's hopeless infatuation with her, despite abundant clues—including the manifestation of three naked, go-go-dancing Gabrielles! At this point, Gabby seems to be in heavy denial regarding Joxer's romantic intentions, going to ridiculous lengths to willfully ignore the obvious. Not that you can really blame her . . .

Speaking of relationships in denial, check out Ares and Gabrielle's uneasy reaction when they catch themselves bonding with each other while reminiscing about the events of "The Reckoning" and "The Furies." Turns out the God of War and our favorite bard have at least one thing in common: an admiration bordering on obsession for a certain Warrior Princess.

Overall, the comic complications escalate in a cleverly logical fashion, except for one little point: Er, why exactly did the peddler head for the caves when he already had the scroll? Beats me, unless he just wanted to scope out the naked Gabrielles for himself.

Not that you can really blame him . . .

Reality Check

The term "barbarians," applied to the unkempt, vaguely Viking-ish raiders in this episode, derives from the original Greek *barbaros*, so called because the sophisticated Greeks thought the crude lingo of certain savage foreigners sounded like inarticulate babbling, as in *"ba-ba-ba."* (Amazing, the things one hears on the History Channel.)

The premise of the enchanted scroll recalls a classic 1943 fantasy story by Anthony Boucher, "We Print the Truth," about a small-town newspaper with the same reality-warping abilities.

Rating: ⅄⅄⅄

Maternal Instincts

WRITTEN BY CHRIS MANHEIM
DIRECTED BY MARK BEESLEY

Come meet your Auntie Callisto.
—You-know-who, back again

What Happens

The return of Gabrielle's Hope brings tragedy, not to mention Callisto. While Xena struggles to protect her son, Solan, from the Warrior Queen's vengeance, Hope herself (with Gabrielle's un-witting aid) murders Solan as part of Dahak's plan to destroy Xena. Hope pays with her life (we think), but the deaths of their children lead Xena and Gabrielle to a bitter parting.

Remarks

The Rift breaks wide open in a literal Greek tragedy that came as quite a shock after the preceding run of comic episodes.

So, I guess we are to assume that baby Hope really did kill that unlucky knight back in Britannia, just as she blithely mur-ders a full-grown Centaur here, not to mention Solan. Is the moral, then, that Gabrielle should have let Xena slice up her newborn baby right away, or are we still free to wonder whether Hope would have grown so evil had she not been de-prived of Gabby's benevolent maternal presence? Having a knee-jerk aversion to infanticide, I lean toward nurture vs. (demonic) nature in this dispute, being inclined to give Hope the benefit of the doubt, but Zeus knows, it gave the gang on the Internet something to argue about.

Still, Gabrielle's blood innocence is undeniably lost at this point. There's so much going on in this episode that it's almost easy to overlook the detail that our favorite bard has now killed for the second time, and this time with cold premeditation, in an ending shamelessly lifted from *The Bad Seed* (1956). (Come to think of it, poisoning the evil little girl in that film didn't work, either.)

As for baby Hope, that was quite a journey her basket took. Gabrielle plunked it in a river in Britannia and somehow she ended up in Greece? Maybe Gabby should have started getting suspicious at that point; by my extremely rough calculations, that's a voyage of at least 1,500 nautical miles, down the coast of Europe, through the Strait of Gibraltar, and up the Mediterranean Sea. (Okay, okay, I suppose she *could* have simply crossed the English Channel and made the rest of the trip overland, but we're still talking 1,000 miles or so.)

Callisto's comeback, as she is liberated by Hope from the now-solid lava pit, is easier to explain, although one wonders why Velasca could not escape through the same fissure. The Warrior Queen gets plenty of opportunities to show off the godlike powers she acquired at the conclusion of "A Necessary Evil," also directed by Beesley—hurling fireballs, appearing out of thin air, surviving mortal wounds, etc. (She does seem to have ditched the white contact lenses, though.) Her pincushion trick, when she flings all the arrows embedded in her immortal body back at the archers who shot them,

---

Xena Invades Pop Culture . . .

"[Singer Paula Cole] is part prom queen, part macrobiotic earth mother, and part Xena." (*Entertainment Weekly*, February 20/27, 1998)

echoes an almost identical stunt performed by the embodiment of Evil, played by David Warner, in the movie *Time Bandits* (1981). A nitpick: Callisto tells Xena that not even godhood allows her to be in two places at once, but Ares did precisely that in "Ties That Bind."

With Solan's death, Callisto finally achieves the vengeance against Xena she has always craved, only to find herself just as tormented as before. Having seemingly lost her taste for revenge, she is strangely melancholy by the end of this episode, raising the question of whether a Xena-style reformation might be in the works for the Warrior Queen? On the other hand, even a depressed Callisto can threaten to butcher a caveful of innocent children, if only for lack of anything better to do. Her eventual fate, being buried alive for the *third* time (not counting the VR game), is both too familiar and too unconvincing. Were we really supposed to believe that a cave-in could hold a god?

Besides Hope and Callisto, "Maternal Instincts" also brings back Ephiny (last seen in "A Necessary Evil"), her son, Xenan ("Is There a Doctor in the House?" and Solan and his Centaur father Kaleipus (both from "Orphan of War"). The top half of Kaleipus is now played, but not for long, by a different actor; it's unknown whether his bottom half is played by the same horse as before. Solan seems to have grown about a foot since his last appearance, which we are explicitly told was one year, two months, and twelve days ago. He never does figure out that Xena is his mother. Xena's cry of rage and despair when she discovers Solan's body both visually and aurally recalls James T. Kirk's reaction to his own son's death in the third *Star Trek* feature film ("You dirty Klingon bastard!"). Despite his tragic demise, Solan, as well as Ephiny, would appear briefly in next week's episode.

More continuity: We finally learn (via Ephiny) that Boadicea defeated Caesar back near the beginning of the season. Ironically, Gabrielle identifies Hope as her daughter by means of the toy lamb, sculpted by Senticles, that Xena gave her in "A

Solstice Carol." Ephiny's son, little Xenan, is also shown to have one of Senticles' toys.

Some Amazon fans on the Net were disappointed that Ephiny had little to do in this episode except give Gabrielle a shoulder to cry on, but the scene where Gabby tells Ephiny about Hope (sort of) is genuinely touching—and a long way from the hostile, adversarial relationship that the women started out with in "Hooves and Harlots."

Apparently Kaleipus's band of Centaurs *is* a different tribe from those led by Tyldus in "Hooves." Early dialogue here implies that the Centaur nation is divided by fraternal conflicts. Also, Ephiny suggests that she and Xenan have traveled a fair distance to get to Kaleipus's camp, whereas the Centaurs in "Hooves" were close enough to the Amazons, also a fragmented community, to argue over territory.

Aside from some of Callisto's one-liners, and the smiles inevitably produced by the sight of the Centaur children, this is the grimmest episode since maybe "The Price," with little or no humor. Hope and Callisto would soon return in "Armageddon Now," an episode of *Hercules*, but the saga of the Rift would be continued next week . . . in a musical?

Reality Check

"Maternal Instincts" draws so much on *Xena* mythology and history that there's scarcely room for any of the real thing. As far as I know, Hope, daughter of Dahak and Gabrielle, was both literally and figuratively born in the Xenaverse.

Rating: ⲭⲭⲭ

The Bitter Suite

WRITTEN BY STEVEN L. SEARS & CHRIS MANHEIM
DIRECTED BY OLEY SASSONE
LYRICS BY JOSEPH LODUCA, PAMELA PHILLIPS, AND DENNIS SPIEGEL
MUSIC BY JOSEPH LODUCA

Alright, Callisto, cut the song and dance. —Xena

What Happens

Somehow, Argo, I don't think we're in Athens anymore . . .
Enraged by her son's death, Xena tries to kill Gabrielle, but a
mysterious force transports them both to the musical land of
Illusia, where they are forced to confront their feelings and
each other.

Remarks

For an entire week, Xena fans waited, torn between antici-
pation and dread. Solan dead. Hope poisoned by her mother's
hand. Xena and Gabrielle driven apart by the most tragic of circumstances. How in Zeus's name did the powers that be in-
tend to undo all this emotional carnage . . . and in a musical,
no less? I admit I winced at the thought of the entire Rift story
line, carefully constructed over the course of the season, being unsatisfyingly wrapped up in some sort of weird novelty
show. An all-singing, all-dancing episode sounded fun, sure,
but couldn't they have saved the idea for something a little less
important?

The great surprise of "The Bitter Suite" was just how well
it worked after all. Yeah, some of the songs were better than
others, and Stephen Sondheim probably isn't quaking in his
boots, but by the time Xena and Gabrielle found themselves
back together, you really felt that some sort of emotional
catharsis had been achieved. Our sundered heroines had
sung their way past the anger and mutual recriminations,
shared their pain and guilt, and come out the other side, still

wounded but healing. Could the show have attained the same result without the musical conceit? I guess we'll never know, but I, for one, don't feel cheated out of a more conventional resolution.

Visually, the episode was a phantasmagorical treat, complete with vibrant colors, a winking handbag, a talking dog, and a sphinx-drawn chariot. Director Sassone, who started the Rift off in "The Deliverer," keeps the momentum going, beginning with a gasp-inducing sequence in which Gabrielle is dragged for what seems like miles behind a galloping Argo. (You know, Gabby never did trust that horse . . .) The musical numbers, by LoDuca and others, come off like a cross between *Les Miz* and Disney. Probably the weakest song was "Hate Is the Star," whose plummy voice and heavy-handed lyrics struck me as being like something you'd hear at the Haunted Mansion at Disney World, quite at odds with the brutality of the torture and crucifixion imagery on the screen. Much better were Lawless's last few numbers, when Xena soulfully forgives first Gabrielle and then herself. I suspect *Xena* fans were getting choked up and misty-eyed all over the world—not that I'd admit to that sort of reaction myself.

It helps, of course, if you've been paying attention to what has gone on before, since the episode makes numerous references, both visual and verbal, to various previous episodes, including return appearances by Joxer, Ephiny, Callisto, Ares, Lila, Caesar, Khrafstar, Ming T'ien, Solan, and even the black-eyed evil "Xena" from "Dreamworker." Only Hope remains conspicuously absent, although she would return on *Hercules* in a week or so.

The burning question of how Xena and Gabrielle got to Illusia in the first place is a bit confusing, and some stretches of portentous, quasi-mystical narration by Hudson Leick only muddy the waters. Was Callisto responsible somehow, as I was convinced for a week or two, or were other forces at work? Close inspection reveals that Solan can take the credit for patching up Xena and Gabby's relationship, but this is easy to miss the first few times around. (Near the end, Gabrielle whispers, "It was him," but neither Xena nor Solan seems to be paying much attention.) How exactly a dead kid pulled this whole extravaganza off, foiling Ares' attempt to harness Xena's anger and grief to his own ends, remains puzzling.

Just as fascinating as the episode itself was the fan reaction. Within twenty-four hours of the show's first airing, the entire libretto had already been posted on the Internet, along with plenty of discussion of almost every aspect of the episode. Trying to keep up with all the commentary and interpretations was practically a full-time job. The symbolism and subtext were analyzed and argued about at length, while another popular topic was figuring out which cast members did their own singing and which were dubbed. (For the record, Lucy Lawless, Kevin Smith, and Ted Raimi tackled their songs themselves, while Gabrielle was sung by Susan Wood and Callisto by Michelle Nicastro—who sounds phenomenally like Hudson Leick at times.)

Interestingly enough, a significant portion of the audience seemed to actively resist the idea that the opening sequence, which was quickly dubbed the "GabDrag," really happened, offering torturous explanations of how Xena's attack on Gabrielle was all part of the illusion, even though it appears fairly obvious that everything prior to the pair's arrival in Illusia, except maybe Gabby's hallucinatory vision of Callisto, is meant to be taken literally. As shocking as the GabDrag was, it certainly seems in character for a crazed Warrior Princess pushed to the end of her tether. Remember, this is a character who only three years ago was casually executing her own lieutenants—and none of them was ever responsible, however indirectly, for the death of her only child. (There were also a few vocal fans out there who thought that the GabDrag was richly deserved.)

On the subtext front, a minor tempest in a teapot erupted when it was reported on the Net that a Boston TV station had censored the brief, bittersweet kiss between Xena and Callisto. Much justifiable indignation resulted, sparking calls for angry letters to the offending network, until it turned out

---

Xena Invades Pop Culture . . .

"[National Book Award nominee Dorothy Allison's] office is filled with books for every conceivable brow and decorated with posters of Xena and of Sigourney Weaver in *Alien*."—Jeff Giles (*Newsweek*, March 30, 1998)

---

that, well, the alleged act of censorship hadn't happened. And another good rumor bit the dust.

"The Bitter Suite" attracted attention from the mainstream media as well. Julie Moran, weekend cohost of *Entertainment Tonight*, flew to New Zealand to film a cameo appearance as a peasant maid who welcomes Gabrielle back to Potidaea, generating publicity both in print and on TV. Singing the verse "We're so grateful you've come back to the place you belong," Moran later informed *TV Guide* that she was slightly disappointed by the nature of her role: "I was envisioning a leather outfit with chains. I figured I could beat the *ET* image where I wear suits. When I get there, I find I'm dressed like a village girl."

Regional news broadcasts ran features on the special musical episode, while the *New York Daily News* called it "a delightfully inventive and wild way to resolve the sudden and severe enmity between X and G. The visuals are outrageous, the music and lyrics are witty, and there's a lot more actual drama than you might expect." Surprisingly, the paper missed the dubbing involved, adding, "It's fairly shocking how many *Xena* regulars have strong singing voices." (2/7/98).

One of the few people disappointed in the show was Danielle Cormack, who admitted at a subsequent convention that she thought Ephiny was as interesting "as a wet rag" in that particular episode. Still, the de facto Amazon queen gets her arm broken attempting to defend Gabrielle from a vengeful Warrior Princess and even manages to save Gabby's life from a flung chakram. It will be interesting to see if Ephiny mentions the incident, and still has her arm in a sling, the next time she runs into Xena and Gabrielle.

The inevitable sound-track album was released only a few months later. A later episode, "Forget Me Not," would reveal that at least one loose end from the Rift remained to be dealt with.

Reality Check

As was quickly pointed out on the Net, much of the imagery of Illusia came straight from the Tarot, more specifically from what is known as the Rider-Waite Tarot Deck. This deck, with its distinctive illustrations, was designed in 1910 by occultist Arthur Edward Waite and drawn by Pamela Colman Smith shortly thereafter. Callisto's colorful costume, for instance, is taken directly from the Rider-Waite portrait of The Fool, complete with the little white dog (who, curiously enough, also appeared on *Hercules* the same week).

These images may seem anachronistic in the context of ancient Amazons and Greek gods, but since Illusia is specifically described as existing outside of time, we'll let this one go.

Rating: ᛉᛉᛉᛉ

One Against an Army

WRITTEN BY GENE O'NEILL AND NOREEN TOBIN
DIRECTED BY PAUL LYNCH

Even in death, Gabrielle, I will never leave you.
                                        —Xena

What Happens

The Persian army invades Greece, more or less on schedule, and only Xena stands between it and an easy conquest. But when Gabrielle is pierced by a poison arrow, Xena must choose between saving her home and saving her friend.

Remarks

After the emotional roller coaster of the Rift, it's good to see our heroines' relationship (whatever it is) back to normal, although things get awful mushy after Gabrielle is wounded. The lengthy deathbed scenes, explicitly recalling Xena's near demise in "The Greater Good," feel a lot like fan fiction, where the "hurt/comfort" theme is a recognized and recurring way of exploring the intimate relationship between two fictional characters. (The Xena fan fiction listing at *www.simplenet.com* even contains a separate listing for hurt/comfort stories about Xena and Gabrielle.) Fortunately, the Warrior Princess (in this episode) ultimately dries her tears just in time for a rousing action finale.

But when exactly does this battle take place? A strong case can be made that the episode actually occurs shortly after "The Debt II" and before "Maternal Instincts." Consider: Xena tries to summon up the Tao magic she used to destroy Ming T'ien's palace but finds she can't achieve that purity of concentration and purpose again, raising the question of why she waited so long to attempt using those powers once more. Furthermore, Gabrielle is still apologizing here for her betrayal in China, but she makes no mention of Hope's or Solan's death. In general, as discussed earlier with regard to "Death in Chains," it seems reasonable to assume that the episodes take place in the order in which they are aired, but in this case I strongly suspect that "One Against an Army" was intended at some point to air before "Maternal Instincts" and "The Bitter Suite," but someone, wanting to reaffirm Xena and Gabby's bond after all the heartbreak of the last couple of episodes, delayed this one until later.

On the other hand, it can and has been argued that Xena knew better than to try to clear her mind when her son's life was at stake (a position that explains why she didn't use the Force against Callisto) and that "Forget Me Not," coming up in a few weeks, reveals why Gabby would still be feeling guilty over China even after her stint in Illusia. It will be interesting to see how the episodes are numbered if and when the third season gets turned into a boxed set of videos.

Besides "The Greater Good," Gabrielle's wound also echoes the injury Xena received way back in "Chariots of War," with the same grisly arrow removal and cauterization process, applied to Gabby this time. In another nostalgic touch, Xena breathes fire for the first time in ages, while her instructions to Argo to stay away from amorous stallions would seem to confirm the horse's gender once and for all . . . unless we're talking equine subtext here.

Reality Check

History takes another beating as *Xena* rewrites the Battle of Marathon (490 B.C.) so that the invading Persians overcome a mixed force of Athenian and Spartan warriors, leaving only the Warrior Princess to defend Greece from the would-be conquerors. In fact, the Athenians *defeated* the Persians at Marathon, and did it without any help from the Spartans, who showed up too late for the battle.

In a funny bit, Xena warns Phidippides, the original marathon runner, to pace himself on his legendary sprint from Marathon to Athens. Who knows whether he took her advice or not.

Rating: ⅄⅄

Forgiven

WRITTEN BY R. J. STEWART
DIRECTED BY GARTH MAXWELL

Oh, no. I knew you were evil, but you were obnoxious, too?   —Gabrielle to Xena

What Happens

A mission to rescue the sacred Urn of Apollo is complicated by a troubled and troublesome young woman who wants to replace Gabrielle as Xena's partner. Can the Warrior Princess knock some sense into Tara's head before Gabby kills the wanna-be sidekick?

Remarks

A distinctly minor, inconsequential episode, but it has its moments. Tara, portrayed as a sort of pre-Mycenaean riot grrl (sic) by Shiri Appleby, reminds Xena of her younger self, giving us a hint of what the Warrior Princess's own stormy adolescence might have been like. (Poor Cyrene!) This portrait doesn't quite gibe with the tamer young woman seen in "Remember Nothing," but perhaps that alternate Xena had already grown out of her rebellious youth.

Many fans objected to the way Tara was able to beat up Gabrielle in their first knock-down, drag-out brawl, but I'm inclined to think that the Amazon Princess got slightly concussed early on and simply never managed to clear her head long enough to fight back as well as she might have. Besides, she nearly died from a poisoned arrow last week; small wonder she wasn't at the top of her game.

The eventual revelation that Tara is in cahoots with at least one of the thieves that Xena is hunting is not too surprising, but it does raise one interesting point: Tara must have really had a lot of (misplaced) faith in her villainous boyfriend's ingenuity—or in Xena's heroism—if she was willing to be buried

> "That would be thrilling . . . everybody would love that."
> —Lucy Lawless on the possibility of singer k. d. lang appearing on *Xena*

up to her neck only inches away from an automatic decapitation device while her suitor looked on. Don't tell me that was part of the plan!

Subtext alert: Please note Gabrielle's indignant insistence that "*I* sleep next to Xena." This soon after the Rift, however, the show's creators mercifully resist the temptation to let Tara come between Xena and Gabrielle in a big way.

The low-key story line is partly redeemed by a provocative conclusion in which Xena, after a moment's indecision, wordlessly rejects a priest's offer of spiritual forgiveness. It's an effective moment, and completely in character for a Warrior Princess who seldom depends on the gods—and who may feel her own sins are too substantial to be washed away by a ritual sip of wine. (Lucy Lawless had described herself as a "recovering Catholic," but I'm hesitant to read too much into this scene; Xena and Lucy are two very different people, after all.)

On a lighter note, the hands-down funniest scene in this episode comes when we discover that Gabby invented Charades! Xena is dubious ("This will never catch on"), but you've got to love Gabby scolding Xena for not paying more attention to contemporary theater. Maybe the next time Xena owes Gabby a favor, the bard should hit the Warrior Princess up for dinner and a show. I hear *Antigone* is still playing in Athens . . .

Reality Check

Apollo, the Greek god of the sun, as well as of archery and prophecy and music, remains conspicuously missing in action in the Xena saga, even though Callisto invaded his temple at Delphi a few years back. The god himself is represented only by some pretty solar imagery at the beginning and end of the episode, and his rites, as depicted here, seem to have a suspicious resemblance to the Catholic ceremony of Communion. Apollo's sacred symbols included the bow and the lyre but not, that I'm aware of, an urn. A teenage Apollo eventually appeared in a flashback episode of *Hercules* titled "Top God."

Rating: ⵣⵣ

Hercules: The Legendary Journeys: Armageddon Now

WRITTEN BY PAUL ROBERT COYLE
DIRECTED BY MARK BEESLEY

Your work's not finished, Callisto.   —Hope

What Happens

Hope returns from the ashes . . . literally, then rescues Callisto, who convinces Ares to free the Sovereign from limbo so she can use the Hind's Blood to kill Strife, then put the Sovereign *and* Hercules back into limbo, and travel backward in time to kill Hercules' mother before his birth. Huh?

Remarks

Apparently that poison Gabby used on Hope wasn't quite strong enough . . .

A quasi sequel to both "Maternal Instincts" and "Stranger in a Strange World," this *Hercules* episode is packed with familiar faces but makes very little sense. There's lots of running around and ranting, but none of the five (!) villains involved seems to have a coherent plan in mind. Ares and Callisto go to great effort to get the Hind's Blood from the Sovereign (who is returned to limbo so quickly that it hardly seems worth freeing him), but why do they need Hind's Blood if the plan is to kill Alcmene, a mortal? And why bother trapping

Herc in limbo if he's just going to be erased from history anyway? Ares comes off looking especially bad, being easily manipulated by Callisto, who is being manipulated by Hope, and standing by helplessly as Callisto murders Strife for no particular reason. (Unlike some fans on the Net, however, I have trouble getting too worked up over the demise of Strife, whose obsequious antics were rapidly wearing out their welcome.) And how come Ares, who was greatly concerned about the advent of Dahak in "The Deliverer," seems completely unaware of Hope's role in Callisto's return?

Poor Callisto. She really does seem to depend on the kindness of strangers; so far she has been liberated from various subterranean prisons by Ares, Hera, and now Hope (twice). A fearsome warrior, I guess, but not much of an escape artist.

Still, the Warrior Queen's character continues to evolve; picking up from her disillusionment in "Maternal Instincts," Callisto now seems more intent on finding some sort of peace of mind rather than on exacting revenge against Xena. Of course, being Callisto, she is still perfectly willing to slaughter whomever it takes to find that peace—as Strife, Iolaus, and Alcmene soon find out.

Nice to know some things don't change, even if the rest of this episode is a muddle.

Reality Check

As a rule, parallel worlds and time travel have more to do with science fiction than with classical mythology. The death of Strife, at the hand of the goddess Callisto, is an event not recorded in the annals of mythology, although the producers of *Hercules* may have considered it to be Strife's just deserts for killing Hercules' wife back in "Judgment Day."

Given that Discord is Strife's mother or sister or something (it's a bit fuzzy), one wonders if she will ever attempt to avenge his death.

Rating: ✕

Armageddon Now, Part 2

WRITTEN BY GENE F. O'NEILL AND NOREEN V. TOBIN
DIRECTED BY MARK BEESLEY

I'm a legend.   —Xena the Conqueror

What Happens

With Hercules both unborn *and* trapped in limbo (go figure), Callisto tries to undo her own tragic past but succeeds only in killing her parents herself. Meanwhile, an unreformed Xena conquers the entire civilized world and crucifies an outspoken young dissident named Gabrielle. Fortunately, Iolaus uses the mystical Chronus Stone (from the animated movie!) to put everything back the way it was, even though Hope, ominously referred to as "the daughter of darkness," is still lurking around in the shadows.

Remarks

The time-travel plot still doesn't make sense, but there's plenty of interesting stuff for Xena fans here. Lucy Lawless gets to play the evil Xena at two different stages in her life: as the wild-eyed, wild-haired warlord who orders her troops to torch Cirra and as the jaded, immaculate empress of Greece, China, Rome, Gaul, and everything else. In a neat touch, we see a silver coin with Xena's profile engraved on it (and if Universal's licensing department is smart, they'll make that coin available to the fans). Even Darphus, last seen in "Unchained Heart," makes a comeback, once again played by Matthew Chamberlain.

The destruction of Cirra, previously glimpsed in a brief flashback in "Destiny," is shown here in more detail. Granted, the anomalous presence of both Callisto and Iolaus means we have to take this version with a grain of chronological salt, but it appears that Xena sincerely gave the women and children a chance to evacuate the village before she had her soldiers torch it; unfortunately, Callisto and her parents chose to hide in a barn rather than flee. Bad decision.

I'm not sure when or how Iolaus learned about Solan, but judging from the evil Xena's reaction to the name, it seems clear that the inferno at Cirra took place after the Warrior Princess gave up her baby at the end of the Centaur War.

There are enough inconsistencies with previous accounts of Callisto's origin to raise questions and provoke plenty of on-line speculation. Like, what happened to the dead sister Callisto mentioned to Xena in "Callisto" and told Gabrielle about in "A Necessary Evil," and when did Callisto's eyes change from blue to brown? Regarding the missing sister, I suppose we should remember that Callisto is hardly the world's most dependable eyewitness; if Xena can give herself an extra brother in "The Warrior Princess," there's no reason why Callisto can't invent a martyred sister or two, especially if she's aware of Xena's guilt over the death of Lyceus and Gabrielle's close ties to Lila.

Even Callisto's mother has changed; she's not the same actress Callisto met in the Underworld at the climax of "Intimate Stranger."

Trying to unravel all the time paradoxes at work here is probably a thankless task, but one has to wonder about the motivations of some of the principal players. I mean, if Callisto prevents her own creation, who does she think will go back in time to rescue her family? And what exactly did Hope seek to accomplish by instigating this whole farrago? By preventing Hercules' birth, and Xena's subsequent reformation, wasn't she negating her own conception? After all, in the world remade by Callisto, Gabrielle ends up on a cross in Greece instead of an altar in Britannia. Was Dahak willing to sacrifice his daughter's very existence to ensure Xena's empire of evil? And how does Ares fit into this, anyway? Don't he and Dahak both want the same thing, namely the rise of Xena the Conqueror?

Given that probably neither Hercules nor Iolaus is familiar with the sad story of Gabrielle's Hope, which Gabby couldn't even bring herself to share entirely with Ephiny, it seems unlikely that either of them will think to connect the darkness behind Callisto to their pals Gabrielle and Xena and pass the news on to our heroines. In other words, *we* know that Hope is still kicking, but Warrior Princess and her bard don't.

The Chronus Stone, introduced in the animated movie (to be discussed later), had revealed its time-warping abilities in an earlier episode of *Hercules*, "The End of the Beginning."

Ultimately, Callisto falls through an interdimensional doorway to an unknown fate, but not before Iolaus reveals that Xena has a secret birthmark on an unspecified part of her anatomy. I suspect we'll see Callisto again before we hear any more about that birthmark.

Reality Check
Er, need I mention that Xena didn't really conquer the known world?

Rating: ⅔⅔

King Con

WRITTEN BY CHRIS MANHEIM
DIRECTED BY JANICE GREEK

Mama needs a new pair of sandals.
—Xena, rolling the dice

What Happens
After Joxer is beaten to a pulp by hired muscle belonging to the ruthless owner of a lavish gambling palace, Xena concocts an elaborate revenge scheme that involves teaming up with two skilled con artists, one of whom bets that he can win a kiss from the Warrior Princess.

Remarks

A rather ho-hum episode, actually, that contains very few surprises to anyone who has already seen *The Sting* (1973). While I suppose it's good to know that Xena's many skills include playing cards and throwing a mean pair of dice, you know you're in trouble when you spend most of the episode wondering what in the world Renee O'Connor has done to her ankle. Gabrielle limps around like Tiny Tim through the whole story without much in the way of explanation. Is this supposed to be the same sprained ankle she got in "Forgiven" or did Gabby attempt another Xena-type flip? (Remember, always lead with *right* foot . . .)

Speaking of physical abuse, Joxer takes quite a lot of it from the gambler's goons—with surprisingly bloody results. One tends to think of him as a live-action 'toon who can absorb an infinite amount of slapstick violence and spring up ready for more, but his comedic invulnerability definitely fails him here. It makes sense, I guess, that Joxer has to get really hurt this time, in order to give Xena sufficient motivation for her campaign of retaliation, but it's still pretty jarring. Look at all the knocks he got in "Been There, Done That" alone. If he can survive that, he can live through anything.

As for the simmering sexual tension between Xena and the better-looking of the two con men, it comes as a bit of a surprise to realize that this Rafe is the first man Xena has shown any interest in all season, not counting the flashbacks to Borias in "The Debt" two-parter. Unfortunately, it's not at all clear what exactly Xena sees in Rafe. As played by Patrick Fabian, he seems a bit young and lightweight for her. One of the reasons, I suspect, that the subtext comes through so persistently on

---

Xena Invades Pop Culture . . .

"[A] leather-clad proto-Xena."—David Browne (*Entertainment Weekly*, ON DIANA RIGG AS EMMA PEEL, APRIL 3, 1998)

Xena is that the male love interests are so seldom convincing, especially when Xena or Gabrielle is expected to fall hard for somebody over the course of forty-five minutes or so. The romantic subplots have worked best when they implied an enduring connection with some history to it, as with Draco and Marcus and Borias and, well, maybe Perdicas.

When Gabrielle knowingly alludes to her partner's predilection for "bad boys," one assumes she has Petracles or Draco in mind, not Ulysses or Caesar.

Still, when you consider that neither of our heroines has come close to getting lucky for more than a year, I guess a small-time grifter like Rafe starts looking better and better after a while.

Reality Check

Gambling on games of chance has been probably going on since the beginnings of civilization, if not before. ("Thog throw bone in air. Call heads or tails.") The Greeks and Romans were playing with dice at least as far back as roughly 300 B.C. Playing cards are, by comparison, a more recent invention, believed to have been first created by the Chinese in 1120 A.D. and imported into Europe around the fourteenth century. Xena appears to be playing a variation on poker, a game developed in nineteenth-century America, but based on older games of unknown origin.

Rating: ⅄

When in Rome . . .

WRITTEN BY STEVEN L. SEARS
DIRECTED BY JOHN LAING

This is no time for you to have a crisis of faith.
—Xena to Gabrielle

What Happens

Xena comes to Rome to rescue a captured Gaulish warrior—
or is she really there to assassinate Caesar? While the Warrior
Princess renews her acquaintance with her old adversary, Gabrielle holds the life of a Roman hostage in her hands.

Remarks

After "Forgiven" and "King Con," one could be forgiven for
fearing that everything after "The Bitter Suite" and the resolution of the Rift would be anticlimactic. Then along came this
episode to prove that the third season still had plenty of dramatic juice to spare.

Thorny moral dilemmas abound and Xena and Gabrielle,
despite their reconciliation, still seem a little wary of each
other. Will Xena's hatred of Caesar cloud her judgment? Will
Gabrielle's moral scruples endanger them both again? And is
it just me, or does Gabrielle look distinctly uncomfortable
when Xena drags Crassus behind Argo, much as she dragged
Gabby only four episodes ago? (Xena herself gets dragged behind a horse before their excursion to Rome is over, establishing some sort of parity, I guess.) The ending, in which
Gabrielle deliberately sends Crassus to his death, is both unexpected and powerful, demonstrating just what a long and
painful road our innocent little Gabby has traveled over the
past three years. Meridian, Hope, Crassus . . . she's getting an
awful lot of blood on her hands this season.

Xena herself claims to be "over" Caesar now, which may or
may not be true. It's unclear to me whether her assassination
attempt and imprisonment in this episode were part of her

master plan to rescue Vercinix, but Xena seems to have her priorities straight—most of the time, that is.

It is surprising that it has taken this long for the Warrior Princess to end up as a gladiator in an arena, given that it's a fairly familiar situation in sword-and-sorcery sagas. Still, Xena acquits herself well before the mob, much to the annoyance of Caesar, even if the colosseum seen in this episode lacks the imperial grandeur that one expects. (What, they couldn't splice in a cast of thousands from *Ben Hur* or something?) Granted, the great Colosseum of Rome was not inaugurated until 80 A.D., more than a century after the capture of Vercinix, but since when has that stopped this show?

As always, the appearance of Caesar raises the nagging question of just how far *Xena* is willing to go in twisting history to its own ends. On the one hand, there's a certain lack of suspense where Caesar is concerned; after all, we all know that he's destined to become emperor, despite anything Xena might do, and that ultimately he will be brought down by a conspiracy of assassins instead of a rampaging Warrior Princess. Then again, this is the show that rewrote the Battle of Marathon only a few weeks ago and has never let anything so annoying as documented historical fact get in the way of a good story, so maybe anything is possible. *Et tu, Xena?*

The cast of "When in Rome . . ." is practically a class reunion. Besides bringing back the ubiquitous Karl Urban as Caesar, the episode is filled with familiar faces playing noted historical figures. Crassus is played by Matthew Chamberlain, previously seen as both Darphus and Orpheus, while his rival Pompey is Jeremy Callaghan (a.k.a. Palaemon in "Blind Faith"). Vercinix, the heroic Gaul, is Tamati Rice, previously seen as one of the besieged Greek soldiers in "The Price." Even Grant Triplow is back as Brutus, briefly glimpsed in "Destiny."

Once again, Poseidon lets Xena sail from Gaul to Syria to Rome and back again, without making so much as a splash.

Reality Check

Starting in 60 B.C., Rome was ruled by a triumvirate consisting of Caesar, Crassus, and Pompey, much as seen in this episode, and Vercinix (usually spelled Vercingetorix) did indeed lead a major revolt against Roman rule in Gaul, which ultimately ended in his capture.

According to "When in Rome . . . ," Crassus was "accidentally" executed in Vercinix's place. A neat trick, considering that Crassus died in battle in northern Mesopotamia in 53 B.C., a year before Rome took Vercinix captive.

It is unknown whether Xena and Gabrielle ever met Vercinix's famous kinsmen, Asterix and Obelix.

Rating: ϫϫϫ

Forget Me Not

WRITTEN BY HILARY J. BADER
DIRECTED BY CHARLES HASKELL

I can help her forget. I'm a very forgettable person.
—Joxer

What Happens

Tormented by memories of the Rift, Gabrielle seeks solace at the Temple of Mnemosyne, where she is sent on a mental journey through the recent past. But while Gabby's mind explores her guilty secrets, accompanied by the figure of Ares, Joxer ends up with custody of her amnesiac body.

Remarks

So that's how Gabby got to China first! Several weeks after "The Debt," this episode reveals that Gabrielle struck a secret deal with Ares to arrive at the Green Dragon's palace before

Xena. One has to wonder: Was this revelation planned all along, or was it merely an ingenious solution to an earlier plot hole?

"Forget Me Not" is another clip episode, reprising scenes from "Maternal Instincts," "The Deliverer," "When in Rome . . . ," "The Bitter Suite," and both parts of "The Debt," but it takes a darker, more dramatic approach than "Athens City Academy of the Performing Bards" or "The Xena Scrolls" (the latter also directed by Haskell), serving as an effective summary of and epilogue to the entire Rift story line. (Still, did they have to recycle my least favorite song from the musical, that dopey "Hate" number?) Gabrielle's ultimate recognition of her own jealousy of Lao Ma goes a long way toward explaining her unexpected betrayal of Xena back in China, while no doubt warming the hearts of subtext fans everywhere. Says Gabby of the Warrior Princess, with remarkable candor, "I hated her for loving someone else."

To my surprise, this statement didn't attract nearly as much attention on the Internet as did this episode's humorous subplot, in which Joxer considers taking amorous advantage of Gabrielle's amnesiac state but ultimately comes clean about the true nature of their (non)relationship. *Alt.tv.xena* was overflowing with posts debating the relative merits and defects of Joxer's behavior under the circumstances—like we were supposed to be surprised that Joxer is a basically decent guy who acts like a jerk sometimes? So what else is new?

The Joxer subplot, which involves the Mighty One reading Gabby's own scrolls back to her in an attempt to jog her absent memory, contains a couple of funny in-jokes, like the fact that the first scroll is titled "Sins of the Past." Gosh, does this mean Gabrielle is responsible for coming up with the names of all the previous episodes? Even "Hooves and Harlots". . . or "Girls Just Wanna Have Fun"?

Gabby also comments on the way her costume keeps shrinking throughout the saga, while her journey through the past is explicitly compared to Xena's trip through the dreamscape passage in "Dreamworker." In the end, our heroines are reconciled once more, but a new loose end remains.

Gabrielle now owes the God of War a favor. When and how will he collect?

Reality Check

Mnemosyne (Memory) was one of the original Titans. She is best known in the myths for being the mother, by Zeus, of the nine Muses, as a bard like Gabrielle would surely know. She has also lent her name to the modern word "mnemonics." (She should not, however, bear any responsibility for the bad Keanu Reeves sci-fi movie *Johnny Mnemonic*.)

Rating: ⚛⚛

Fins, Femmes, and Gems

STORY BY ROB TAPERT & ADAM ARMUS & NORA KAY FOSTER
WRITTEN BY ADAM ARMUS & NORA KAY FOSTER
DIRECTED BY JOSH BECKER

Fish don't just catch themselves! —Xena

What Happens

Something fishy is going on when, thanks to Aphrodite, Xena and friends succumb to a variety of obsessions. Joxer becomes an ape-man, Gabrielle falls in love with herself, while the Warrior Princess becomes determined to land the one that got away. And, sure, there's this mystic diamond, too.

Remarks

Somebody at Renaissance Pictures really thinks fish are funny. Consider: You've got the nude fishing gags in "Altared States," Gabby getting fish in her face in "A Day in the Life," Xena repelling an army with a cartload of fish in "The Quill is Mightier . . ." and so on. Even the otherwise harrowing "The

Price" begins with a humorous fishing scene. Gods above, this is the *second* time this season (after "Quill") that the Warrior Princess has been gripped by a sorcerous compulsion to go fishing. (Ah yes, the old magical-fishing-compulsion plot. Works every time.)

Various evidence suggests that this piscatorial predilection swims straight down from the top, namely Rob Tapert and Lucy Lawless, both reported to be avid anglers. Tapert's mania for fishing was extensively parodied in "Yes, Virginia, There Is a Hercules," while their real-life wedding cake was crowned by figures of Poseidon and a mermaid. Can a Xenaized version of "The Old Man and the Sea" be very far behind? And are we surprised that this episode was originally announced as "Fish Shticks"?

Gills and scales aside, this is an extremely silly episode which basically consists of the cast goofing around on the shore of a picturesque lake. Fannish response was distinctly divided between those who thought it was the funniest thing since the dancing go-go Gabbys and those who considered it a colossal waste of time. Put me squarely in the first camp; it took me over an hour to watch this ep the first time around because I kept rewinding the tape to laugh at the most hilarious bits again. As is usually the case with the better comedy episodes, there are too many good gags to mention them all, but some of the laugh-out-loud highlights include Gabrielle's narcissistic paean to herself (sung to the theme song of *The Beverly Hillbillies*), Xena humming her own theme song as she fishes, and the sad-eyed, puppy-dog pout the Warrior Princess employs to get Gabby to part with a lock of her precious golden fleece. A lot of the fun comes from the giddy, gleeful, childlike enthusiasm and creativity the spell brings out in the frequently somber Xena; we even get an unprecedented flashback glimpse of lil' Xena, played a child actress (Renee Schuda) who certainly looks the part.

Parental advisory: As in the brothel episode, the humor gets pretty racy here, ranging from an extended double entendre about a would-be archer's "shaft," to a tour of the

XXX-rated pictographs in Aphrodite's temple, to Gabrielle's immortal line "You want me to fist a fish?" Not to mention the frightening concept of a nearly naked Joxer. (Still, given how often Xena and/or Gabrielle have shed their clothes this season—in "The Furies," "The Debt," "The Quill is Mightier . . . ," "The Bitter Suite," and "Forget Me Not"—a nude Ted Raimi was probably inevitable, if not terribly appetizing. The sight provoked much Internet speculation and commentary regarding Joxer's conspicuously pallid complexion and absence of body hair, proving that no subject was, er, beyond the pale of the gang at *alt.tv.xena*.)

Furthermore, while the fish may not be biting much, the subtext definitely rises to the surface. Homoerotic hinting doesn't get much more blatant than the moment when an entranced Gabrielle stares soulfully at her longtime companion and declares, "I looked into your eyes and, Xena, I finally realized there can only be one person for me . . . me!" The expression on the Warrior Princess's face, as she swings from misty-eyed expectation to abrupt disappointment before stomping off in a huff, speaks more than all the scrolls in Athens.

Department of Déjà Vu: Gabrielle gets clobbered by Xena's infamous "flying parchment," just like she did in "A Day in the Life."

Last seen in "Quill," Alexandra Tydings makes a brief but effective appearance as Aphrodite, complete with an anachronistic Walkman done up in her trademark seashell motif. Lawrence Makoare, who played the chief barbarian in "Quill," returns as a murderous warrior who makes the mistake of interrupting Xena just as she's about to catch her fish. Bad idea.

As for the nominal plot of the episode, something about returning a mystic diamond to the heavens before nightfall, why should we worry about it any more than Xena does?

Reality Check

As emulated by Joxer, Attis the Ape-Man seems to bear more resemblance to Tarzan of the Apes (or maybe George of the Jungle) than to the mythological Attis, a Phrygian deity whose triumph over death was celebrated each spring. Probably it was just as well Joxer got the story wrong: The real Attis is perhaps best known for castrating himself, which seems to be the last thing the Mighty One has on his addled mind. (For the record, Tarzan was created by writer Edgar Rice Burroughs in 1914 A.D.)

Gabrielle's obsession, on the other hand, echoes that of Narcissus, who also fell in love with his own reflection. Intriguingly, Narcissus' condition was brought on by the goddess Nemesis because he scorned the love of another. Could there be a further parallel here? I leave it to others to argue whose unrequited passion Gabby may be most oblivious to, Joxer's or Xena's. Unfortunately for the original Narcissus, there was no Warrior Princess around to snap him out of his fatal self-love.

Although the precise location of this episode is never specified, Xena's childhood memories suggest that this particular lake cannot be far from Amphipolis. So what's with all that stock footage of elephants, hippos, lions, monkeys, and giraffes? Since when did Xena grow up next to a jungle? Or did Cyrene and family routinely take summer vacations to Africa?

Finally, this episode does to astronomy what *Xena* routinely does to history. The North Star, which Xena uses to anchor a brand-new constellation commemorating her catch of the day, is actually part of the Little Dipper or *ursa minor*, whereas in the Xenaverse, Solares the fish shines brightly for all to see.

And poor Aphrodite! She never did get her own constellation, as she intends here, but had to settle for having the planet Venus named after her Roman incarnation.

Rating: ꓘꓘꓘ

Tsunami

Written by Chris Manheim
Directed by John Laing

We're trapped inside a sinking ship and you're making like the Argonauts! —a drowning convict

What Happens

Xena and Gabrielle get wet for the second week in a row. When a gigantic tidal wave capsizes an unlucky ship, our heroines are trapped in the sinking, overturned vessel with a handful of survivors, including a dangerous convict and the King of Thieves.

Remarks

I'm not saying this episode bears a distinct resemblance to the 1972 disaster flick *The Poseidon Adventure*, but I was humming "The Morning After" for hours afterward. Too bad they couldn't work in a surprise guest appearance by Shelley Winters, perhaps as part of the chain gang?

Seriously, perhaps the producers should think twice about rehashing old movies this shamelessly. Possibly the least inspired episodes this season, "King Con" and "The Dirty Half Dozen," were the ones recycling plots from the Late Late Show. "Tsunami" is better than "King Con," being a straightforward disaster yarn with a few tense moments, but rather too much time is spent on the soap opera-ish personal problems of the various guest-stars treading water with Xena and Gabrielle; if I want to watch a boring couple work out their marital difficulties while trying not to drown I can always watch *Baywatch*. Particularly wasted is Autolycus, last seen in "King of Assassins," who is given little opportunity for the sly humor and derring-do that one expects from the King of Thieves. A serious Autolycus, weighed down by uncharacteristic guilt and angst, proves that all work and no play makes

Bruce a dull boy. Fortunately, he would be back in form next episode.

At least Xena and Gabby are being themselves, with the Warrior Princess taking command of the situation in a typically impressive fashion. She also uses the same spectacular technique she employed in "Lost Mariner," although repetition renders it slightly less surprising this time around. Meanwhile, Gabrielle has that pressure-point trick down to an art now, displaying not a trace of seasickness even when the boat flips all the way over.

Curiously, Poseidon misses another really good opportunity to get revenge on Xena, even though his name is frequently invoked by the most panicky of convicts. Guess he wasn't listening.

Fans on the Internet spent an awful lot of time dissecting the practical logistics of this episode, mulling over such issues as the likelihood of watertight compartments on a leaky slave ship, the (non)use of rudders in ancient Greece, the practicality of empty wineskins as scuba equipment, and just why nobody got the bends. Since I can barely tell port from starboard, I won't presume to pass judgment here, although perhaps the most damning nitpick was the most simple one: Where in the sealed hold of a submerged ship was the light coming from? Frankly, I wouldn't be at all surprised to find out that Xena can see in the dark, but what about the rest of the mere mortals trapped aboard?

More familiar faces among the guest stars. The surly convict Macon is played by Todd Rippon, previously seen as Goliath in "Giant Killer," while the rich merchant is none other than Stephen Tozer, a.k.a. Mezentius in "The Path Not Taken" and "Remember Nothing." The May-December casting of the merchant and his pregnant bride puzzled me at first; for most of the episode I thought they were father and daughter rather than husband and wife.

Reality Check

Mount Etna, the volcano that sets off the tidal wave, has a number of intriguing mythological and historical connections. Located in eastern Sicily, the peak was said to be the foundry of Hephaestus, where he presumably hammered out the magical metals mentioned in such episodes as "Prometheus" and "The Dirty Half Dozen." Both the giant Enceladus and the monster Typhon, defeated during the war on the Titans, were confined beneath Etna, where their writhings produced frequent eruptions.

But when was the volcanic outburst that swamped Xena's ship? Well, history records that a major eruption in 49 B.C. coincided with the outbreak of civil war in Rome between Caesar and Pompey, seen plotting against each other earlier this season. Sounds right on target to me.

Rating: ⅄⅄

Vanishing Act

WRITTEN BY TERRENCE WINTER
DIRECTED BY ANDREW MERRIFIELD

You are the second-best thief I ever met.
—Autolycus to Xena

What Happens

The King of Thieves finds his title in jeopardy when another culprit steals an immense golden statue under the cover of night. To recover the statue (and Autolycus' reputation), Xena and Gabrielle go undercover . . . and then some.

Remarks

Not as sublimely silly and ingeniously clever as the best of the comedy episodes, like "Been There, Done That," or "A

Day in the Life," but a lot more amusing than "Tsunami," most of the fun coming from the outrageous disguises (and accents) assumed by our heroic trio.

Who knew the Warrior Princess could do a flawless Queens accent, coming off as the Fran Drescher of the ancient world? Lucy Lawless adds to her gallery of characters as a blowsy dealer in stolen goods, with voice and mannerisms straight out of Flushing. For a few moments, I actually thought that "Esra" might be yet another lookalike until Xena discreetly tips her hand to Gabrielle, who is amusingly preoccupied with the ugly mole on her companion's chin. The fact that Xena feels obliged to go undercover says a lot about her improved reputation over the last few years. In the first season, she would have just shown up as herself, counting on her notoriety as an unscrupulous warlord to justify her presence in this den of thieves. How things have changed.

As "Myopia," Gabrielle affects a haughty Eastern European persona along the lines of her impersonation of the Marquessa in last year's beauty contest episode. "I do not pay for goo," she says huffily, while Autolycus poses, for no particular reason, as a one-eyed hunchback named Bentley. The King of Thieves' backstory is fleshed out by the revelation that he first turned to stealing to avenge the death of his brother Malachus, a merchant murdered by a sinister rival who just happens to be behind the theft of the statue as well.

Besides the ridiculous costumes and voices, a certain amount of humor is successfully derived from Xena's efforts to curb her warrior instincts so as to handle matters "the Autolycus way." Gabrielle also produces a few chuckles by apprehensively ticking off the seconds during a protracted pinch interrogation.

And what's with that weird, squishy sound effect when Autolycus winks at the corrupt wharfmaster? It sounds like the whoosh machine has sprung a leak.

Reality Check

Pax, the divine subject of the stolen monument, was the Roman goddess of peace, known to the Greeks as Eirene. The feast of Pax, which is taking place as this episode begins, was celebrated on January 3rd of each year.

The precise location of the statue is not specified, but since it is apparently only a short sea voyage from the isle of Mykonos, I would guess that the vaguely Middle Eastern port seen here is somewhere on the coast of Turkey, only six thousand nautical miles from Queens, New York.

That Xena, she really gets around.

Rating: ☟☟☟

Sacrifice I

WRITTEN BY STEVEN L. SEARS
DIRECTED BY DAVID WARRY-SMITH

You should have been my child. —Callisto to Hope

What Happens

The Fates' threads begin to come together as Xena and Gabrielle try to stop the deluded worshippers of Dahak from bringing about the rebirth of Hope. But while Callisto protects the daughter of darkness, whose side is Ares on anyway?

Remarks

Ironically, "Sacrifice" first aired in New York on Mother's Day 1998, but Gabrielle could hardly expect a card or flowers from the demon-child she poisoned back in "Maternal Instincts." Instead there's more guilt for Gabby as a former friend, now a devout follower of the goddess Hope, names her "The Betrayer" and tries to convince Gabrielle that she should have never abandoned the hell-spawned baby in the first place. The episode teases viewers with the possibility that Gabby might choose Hope over Xena once more, but the un-happy sidekick proves ready to destroy Hope again if needs be. Her life gets more complicated, however, when Ares calls in his debt from "Forget Me Not" and informs Gabrielle that Xena's own life will end if the Warrior Princess slays Hope, forcing Gabby to save Hope from Xena again—for Xena's sake this time.

Yikes, what a mess. Unlike that "Armageddon Now" tangle, though, "Sacrifice" actually makes sense, with the complica-tions arising naturally from the characters' complicated pasts. Xena wants revenge for Solan's death, Callisto wants the peaceful oblivion promised her by Hope, and Gabrielle just wants to do the right thing, no matter how much it hurts. Only Ares' motives are unclear, and that is obviously deliber-ate; the show's creators are clearly withholding one vital piece of the puzzle, perhaps until next week. Revenge for the death of Strife, which is mentioned a couple of times, may be a key factor.

From a strict continuity perspective, exactly why Hope needs to be reborn is obscure since she was up and about, if slightly charbroiled, in "Armageddon Now." I can only assume that this whole larval cocoon stage is part of the unnatural lifecycle of a growing demi-demon. The shocking cliffhanger, in which the revitalized Hope turns out to be a dead ringer for Gabrielle seems inevitable in more ways than one. It's about time Gabby got her own look-alike in the Xenaverse (not counting the three naked Gabby dancers).

And what did happen to that pendant full of Hind's Blood that Callisto snatched several weeks back on *Hercules*? She doesn't appear to have it on her when she escapes from the interdimensional vortex that captured her at the conclusion of the "Armageddon" storyline. Interestingly, Xena seems fairly well-versed in what happened to Callisto and Strife on the sibling series, although (as discussed earlier) it's unlikely that she found out about Hope's involvement in Callisto's time-travel scheme.

Believe it or not, Callisto gets buried alive for the *fourth* time, even though I'm still not sure how a simple cave-in can confine a full goddess. Can't she just teleport herself free? Maybe she's simply a sucker for tradition; this is starting to feel something like a running gag between her and Xena.

For the record, this is the Warrior Queen's first appearance on *Xena* since "Maternal Instincts," although Hudson Leick played an illusory role "The Bitter Suite." The Fates, last seen in "Remember Nothing" (and "Judgment Day" on *Hercules*), return as well, spinning the thread of Xena's life.

Would that thread be cut next week? It seemed like a terribly long time to wait to find out.

Reality Check

Gabrielle's childhood friend, now Hope's willing sacrifice, is named Seraphin, no doubt derived from the Hebrew word *seraphim*, referring to the highest order of angels. Given that Gabrielle's own name has Hebrew (and angelic) roots, one has to wonder what sort of Biblical influences are at work in humble Potidaea?

Rating: ⵣⵣⵣ

Sacrifice II

Written by Paul Robert Coyle
Directed by Rick Jacobson

You are so not like your mother.   —Ares to Hope

What Happens

The season cliffhanger turns out to more of a volcanic pit-
faller as Gabrielle and her pregnant demon daughter take a
shocking plunge to certain doom (yeah, right), while Xena finally brings her bloody dance with Callisto to a brutal close.

Remarks

Rumors had been circulating for weeks about Callisto's
possible demise. "Personally, I think it's time for Callisto to
die," Hudson Leick told *Starlog* magazine in an issue that
went on sale shortly before the fatal episode, and certainly
Callisto was starting to repeat herself. In this episode alone,
the Warrior Queen switches sides again, just as she did in "A
Necessary Evil," and, hilariously, gets buried alive for the *fifth*
and hopefully final time. I had expected her to go out nobly,
with some sort of heroic redemptive sacrifice along the lines
of Darth Vadar in *Return of the Jedi*, and was pleasantly surprised to discover that, nope, Callisto stays true to her own
psychotic self, remaining fascinatingly perverse and problematic right to the end. Debate still rages on whether Callisto deliberately provoked Xena into killing her or if she truly wanted
to live after witnessing Gabrielle's apparent death. I kind of
like the latter idea, but lean toward the former. (Memo to future villains: *Don't* taunt Xena at a vulnerable moment. Look
what happened to Ming T'ien and Callisto.)

And what about Hope and Gabby's fiery plunge? Well, considering that Hope has already survived her own cremation
earlier this season, a lava pit is hardly likely to do her in. Justifying her mortal mother's survival is going to be a little

harder; I wouldn't be surprised if the Warrior Princess has to make a special trip to Hades to retrieve her bard. (But how will she know it's *really* Gabby and not Hope?) Still, Gabrielle's impulsive sacrifice would have been more shocking had not the climactic scene shown up in all the "coming soon" teasers for the episode. (What *were* they thinking?)

Just about everybody shows up for the big season finale: Xena, Gabrielle, Hope, Callisto, Seraphin, Ares, Joxer, the Fates, and even Dahak in the form of a grumbly gout of flame. With so many storylines and characters to service, this had the potential to turn into another confusing free-for-all like "Armageddon Now" (also written in part by Coyle), but thankfully "Sacrifice II" manages to stay (mostly) coherent while still giving all of the featured players a chance to shine, including a long-overdue mother-daughter reunion between Gabrielle and you-know-who.

Hope as played by Renee O'Connor is a lot more evil fun than her previous incarnations as a bratty child and crispy zombie. Besides a creepy reptilian stare, the new Hope shows glimmerings of an actual personality behind her symbolic persona as the embodiment of evil, including some trenchant abandonment issues to deal with. For those of us who still think the poor kid might have stood a chance at goodness if Xena hadn't forced Gabrielle to send Hope down the river back in "Gabrielle's Hope," these traces of emotion make Gabrielle's torment all the more complicated and poignant. Is it too much to hope that, with Hope's upcoming offspring, Gabby might get a second chance at parenting? Alas, Ares' ominous prophecies about the "Six Destroyers" don't offer much hope along those lines.

Speaking of parents, if Ares really is Xena's father, as this episode continues to hint, does that make her the half sister of Gabrielle's grandchild? Impregnating Hope and casting his lot with Dahak (at least for the time being), Ares certainly seems willing to sacrifice one child (Xena) for another. Maybe that's what he really meant when he called this latest scheme a "win-win" situation: He's pitting his children against each other, winner take all.

Meanwhile both Joxer-phobes and Joxer-philes can claim partial victories as well, with Xena giving the Mighty One a vicious tongue-lashing (echoing the sentiments of many in the audience) before allowing him to play a vital role at the conclusion. His scene with Hope, when the disguised daughter of darkness puts him on the spot about his true feelings for Gabrielle, is memorable as well. I guess it's going to be at least next season before the real Gabrielle catches on, though.

Although enjoyable and dramatic overall, with Callisto getting most of the good lines, "Sacrifice II" is not without its faults. I've watched the darn thing three times now and I still can't figure out when or why Xena hid the Hind's Blood dagger (the Olympian version of kryptonite) in the Temple of Dahak. And how come Callisto is now convinced that the Hind's Blood alone can send her to oblivion and not Tartarus, where she spent most of "Armageddon Now" (parts one *and* two) carrying around a pendantful of the stuff? And what happened to that pendant anyhow?

Also, a subplot involving some manner of mystical link between Hope and Seraphin falls by the wayside, unless the Powers That Be are planning to do something with it next season. Ironically, the would-be sacrifice manages to stay alive throughout, even while the rest of the cast is dropping like flies.

A minor point: While the tragic death of Solan is frequently invoked, it seems odd that Callisto meets her end without a single soul, not even Gabrielle, bringing up the little matter of the murder of Perdicas. Granted, she paid for that crime with her life (twice), but I'm surprised that both our heroines seem to have put that particular grudge aside.

Finally, was it a subtle joke on the part of the show's creators that this third season cliffhanger includes a scene of Xena literally hanging from a cliff?

Reality Check

Opposing mythologies meet and mingle as a Greek deity mates with the half-human daughter of a Persian devil to spawn a new hybrid pantheon born of diverse and contradictory religious traditions, which may not be a bad metaphor for the creation of the Xenaverse itself. And will these prophesized new gods and monsters bear any resemblance to authentic figures from myth or history?

We'll find out next season, I guess.

Rating: ⵣⵣⵣ

Hercules & Xena:
The Battle for Mount Olympus

SCREENPLAY BY JOHN LOY
PRODUCED AND DIRECTED BY LYNNE TAYLOR
FEATURING THE VOICES OF KEVIN SORBO (HERCULES), LUCY LAWLESS (XENA), MICHAEL HURST (IOLAUS), RENEE O'CONNOR (GABRIELLE), KEVIN SMITH (ARES), ALEXANDRA TYDINGS (APHRODITE), JOSEPHINE DAVIDSON (ALCMENE), JOY WATSON (HERA), PETER ROWLEY (ZEUS), JOSEPHINE DAVIDSON (ARTEMIS), DAVID MACKIE (PORPHYRION), ALISON WALL (TETHYS), TED RAIMI (CRIUS), ALISON WALL (MNEMOSYNE)
"ACROSS THE SEA OF TIME," "TITAN'S SONG," AND "XENA'S SONG," WRITTEN BY MICHELLE BROURMAN & AMANDA MCBROOM

> *Try and stop me, goat-breath.*
> —Xena to cartoon satyr

What Happens

When Zeus brings Hercules' mom, Alcmene, to live on Mount Olympus, Hera throws a serious hissy fit and frees the four Titans from Tartarus. Still on the outs with his father, Herc refuses to take sides in the coming battle between the

Olympians and the Titans, so the gods enlist Xena instead,
changing Gabrielle into a giant eagle (!), the better to get Xena
to the top of Mount Olympus. Despite her efforts, the Titans
take over Olympus, turning on Hera and transforming the
other gods into barnyard animals. Zeus becomes a mouse, Ares
is a goat, Aphrodite a cow, and Artemis a bunny. In the end, no
surprise, all concerned put aside their differences and team up
to retake Mount Olympus. The gods are restored, Gabrielle becomes human again, but everyone's still badly drawn.

Remarks

What, no Joxer? They did a musical cartoon without the
Mighty One and his theme song? Horrors! (Although Ted
Raimi does provide the voice of the most clownish Titan, as
well as various ruffians who are thrashed by Xena).

> "She-Ra, my ass!" —Lucy Lawless, in response to a compari-
> son between Xena and the cartoon heroine. (New York Con-
> vention, September 28, 1997)

Beyond that, it helps to come to this, *The Animated Movie*
(TM), with seriously diminished expectations, especially
where the visuals are concerned. The artwork is astonishingly
crude; we're talking bad Hanna-Barbara here, not Disney or
even Ralph Bakshi. Hercules, in particular, looks more like the
Frankenstein monster than Kevin Sorbo. Xena fares somewhat better, although she sometimes seems to have the
shoulders of a linebacker. Gabrielle gets off easy, spending
most of the video covered with feathers, even if our favorite
bard would doubtless consider this adventure one for the
birds. Perhaps not surprisingly, of all the characters from the
live-action shows, Aphrodite translates most easily into a
'toon, sledding down the besieged mountain in her trademark shell.

The vocal characterizations, performed by many of the

actors from the two series, do their best to bring the story to life, and everybody is more or less in character. Xena even finds time to mention the events of "The Reckoning" and her bumpy history with Ares, although the Titans seen here bear little resemblance to the ones in "The Titans." *Hercules* fans may wonder why the animated Alcmene is not happily married to Jason like her live-action counterpart.

On a mythological level, Olympus seems a bit underpopulated, inhabited by only five deities when the Titans attack. Apollo and Athena are among the missing, as usual, but Artemis plays a large part in the proceedings, something of a surprise given her relatively low profile on the television shows. She comes off as Ares' slightly bratty, know-it-all little sister and gets on Xena's bad side by being the one who actually changes Gabby into a bird. (A note on casting: Neither Hera nor Zeus is voiced by the same actors who have portrayed those characters on the shows.)

Musically, the video hits some sort of low point (or high, depending on your point of view) with a so-bad-it's-good number by the Titans, rhyming "worst" with "perverse-t," that makes Xena's later ballad sound like a Top Ten hit by comparison. "Xena's Song," sung by Lawless herself, is full-bodied enough and will probably have to do for those of us who are still ticked off that they didn't put out a recording of Lucy's performance in *Grease*—at least until "The Bitter Suite" CD came out.

All in all, *The Animated Movie* (TM) is best suited for completists and undemanding children, but if you're a true *Xena* fan you probably have to see it at least once. Rent it first, before you even think of adding it to your permanent video library. Beware, *Entertainment Weekly* thought even less of the video, giving it a "D" rating and complaining that the animated movie was "not nearly as vivid a cartoon as the live-action series."

A nagging question: How come the opening number, "Across the Sea of Time," sung by a quartet of pastel naiads, praises Hercules to the skies but doesn't mention Xena? Hmmph!

What, no funny disclaimer either? What a gyp!

Reality Check

Artemis, known as Diana to the Romans, was the virgin goddess of the hunt and, according to *Xena* lore, the patron goddess of the Amazon Nation. She was the daughter of Zeus and Leto, as well as the twin sister of Apollo. She is often depicted, as she is here, with a bow and arrows. To date, she has only made one brief appearance on *Hercules* ("The Apple"), and none in *Xena*. Although challenged by Velasca in "A Necessary Evil," she failed to appear.

Hera, a.k.a. Juno, was Zeus's jealous wife and Hercules' number one foe. (Kind of odd, isn't it, that the story line of this kid-friendly video is sparked by the king of the gods' adulterous love for Alcmene? You know, there was a reason the Disney version left that part out . . .) Xena and Hercules defied Hera together in "Prometheus," and she later brought Callisto back to life in the *Hercules* episode "Surprise." Hera is represented on the live-action shows only by a pair of ominous eyes accented with peacock feathers, but here she looks more like your standard cartoon evil queen, high cheekbones and all.

Porphyrion, Crius, Menemosyne, and Tethys are indeed the names of four of the Greek Titans, although they seem more like elementals in this cartoon, embodying between them Earth, Air, Fire, and Water. Traditionally, there are at least twelve different Titans, including the three seen earlier in "The Titans," one of whom was also named Crius. The "Chronus Stone" which the gods use to defeat the Titans in the video is presumably named after Chronus, the deposed ruler of the Titans and father of both Zeus and Hera.

Rating: ⰽ

"MAY I HAVE THE PAPYRUS, PLEASE...?"

The Top Ten Episodes of *Xena: Warrior Princess* (in chronological order)

1. "Hooves and Harlots." Centaurs, assassins, and Amazons . . . oh, my! Plus, Gabby gets her stick.

2. "Mortal Beloved." A trip to the Underworld, great Harpies, *and* a tragic love story.

3. "Callisto." Enter you-know-who (hiss!) and Joxer, too. Plus, that fight on the ladders.

4. "Is There a Doctor in the House?" Lucy Lawless's favorite episode, and who are we to argue?

5. "A Day in the Life." One priceless moment after another. Plus, Xena discovers electricity!

6. "The Price." Not a lot of laughs, but intense and scary. (And that's just our heroine . . .)

7. "A Comedy of Eros." I'm not sure what's funnier, Joxer and Gabby singing his theme song together, or Xena's horrified reaction when she catches herself calling Draco "sweetie."

8. "Been There, Done That." Ingenious and hilarious. The dead rooster gets me every time.

9. "The Bitter Suite." By Zeus, they pulled it off. A daring experiment that actually succeeds on most every level. The sound track's not bad, either.

10. "Sacrifice II." A bit cluttered, but an effective windup to a tumultuous season. Plus, Callisto goes out in style.

Honorable Mentions:
"Dreamworker," "The Greater Good," "A Solstice Carol," "A Necessary Evil," "The Debt (both parts)," "The Quill is Mightier . . ."

CHAPTER V

XENA: THE PHENOMENON

It's clear that the Warrior Princess can no longer be confined to a weekly hour of television. Growing even faster than Gabrielle's demon baby, Xena fandom and merchandising are expanding by leaps worthy of the warrior herself: conventions, fan clubs, comic books, novels, fan fiction, Web sites, and even a special attraction at Universal Studios Theme Park in Orlando, Florida. Alas, time and budgetary limitations prohibited me from sampling said attraction, "Hercules and Xena: Wizards of the Screen," in person, but what follows is a survey of the many and varied ways today's Xenaphile can scratch that Warrior Princess itch during the dark days of re-run hell.

Xena Between Covers: The Novels

To date, four full-length novels starring Xena and Gabrielle have been published in the United States by Boulevard Books, an imprint of the Berkley Publishing Group, with more to come. These books are licensed by MCA, which controls the publishing rights to Xena, and written by authors who often have little direct contact with the producers of the television show. Knowing full well the difficulties under which TV tie-in writers work, usually kept completely in the dark as to future developments on the series, I would feel churlish and a bit cruel to point out the occasional continuity glitches, although one is surprised that Xena's weapon of choice is consistently misspelled as a "chakra" throughout the first four books.

In general, the novels tend to be straightforward historical fantasy, packed with figures out of Greek history and mythology, but never quite as engagingly goofy as the TV version is capable of getting. A scene in the first novel, in which Gabrielle indulges in a little girl talk with Circe, offering the legendary sorceress helpful advice on how to deal with men besides turning them into pigs, probably comes closest to catching the irreverent tone of the TV series. A running gag about Gabby's dubious abilities as a seer is so prevalent in all the books to date that I suspect that it had to have been mentioned in an early writers' bible.

In sequence, the novels are as follows:

The Empty Throne, by Ru Emerson. Sometime between the events of "Beware of Greeks Bearing Gifts" and "Ulysses," our heroines defend the island of Ithaca from the warlord Draco, as well as from Odysseus' jilted lover Circe.

The Huntress and the Sphinx, by Ru Emerson. Shortly after the preceding book, Xena and Gabrielle arrive in Athens, where they encounter a number of mythological figures, including Atalanta, Arachne, the Sphinx, and Nausicaa, the latter yet another character from *The Odyssey*. Gabby is reunited with her old friend and fellow bard Homer, while we learn that Xena has a somewhat acrimonious relationship with the legendary female athlete Atalanta.

The Thief of Hermes, by Ru Emerson. Picking up more or less where the previous book left off, Xena and Gabby's departure from Athens is complicated by a young thief who may or may not be the son of Hermes, messenger of the gods. Also making an appearance are King Theseus and his wife, Hippolyta.

Prophecy of Darkness, by Stella Howard. A precocious twelve-year-old prophetess foretells a coming disaster that only Xena can prevent, leading to a finale that pits Xena against the unleashed fury of Cerberus, the snarling three-headed dog of legend. Howard's novel feels more young-adult than Emerson's books, with Gabrielle coming off as even more wide-eyed and naive then usual. The round killing thing is still called a "chakra," though, while Xena's horse is inexplicably named "Argos" throughout. (I thought that was Ulysses' dog instead.)

Emerson is currently working on at least three more volumes about the Warrior Princess. There are also two children's picture books by Kerri Milliron, *Princess in Peril* and *Queen of the Amazons*, based on "The Path Not Taken" and "Hooves and Harlots," respectively.

Brightly Colored Scrolls: The Comics

As on television, Xena originally entered the world of comic books by way of Hercules, guest-starring in issues #3–5 of the official *Hercules: The Legendary Journeys* comics series, in a story appropriately titled "The Warrior Princess." Despite that familiar title, this was *not* an adaptation of Xena's villainous debut on the TV series, but an original adventure that finds Xena and Gabrielle in pursuit of a murderous Hercules imposter. (A five-page comic story in the June 15, 1996 issue of *TV Guide*, teaming Herc and Xena, actually preceded their first full-length comics team-up by a few months. That short piece and those three issues of *Hercules* featuring Xena have since been collected in one volume as *Xena: Warrior Princess*, a trade paperback.)

Once again, the Xena tail was soon wagging the Hercules dog, with the Warrior Princess graduating to her own comic, or, more precisely, a string of multipart *Xena* miniseries, published somewhat irregularly by Topps Comics. Roy Thomas, the man who introduced Red Sonja to comic book readers two decades ago, has written the majority of the stories, although other scripters have included Aaron Lopresti, Tom & Mary Bierbaum, and even Robert (Salmoneus) Trebor. The visuals, by a wide variety of guest artists, have been uneven, but good work has been done by such comics illustrators as Ron

Lim, Joyce Chin, and Robert Teranishi. (Who in Zeus' name, though, approved that grotesque cover illustration of Xena and Gabrielle on the very first issue of Xena's own comic?) Unlike the novels, the comics tend to emphasize the humorous aspects of the show; with lots of colorful monsters and funny banter, they seem deliberately skewed toward the younger end of the comics market. Characters crossing over from the TV episodes have been Joxer, Callisto, Salmoneus, Orpheus, Cyrene, King Gregor, Pandora, Hercules, Ares, Aphrodite, Hades, Cupid, the Fates, the Sirens, some Amazons, and, of course, Argo, while new mythological guest stars have included Perseus, Gilgamesh, Cassandra, Persephone, the Gorgons, Oedipus, Pegasus, the Hydra, and Cerberus again (twice). Short Xena comics show up regularly in the official Xena magazine, also published by Topps, as well as in the August 9, 1997 issue of *TV Guide*. Perhaps the oddest curiosity among the comics was something called *Xena: Year One*, written by Thomas and drawn by Yanick Paquette and Armando Gil, which purports that Cyrene's long-missing husband, and Xena's apparent father, was a Spartan nobleman named Nelo. Come again? Does Ares know about this? *Year One* also reveals that it was the God of War who initially inspired Xena to destroy Hercules, shortly before her first appearance on television.

More Xena comics are in the works, including a rumored *Xena/Wonder Woman* team-up, to be published jointly by Topps and DC Comics. Who knows, we may finally get an answer to the question Does a Warrior Princess beat an Amazon princess? Me, I'm holding out for the inevitable Xena/Catwoman crossover. Or maybe Xena vs. Vampirella? (Sadly, no one is yet publishing any *Buffy the Vampire Slayer* comics, making that crossover unlikely . . . except in the realm of fan fiction.)

More for Your Dinar . . .

It's almost impossible to keep up with all the authorized Xena merchandise being churned out these days by the con-

---

Where Can I Find the Light-Switch Cover?

"Lawless's nine-year-old daughter, Daisy, favors Xena earrings. Lucy is partial to the plastic light-switch cover." (*TV Guide*, December 20, 1997)

---

temporary equivalents of Salmoneus. The next time Gabrielle wants to "squander a few dinars," as she did right before being abducted by Palaemon in "Blind Faith," she might consider such Xena-related tchotchkes as the official mug, beer stein, posters, calendar, postcards, CD-ROM's, action figures, dolls, journal, diary, key ring, costumes, trading cards, pewter figurines, role-playing game, sound-track albums, memo board, life-size cardboard stand-up, map, scripts, bookmarks, and even a collectible chakram of her very own. Wondering what to wear to your next bacchanalian revel? Might we recommend a matching ensemble of *Xena* jacket, T-shirt, cap, wristwatch, earrings, pin, and pendant. Vidalus, fashion consultant to the future Queen Gabrielle, would surely term it "a bold choice."

More paraphernalia is undoubtedly under consideration by Universal's busy licensing department. I figure it's only a matter of time before the Hallmark Solstice ornaments will be available . . .

Amazons, Unite! The Conventions

If you'll indulge me a moment of fannish snobbery, the Official Hercules/Xena Conventions put on by Creation, a California-based company specializing in marketing science fiction media, are not *real* conventions in the sense of, say, the annual World Science Fiction Convention but are more like staged theatrical events. Instead of taking part in panels and parties, as an active participant in the proceedings, you buy a ticket and take in a show.

That being said, an afternoon spent at a Creation con provides you with a chance to mingle with like-minded souls, see various cast members live and in person, and score all the goodies you can in the dealers' room. (Warning: The Xena stuff sells out much faster than the Hercules products.) The usual itinerary of programmed entertainment consists of selected film clips, previews of upcoming episodes, blooper reels, a trivia contest, and a costume competition . . . all of which is mere padding for what everyone has *really* come to see: the flesh-and-blood manifestations of such figures as Kevin Sorbo, Michael Hurst, Ted Raimi, Hudson Leick, Danielle Cormack, Robert Trebor, Karl Urban, and maybe even Renee O'Connor or Lucy Lawless, who generously answer questions from the audience, cope with the inevitable squeals and hugs of overwrought fans, and sign autographs until their hands are surely ready to fall off. (Faced with the unchecked enthusiasm of their fans, the featured celebrities often seem torn between amazement and utter terror, especially if it's their first convention). The fans themselves are an admirably diverse lot; at the last couple of Manhattan conventions the attendees ranged from East Village lesbians to adorable five-year-olds in their homemade Xena costumes, as well as Gabrielles and Amazons of all ages, and even a Joxer or two.

Such gatherings can take on the tone of an old-time revival meeting, especially if Lawless herself shows up. "What do *you* like about the show?" she asked the fans on one occasion, eliciting a stream of heartfelt testimonials about the redemptive nature of Xena's triumph over her damaged past, the importance of the Warrior Princess as an empowering female role model, and the strength of the friendship between our two very different heroines. All of this is undeniably true, but I admit that, after listening to the umpteenth fan trek up to the microphone to declare What Xena Means to Me, I wanted to leap out of my seat in the back row and shout, "But the show is also fun! Why is no one mentioning the fun?"

Instead I kept my mouth shut and wrote this book.

Bards and Sages: The Fan Connection

Beyond the world of licensing products and shows there exists an entire alternate Xenaverse of fannish activities, in which devoted Xenaphiles of every persuasion connect with each other and make their own entertainment. From a women's basketball team in Washington, D.C., called "Xena's Posse" to the innumerable fan-maintained sites on the World Wide Web, Xena enthusiasts (like generations of Trekkies and other science fiction fans before them) do more than passively watch the series and consume Xena products. They analyze, debate, and elaborate on every aspect of the Xenaverse.

The Internet, in particular, is a wine-dark sea of commentary, conversation, and creativity into which one can plunge for hours without ever coming up for air. Literally hundreds of fannish Web sites exist as tributes to one aspect of the series or another, of which perhaps the best is *http:// whoosh.org.*, entry into the voluminous archives of the International Association of Xena Studies. At *whoosh*—named after one of *Xena*'s favorite sound effects—you can find obsessively detailed synopses of every episode of *Xena* and *Hercules*, production credits and cast lists, and, naturally, lots of opinionated reviews of each episode, as well as quasi-scholarly articles on such burning topics as, for example, the thematic similarities between Xena and *Deep Space Nine*'s Major Kira.

Meanwhile, over at newsgroups like *alt.tv.xena*, they're still arguing over whether Gabrielle should have killed that damn demon baby when she had the chance, along with numerous other issues. Every day fans operating behind a variety of colorful aliases weigh in with their opinions on everything from the fine points of Greco-Roman mythology to the horrifying possibility of Joxer/Gabrielle subtext. ("Forget Me Not" kept that one going for days.)

Which brings us invariably to the fan fiction. Not content to eke out what they can from the sixty-eight episodes of *Xena: Warrior Princess* that have aired so far, dozens if not hundreds of fannish writers, with varying degrees of talent and productivity, have created their own tales of Xena, Gabby, Callisto, and the rest, then sent them out onto the Net for all the world to read. There are spoofs and parodies, character studies, flashbacks to unrevealed chapters of Xena's past, hopeful projections of the Warrior Princess's future, crossover sagas blending the Xenaverse with other popular fictional universes such as those of *Star Trek* or *Highlander*, and enough erotica, hetero and otherwise, to fill all of Aphrodites' temples and still have some left over to the fuel the fantasies of frustrated Hestian virgins. Just skimming lightly over the surface of this bottomless reservoir of fan-generated fiction, I found such bizarre and intriguing oddities as a Xenafied version of *Monty Python and the Holy Grail*, not to mention a three-way *Xena/Star Trek/Knight Rider* crossover!

One of the better fan fiction listings, *www.xenafiction. simplenet.com* has its extensive library broken down into a wide variety of categories, including Amazons, Crossover, Hurt/Comfort, Characters, Adventure, Drama, Humor, Horror, Mystery, Romance, and Romance (Alternative). Concerning the last, you could probably fill several bookshelves with all the stories in which the subtext is energetically un-subbed, not just between Xena and Gabrielle, but also Xena and Callisto, and Xena and Lao Ma, and Hercules and Iolaus, and various combinations thereof. (Like, say, Gabrielle and Xena-in-Callisto's-body.) An unscientific survey of the lesbian fan fiction, much of which can also be found at *www.obsession14. com*, suggests that a large percentage of these particular stories revolve around the long-awaited First Time, when the scales finally fall from our heroines' eyes, when long unvoiced desires are finally spoken aloud, and the Warrior Princess and her bard do all the things they will *never* do on prime-time TV.

As stated before, this is nothing new. Just about every cult TV program from *Dark Shadows* to *Beauty and the Beast* has generated this kind of feverish erotic speculation, except that the steamy stories used to be stapled and xeroxed instead of posted on-line. What's distinctive about *Xena* is just how well the actual show lends itself to this sort of thing. As a perceptive friend once observed, blurring the line between what is authorized canon and what is not, "*Xena* is its own fan fiction."

How Do You Spell Khrafstar?

One final note on this subject: The bane of Xena scholarship and storytelling is the problem of how do you spell all those exotic and archaic names, anyway? Since the credits on the original episodes seldom list the major characters by name, one invariably encounters wide variations in nomenclature. Wherever possible, proper names in this book have been checked against authorized sources, but even that is no guarantee of consistency. *The Official Guide to the Xenaverse,* published early this year, managed to identify Gabrielle's Amazon nemesis both as "Velasca" and "Velaska." And don't get me started on Potidaea. Or is that Poteidia? Or Poteidaia?

Thank the gods that everyone (except Meg) spells "Xena" with an *X*!

CHAPTER VI

"HER COURAGE WILL CHANGE THE WORLD"

As we eagerly anticipate the fourth season of *Xena: Warrior Princess*, the future looks bright for the Warrior Princess and her legions of fans. Both *Hercules* and *Xena* have been renewed through the year 2000, while nightly reruns on the USA Network are carrying the early chapters of our heroine's career to a new audience of initiates. Lucy Lawless has married executive producer and fishing partner Rob Tapert, guaranteeing (we hope) years of harmonious relations between management and star. Meanwhile, sketchy reports creep out of New Zealand about a mysterious spin-off series called *Amazon High*, rumored to involve a teenage girl from the twentieth century who suddenly finds herself among Ephiny and Amazons. A cross between *Xena* and *Buffy the Vampire Slayer*? We can only hope.

So what does it all mean? I suspect we won't know the full impact of the series until all the little six-year-olds watching the show now grow up to be warrior princesses and bards and, yes, even warrior princes in their own rights. In the meantime, the success of the series is proof that, once in a while, energy and enthusiasm and quality in execution win out in the end. *Xena: Warrior Princess* may have hit some sort of nerve in the cultural zeitgeist of the late nineties, but the series would not have found as large an audience as it has if it were not so consistently and superlatively written, directed, and acted. As one of those rare confluences of diverse talents and imaginations working together at the top of their game, *Xena* is a gift from the gods, and one I'm not inclined to take for granted.

Battle on!

BIBLIOGRAPHY

BOOKS

Crenshaw, Nadine. *Xena X-Posed: The Unauthorized Biography of Lucy Lawless and Her On-Screen Character.* Prima Publishing, 1997.

Fuller, Edmund. *Bulfinch's Mythology: A Modern Abridgment.* Dell, 1959.

Grun, Bernard. *The Timetables of History.* Simon & Schuster, 1991.

Haining, Peter. *The Leprechaun's Handbook.* Harmony Books, 1980.

Hamilton, Edith. *Mythology: Timeless Tales of Gods and Heroes.* Little, Brown, 1940.

Hull, Edward. *The Wall Chart of World History.* Barnes and Noble, 1995.

Jackson, Beverly. *Splendid Slippers: A Thousand Years of an Erotic Tradition.* Ten Speed Press, 1997.

Johnson, Rossiter, editor-in-chief. *Mythology* (*Authors Digest,* vol. 18). Authors Press, 1908.

Mercatante, Anthony S. *The Facts on File Encyclopedia of World Mythology and Legend.* Facts on File, 1988.

Van Hise, James. *Hercules and Xena: The Unofficial Companion.* Renaissance Books, 1998.

Weisbrot, Robert. *The Official Guide to the Xenaverse.* Doubleday, 1998.

——. *Hercules: The Official Companion.* Doubleday, 1998.

ARTICLES

Bay, Gretchen J. "Small-Screen HEROES." *3D Design,* September 1997.

Brady, Erik. "In This Corner, in Red Trunks, St. Nick!" *USA Today,* December 23, 1997.

Cassata, Mary Anne, and Ian Spelling. "I, Xena." *Legendary Heroes,* October 1997.

Clehane, Diane. "The Big Bang Theory." *TV Guide,* December 13–19, 1997.

Damarell, Steve. "Instant Guide to Xena, Warrior Princess." *Cult Times,* November 1997.

DeCaro, Frank, Hilary De Vries, and Mark Lasswell. "TV's Top 20 Sexy Stars." *TV Guide,* November 22–28, 1997.

Dovlin, Rod. "Warrior of the Soul." *Axcess,* March 1997.

Evans, Cleveland Kent. "From Lisa to Jaleesa." *TV Guide,* June 21, 1997.

Fagan, Gary. "Singing a Different Toon." *TV Guide,* June 28, 1997.

"The 50 Most Beautiful People in the World." *People,* May 12, 1997.

Finch, Amanda. "The Most Intriguing Women in Science Fiction." *Sci-Fi Universe,* September 1997.

Findley, Heather. "Xena-Philia!" *Girlfriends,* April 1998.

Flaherty, Mike (with additional reporting by Tricia Lane). "Xenaphilia." *Entertainment Weekly,* March 7, 1997.

Gonzalez, Desiree, "Renee O'Connor." *Sci-Fi Universe,* September 1997.

Hockensmith, Steve. "6 Degrees of Xena." *Cinescape,* July/August 1997.

Jacobs, A. J. "Toys in Babeland." *Entertainment Weekly,* November 24, 1995.

Kloberdanz, Kristin. "X-Siting." *Cinescape,* July/August 1997.

Martinez, Jose A. "*Xena*'s Naughty Nymph." *TV Guide,* May 3–9, 1997.

McCaughey, Brian F. "Fight On!" *Axcess,* March 1997.

Miller, Craig. "The Official Hercules/Xena Convention." *Spectrum,* May 1997.

———. "Xena: Warrior Princess." *Spectrum,* September 1997.

Miller, Craig (with John Thorne). *Spectrum Special Edition #2,* November 1997.

Minkowitz, Donna. "Xena: She's Big, Tall, Strong—and Popular." *Ms.,* July/August 1996.

Nazzaro, Joe. "Budget Dragonheart." *SFX,* Christmas 1996.

———. "Savage Sword of Xena." *Starlog,* January 1996.

———. "Myth Directions." *Starlog,* March 1997.

———. "Xena, Warrior Princess." *Starlog,* April 1997.

———. "Story-telling Sidekick." *Starburst,* August 1997.

———. "Heroic Renaissance." *Starlog,* December 1997.

———. "Dreamworker." *Starlog,* January 1998.

Perez, Dan. "Hudson Leick." *Realms of Fantasy,* April 1998.

———. "Xena's Zeitgeist." *Sci-Fi Entertainment,* June 1998.

Reid, Craig. "Xena, Warrior Princess." *Sci-Fi Universe,* January 1997.

Rensin, David. "Lucy Lawless, the Woman Behind the Warrior." *TV Guide,* May 3–9, 1997.

Rudolph, Ileane. "Lawless in Love." *TV Guide,* February 21, 1998.

Scapperotti, Dan. "Sword and Sorcery EFX." *Cinefantastique,* December 1997.

Schaefer, Stephen. " 'Xena' Takes on Broadway." *USA Today,* August 26, 1997.

Schindler, Rick. "Eye to Eye to Xena." *TV Guide,* December 13–19, 1997.

Seligmann, Jean, and Karen Schoemer, with T. Trent Gegax. "Her Cup Runneth Over." *Newsweek,* May 19, 1997.

Shapiro, Marc. "Myth Maker." *Dreamwatch,* December 1997.

Spelling, Ian. "Legendary Journeys." *Starlog,* May 1997.

Stanton, Gabrielle, and Harry Werksman. "Lucy Lawless." *Sci-Fi Universe,* September 1997.

Stewart, Susan. "Xena vs. Hercules." *TV Guide,* January 20, 1996.

Thomas Roy. "Hercules, Xena and Me." *Hercules: The Legendary Journeys #3,* Topps Comics, August 1996.

Tresniowksi, Alex, and Craig Tomashoff. "Lawfully Wedded." *People,* April 13, 1998.

Tucker, Ken. "Gimme Some Skin." *Entertainment Weekly,* November 24, 1995.

Wald, Kevin. "Heroine Barbarian." *Comics Buyer's Guide,* July 25, 1997.

Weisel, Al. "The Importance of Being Xena, Warrior Princess." *US,* October 1997.

Wilson, Steve. "Myth Understanding." *Time Out (New York),* February 20–27, 1997.

Zuritsky, Elisa. "Two Who Trounced *Trek*." *TV Guide,* May 3–9, 1997.

XENA-RELATED PUBLICATIONS AND PERIODICALS

The Official Xena: Warrior Princess Magazine. Published quarterly under license by the Topps Company, Gary Gerani, editor-in-chief.

The Chakram: The Newsletter of the Official Xena: Warrior Princess Fan Club. Sharon Delaney, editor.

Various *Xena; Warrior Princess* comic books published irregularly by the Topps Company.

ABOUT THE AUTHOR

GREG COX is a best-selling writer and an enthusiastic fan of science fiction and fantasy media. His first reference book, *The Transylvanian Library: A Consumer's Guide to Vampire Fiction*, was praised by *Locus* as "both amusing and informative . . . a delightful book for browsing" and by the *Science Fiction Research Association Review* as "a comprehensive study that belongs on the short list of essential books on the subject." He also coedited two anthologies of vampire and werewolf stories: *Tomorrow Sucks* and *Tomorrow Bites*.

He is the author of several media-related novels, including *Star Trek: The Next Generation: The Q Continuum*, *Star Trek: Assignment: Eternity*, *Star Trek: Voyager: The Black Shore*, *Iron Man: Operation A.I.M.*, and *Iron Man: The Armor Trap*, as well as the coauthor of such books as *Star Trek: The Next Generation: Dragon's Honor* and *Star Trek: Deep Space Nine: Devil in the Sky*.

He lives in New York City and considers 9 P.M. Saturdays (Xena time) to be sacred.